Africana

Lerato Umah-Shaylor

Africana

MORE THAN 100 RECIPES AND FLAVORS INSPIRED BY A RICH CONTINENT

AMISTAD

An Imprint of HarperCollins*Publishers*

HarperCollins books may be purchased for educational, business, or sales promotional use. For information, please email the Special Markets Department at SPsales@harpercollins.com.

Originally published as *Africana* in the United Kingdom in 2023 by HQ Non-Fiction, a division of HarperCollins Publishers.

FIRST AMISTAD HARDCOVER PUBLISHED 2023

Photography: Tara Fisher
Food Styling: Esther Clark
Prop Styling: Tabitha Hawkins
Design & Art Direction: Anita Mangan

Library of Congress Cataloging-in-Publication Data

Names: Umah-Shaylor, Lerato, author.
Title: Africana : more than 100 recipes and flavors inspired by a rich continent / Lerato Umah-Shaylor.
Description: New York : Amistad, an imprint of HarperCollins Publishers, 2023.
Identifiers: LCCN 2022044386 (print) | LCCN 2022044387 (ebook) | ISBN 9780063277496 (hardcover) | ISBN 9780063277502 (trade paperback) | ISBN 9780063277519 (ebook)
Subjects: LCSH: Cooking, African. | LCGFT: Cookbooks.
Classification: LCC TX725.A35 U43 2023 (print) | LCC TX725.A35 (ebook) | DDC 641.596—dc23/eng/20220913
LC record available at https://lccn.loc.gov/2022044386
LC ebook record available at https://lccn.loc.gov/2022044387

---

23 24 25 26 27 LBC 5 4 3 2 1

Contents

Introduction

Africana is a celebration of modern African cookery, a love letter to a rich heritage and an enduring people. With whispered recipes from ancestors and generations past, memories of Mama's sumptuous cooking, soup-stained scribbles and inventive recipes for delightful home cooking, this book is my invitation to you to look to Africa for cultural and culinary enrichment, for an adventure filled with wanderlust and excitement. Bringing people together to share the joy of honest food with family and friends.

Imagine plucking fragrant and beautifully ripened mangoes, sinking your teeth into the sweetened flesh and saving the harvest for recipes such as mango piri piri or a cooling tropical salad with hibiscus syrup. **Listen** to the soothing ocean waves crashing on the seashore in harmony with the sound of crackling fires, as you roast a fresh catch basted in apricot glaze, perhaps with a paste of makrut lime leaves and chilies, or the enthralling perfume of vanilla beans and rum.

Feel the comfort of stirring slowly as you mother a pot of luscious greens, or a sumptuous stew. **Savor** the spellbinding flavors of spiced tea, coffee and the pure decadence of delicious dark chocolate. This is the story of **Africana**, bringing the magic and beauty of vibrant African cooking into your home, wherever that may be, and transporting you to paradise.

This book tells the story of where I have come from and where I have been. You will discover the secrets of African cooking—its rich diversity and shared traditions, its influence on world cuisine and its adaptability to your lifestyle, whether you are an amateur cook, a seasoned chef or a busy bee in need of vibrant ideas. I hope to inspire you with wondrous flavors and stories of passionate traditions as we travel across the continent one dish at a time.

My African Food Journey

Food has always been about much more than nourishment for my body; it is nourishment for my soul and a constant sensual adventure. From a young age, I was curious about flavors and this intensified as I ate my way through a colorful childhood to an even more exuberant adult life, with food taking center stage.

Growing up in Nigeria, food represented family; it was our favorite shared experience, at home, with friends, at celebrations and even in sad times. We show affection through food, and rejection of our food is often taken as rejection of our affection. Our feasts were never quick and simple; they were almost always lengthy and ceremonial, more so when we had guests. Food was often prepared with the neighbors in mind or an uninvited guest, of which there were many. A guest in an African home is treated like royalty, fed the best cut of meat, with the best crockery. As a child I thought our guests were utterly and annoyingly spoiled, until I realized we enjoyed this regal treatment as guests in the homes of others. I began to understand "African hospitality"—the true value of sharing with others, the essence of togetherness and the personal reward found in making others happy, be it family, friends or strangers. As I traveled and explored more cultures, I also learned that this great pleasure in feeding others is not unique to Nigeria but is a way of life for many across Africa. In Senegal, for example, this sense of generosity and community is known as *teranga*.

If you see a man in a gown eating with a man in rags, the food belongs to the latter
FULANI PROVERB

My mother is the quintessential *Africana*, someone who beautifully embraces and celebrates cultures from across the continent.

Although I am West African, from Nigeria, my mother gave me a Southern African name. *Lerato* means love in *Sotho-Tsawna*, a Southern Bantu language predominantly spoken in Lesotho, Botswana, and neighboring countries, and also one of eleven official languages of South Africa. Knowingly or unknowingly, she was preparing me for the pan-African life that I fully embrace. My brother and I spent a considerable amount of time living with family friends in the Republic of Benin, a francophone country just west of Nigeria, and we also traveled with Mum exploring and eating our way across Africa. We were raised mainly by our mother and spent some holidays and weekends at our father's house in Lagos. Mum's house was structured with daily meal plans, including an exciting variety of foods from across the world. Food was abundant and wonderful, which we thoroughly enjoyed. But what my mum called "outside food," or street food, was completely off-limits. In Dad's house, we had little or no structure; we ate lots of "take away" and street foods, which Mum would have found utterly horrific—marvelous food like **Sizzling Suya** (see page 116), with sides of crispy yam chips for dinner, or *Ewa Agoyin* **Black-Eyed Pea Mash with Blackened Red Pepper Sauce** (see page 52) and the most incredible fluffy cloud bread for breakfast. Although she didn't think so at the time, Mum admits now that it was a great experience for me, as it allowed me to explore beyond the food we ate at home. My mother's approach to fresh, home-cooked food has shaped my cooking style, but the freedom to explore beyond the home allowed me to discover and learn much more.

My mother was running a restaurant in her early twenties—carrying me wrapped around her back—and I realize now that the apple didn't fall far from the tree! From a very young age, I started to develop an interest in food, beyond just eating it. I was so curious about how different ingredients could come together to create something truly wonderful. Even though my mother banned me from the kitchen until I was about 10 or 11 years old for fear of accidents, I never passed up an opportunity to sneak in there to dip my finger into the pots, risking a few burns just to taste what was to come. Papa, our family cook, put me to work, too, practically giving me my first job as his assistant chef, after much insistence on my part. I learned to cook intuitively, measuring by eye, by touch—feeling every grain of salt crushed between my fingers—by taste and trusting my palate. My mother worked and traveled a lot, cooking mainly on the weekends. By my early teens, she finally invited me to cook with her, stressing the importance of learning to feed myself. But she was a little late—I was already convinced about the importance of cooking and was well equipped to cook an entire meal for the family, much to her amazement. Papa had taught me the basics of cooking rice and sauces and using the delectable curry spices and seasonings he sprinkled into the pots. Mum went on to teach me to cook more traditional Nigerian recipes, like **Bean Tarts** *Moin Moin* (see page 56), *Egusi* **with Pounded Yam** (see page 74) and, my absolute favorite, **Bejeweled & Aromatic Fried Rice** (see page 210), inspired by Nigerian fried rice.

When I started university in London, I was finally free to burn as many fingers as I wanted. I lived just by the South Bank in Waterloo and could be found almost daily crossing the bridge to dine in Covent Garden. I would eat out, come home and try to recreate what I had enjoyed, adding little twists here and there. Further south and a quick hop on the bus took me to Elephant and Castle, Camberwell and Peckham, where I would stock up on plantains, dried beans and spices. My parents practically bankrupted themselves to give me the best education, surely with the hope that I would make something of myself by becoming a world-renowned economist, which was the most natural expectation after graduating with a degree in economics, and with my keen interest in development. Although my mother was perplexed when I decided to immerse myself in the world of food instead, she has always been thoroughly supportive, even when it hasn't always been clear where this path would lead.

After university, I embarked on many unexpected adventures, from presenting breakfast television and hosting a cookery show, to writing a food column for *The Guardian* in Nigeria—one of the most popular national newspapers—and starting a catering business. Since then, I have been sharing a taste of Africa at supper clubs, live cooking shows and cookery classes. The cookery classes and supper clubs have become an important hub for discovering and learning about African foods, and provide great opportunities to bring people together. At the time, it seemed like an odd thing to do, especially when hosting strangers in our home, but what a wonderful experience it has been to dine with so many people over the years, to share something unique and special, not knowing if or when we would ever have that opportunity again.

Now living on the Sussex coast, I am closer to flocks of British sheep than tropical mango trees, but there is a fire in my belly that can never be quenched—an undying love for Africa, a passion for adventure and discovery, and a desire to share the beauty and generosity of African hospitality. Although one cookbook cannot sufficiently do justice to this extraordinary and diverse cuisine, I hope it will inspire you to start your own journey. Food is the lens through which we can better understand the land, her people and her cultures. I want you to cook your way through Africa, with me firmly holding your hand.

Lerato

PS: It brings me great joy to see your delicious creations. Don't forget to tag your photos @leratofoods with #AFRICANACOOKBOOK

African Threads

Africa is a mysterious and wonderful paradise with vibrant cultures, languages and passionate people. The continent's large expanse includes vast savannas and tropical forests, with some of the world's most-admired animals. With coastlines along the Atlantic Ocean in the west, the Indian Ocean in the east, and the Mediterranean Sea in the north, the fishing communities thrive, and people and produce have traveled far and wide. Ecosystems vary, from the snow-capped Atlas Mountains with their rich flora and vegetation on their slopes, that include olives, date palms and wild mushrooms, to the banana-filled tropical highlands of Ethiopia, Uganda and South Africa. As well as the continent's two highest peaks Mount Kenya and Mount Kilimanjaro in Tanzania, these varied ecosystems influence the way of life and the resources available to each region. We are such a diverse people that attempting to define us is a near-impossible task. Yet I find comfort in identifying as an African. To me, Africa is much more than a physical place, it is also a feeling, a belonging to something otherworldly and yet worldly.

From little date seeds, great things are born

NAMIBIAN PROVERB

Our food is vibrant and varied, arresting and comforting but, most importantly to me, it is also timeless. The migration of our ancestors, through slavery and colonialism, spearheaded its influence on the diversity of food and culture in other parts of the world. From black-eyed peas to okra and sesame seeds, many foods are shared not only by Africans on the continent, but have traveled with our ancestors who planted seeds from their home lands in the soil of new countries and in the hearts of the people—from South America and the Caribbean, to the USA. You don't have to look too hard to see the strong threads that bind us—Afro-Caribbeans, Afro-Latinos and African Americans, who nurture and celebrate their African origins.

While enduring challenging food systems, we also continue to feed the world abundantly with our daily produce, from string beans and watermelons to pumpkins and gourds with edible seeds, and two of the world's most popular beverages originate in Africa—cola, made from kola nuts, and coffee, which was discovered in Ethiopia. Produce from different parts of the world have also made their way into Africa, like cocoa, now a major West African export, and peanuts and chilies, emblematic of a lot of African cooking, all of which originally come from South America.

Secret Whispers

Centuries-old customs continue to live on and evolve through food. Each meal, whether in good or bad times, represents not just sustenance, but an opportunity for conviviality, healing and sharing with family and friends. Our daily food rituals are steeped in rich tradition, with a strong sense of seasonality, sensuality, tribal affinity and family legacy. These rituals live on through celebratory harvests, such as the New Yam festivals in Nigeria, Ghana and beyond. The harvests are considered an important show of appreciation to the gods for a rich bounty. The enchanting daily coffee ceremonies in Ethiopian and Eritrean homes are another of such rituals, generously welcoming friends, neighbors and family to immerse in a sensory experience, from the roasting of beans to tasting your first sip.

Coffee is our bread

ETHIOPIAN PROVERB

Even the daily meals we cook at home can be ceremonial, with often lengthy preparations and the cook in constant motion, stoking flames for a South African *braai* (barbecue), grinding peppers and aromatics, or clinking pots and tapping spoons while making stew. Once the feast is ready, mmming and aahing follow as eager and hungry mouths taste the finished product. Finally, there are cheers of appreciation for the cook's efforts as plates are wiped clean.

This performance of feeding others, with its shared offering of love and gratitude, is a practice I enjoy immensely. I love to eat, but not nearly as much as I adore cooking for others. I love the journey to completing each dish, unplugging memories and creating new traditions as each recipe evolves.

We must seek the past in order to forge ahead

SANKOFA

The recipes in this book represent this journey of "going back to move forward." The essence of *Sankofa*, a word in the Akan dialect of Ghana. Beyond a celebration of our identity, teaching both traditional and modern African recipes has given me the opportunity to engage in an oral and written performance. Like *griots* in West Africa, who breathe life into tales of history and culture, African recipes have remained secret whispers, passed from generation to generation, adapting with migration, technology and socioeconomics, while continuously looking back, never to forget ancestors and their stories.

A lot of my recipes have been written from memory and firsthand experiences. They come from stories told to me by family, friends and the wonderful people I have met traveling across the continent. It was only in 2016, when I wrote **Going to a Lagos Market** (see page 14) and **Under the Mango Trees** (see page 108)

that I realized just how many stories and memories I had collected, and how much more there was to learn. I'd spend time chatting to the mamas and street-food hawkers, who initially found it strange that I was asking a lot of questions. But, once I had explained my agenda, they welcomed me with open arms and poured out stories upon stories. I learned so much from them, about origin and seasonality of produce, cookery tips and more. And, of course, I would buy their wares, not only to show my appreciation but to enjoy their lush produce and report back with delicious news.

Although I have eaten many of these glorious foods, I still had to translate these recipes with little or no official measurements. Neither my mother, my late grandmother, nor the mothers and grandmothers of my friends, have given specific and complete measurements or instructions for the recipes in this book. This is the African way. Learning about food from stories, years of watching and cooking with your senses and intuition.

While I encourage you to follow my recipes, especially as they will be new territory for most of you, I urge you to consider dipping your toes into the camp of the intuitive cook. There is room to make each dish your own— with a dash of lime here, a handful of scented leaves there—that is how I was taught to cook. If you connect with your food beyond prescribed measurements, it can help you become a better cook. You will evolve and improve, as you listen to what your taste buds tell you. You will be quicker on your feet on those days when you need to swap ingredients at a moment's notice. You will understand your food enough to correct it when you make mistakes and when mistakes are out of your control. I have never let go of the natural desire and instinct of an intuitive cook. Let the recipes guide you but not enslave you. As you cook your way through the book, listen to the whispers that were passed from generation to generation—let them inspire you to discover Africa.

Seasonality & Sustainability

African cooking is seasonal and sustainable, in essence. In all the African countries I have lived, the food is always freshly cooked with the best available seasonal produce. This is our way of life. We eat mangoes only in the mango season, for example. We have always cooked nose to tail, using every possible inch of each ingredient. A farm-to-table lifestyle (often garden-to-table) is most prevalent.

Across Africa, produce like banana leaves are used to store and to cook foods, such as in *liboké de poisson*, popular in the Congo Basin, and **Fragrant Fish in Banana Leaves** (see page 152). I have also found them to be a great alternative for grilling or roasting instead of using foil. Recipes such as **Tunisian Tagine** (see page 64) are a great way to use the inevitable leftover parsley and herbs, which can also be frozen, while recipes such as **Pumpkin Pepper Soup** (see page 71) or **Ras el Hanout Rainbow Roast** (see page 102) are perfect for any leftover spuds and vegetables you may have lying around.

For many of us cooking at home, it may not always be easy to find the freshest seasonal produce and my recipes do not ignore that, offering swaps and alternatives where possible, and I encourage my cooks to make do with what they have. Substitutes are highly encouraged and suggested, from using different types of chilies, swapping seasonal spuds, greens and more. While this book includes lots of plant-based recipes, I have also shared tips for vegan and vegetarian variations where they are not. Feel free to play around with substitutes that work for you. By cooking with the best of what the season has to offer and the magic of what you have at home wherever you are in the world, you can make each dish new and interesting every time.

At the back of the book you will find treasured recipes for sauces, spice blends and marinades, which will not only come in handy across the book but will serve as useful condiments to add a burst of sunshine to your plate. The ingredients used here are accessible from a variety of food providers, such as your local farmers' markets, African, Asian, Middle Eastern or Indian neighborhood grocers, in supermarkets or just a click away online. See **Africana Produce & Pantry** on page 16 for more.

Kola nuts last longer in the mouth of those who love them

AFRICAN PROVERB

Going to a Lagos Market

OYINGBO MARKET, LAGOS

A trip to one of the bustling markets in Lagos, Nigeria, is not for the fainthearted. It is the most populous African city, with over 20 million people, and is like nothing you have ever experienced—organized chaos at its best. With a rush of loud people and vibrant food in a large, confined space and narrow passages for entry and escape, if you are not quick on your feet, you will be pushed around, and I don't just mean metaphorically. You must be prepared in mind, body, spirit and on paper. Write a list to ensure that you buy only what you need. Dress appropriately, nothing too lavish, or this may affect your haggling power.

I didn't visit the markets until my early teens when my mum decided to take me as a sort of "field trip" before I fled the nest to boarding school. She said, "Let's go to the market so you see where all the food comes from." This was also a "field trip" for her, as she rarely visited the market herself. I was as mesmerized as I

was frightened. We went to Lagos Island market where droves of people squeezed between one another, all pushing in opposite directions. Traders called out, "sister," "my wife," "fine girl," "fine boy" to me and everyone else to come buy their goods. Customers were treated to an almost theatrical welcome. I enjoyed the performance but also learned that making eye contact suggests a sort of commitment. There are quite a few other rules of engagement for a successful trip to the market. You must only touch the food and engage the traders if you are truly interested in their goods—do not touch what you don't intend to buy!

My mother is a great haggler; she is stern with some of the market traders and friendly with others. I have since learned that she was stern to haggle efficiently, and friendly to her "customers." Yes, the seller is also called a customer. She would say, "Ah, my customer!" to those traders she recognized. They would find it endearing and would be more likely to give a discount. I noticed that this is a very important part of shopping in the market because your "customer" can help you traverse the market, bagging goods for much less from their fellow market traders. In my attempt to buy some peppers, I politely asked for a small tin stacked with scotch bonnets, but my mother jumped in and said, "Don't be so soft, they will cheat you!" Being "too polite" can be to your disadvantage. One must be assertive and insistent. You must appear to know how much the peppers should be, and be prepared to haggle.

Food in the market is sold by volume and not weight. Grains, fruits, vegetables and spices are stacked as pyramids in baskets, buckets and trays of varying heights and sizes. Rice, millet and garri (dried and ground cassava), beans, spices and more are measured with different-sized old tomato and milk cans. Chatting to the market men and women is one of the best ways to learn about your food. They are the key to a lot of knowledge and a lot of what I know about seasons, provenance, species and different characteristics of foods. After a colorful day at the Lagos market, with an abundance of fresh peppers, tomatoes, yams, beans and lush greens, like amaranth, wild spinach, bitter leaves and okra, you have to run the gamut past the market men and women on your way out, as they continue to shout, "Welcome, fine girl!," "fine boy!," "sister!," "my wife!," greetings showered at you and everyone else, coming and going, until next time.

Africana Produce & Pantry

I have put together a selection of some of my store-cupboard favorites, staple produce and essentials that you will need to prepare the recipes in this book. While you may already have most of these in your kitchen, some others will be wonderful new discoveries that will add sunshine to a variety of your dishes. To make sourcing some of the ingredients easier, I have curated a list of suppliers on my website—see www.leratofoods.com.

OILS & VINEGARS

Many recipes in this book begin with a drizzle of oil into a pan or finish with a drizzle of oil over a plate of food. I love to cook most dishes with British **cold-pressed rapeseed oil**. Feel free to use whatever you love. I often use stronger flavored oils, such as **extra-virgin avocado** or **extra-virgin olive oil** for eggs, salads and dressings. **Organic cold-pressed virgin coconut oil** is wonderful in banana bread, curries, stir fries and cakes. Other oils, such as **vegetable**, **sunflower**, **grape-seed**, or **peanut**, can be used in many of the dishes across this book. Peanut oil is most used in West African cooking.

ARGAN OIL

This celebrated oil is extracted from the kernels of the argan trees native to Morocco. Because of the difficult processing methods and the labor-intensive picking and cracking these kernels require, it is an expensive oil and often reserved for salad dressing or dips. There is cosmetic-grade argan oil and culinary-grade argan oil. I love serving it with freshly baked **Medina Bread** (see page 194) for dipping, or blending it into *Amlou*—**Almond & Honey Paste** (see page 265) for pancakes and pastry.

RED PALM OIL

To quote the great Nigerian author Chinua Achebe, author of *Things Fall Apart*, one of my favorite books, "Proverbs are the palm oil with which words are eaten." Red palm oil is an essential part of West African culture and identity, and the same is true further afield in the African diaspora, from Brazil to Haiti. The trees offer shade, the stem produces palm wine, while the fruit is crushed for red palm oil and used in soups.

While palm oil has a troubling reputation, I have the privilege of having learned about where red palm oil comes from in Africa and its importance to the farming culture of the people. In the good fight for more sustainable living, sometimes a lack of education leads to over-simplified opinions and choices by one group of people on behalf of the rest of the world. These can ignore facts, culture and the reality for the people it affects. While the growing demand for palm oil has encouraged the rise of large corporations and governments amassing land to produce more palm oil, the livelihood of small-scale farmers in West Africa wielding their cutlasses to produce oil for a modest income is in question. While we all work toward a more sustainable environment, land rights, deforestation and its effect on climate change are important issues that I believe can be addressed by also considering individual circumstances and needs of the people who produce and use palm oil.

With that said, I use palm oil more sparingly than it would be traditionally used. My mum religiously measured the amount of any oil—including palm oil—in her cooking, and a little drizzle was just right. Red palm oil from local African farms is sold in specialist/ethnic grocers and supermarkets, as well as by new sustainable brands. I have included a recipe for **Red Oil** (see page 262), which I love as a finishing oil and for those moments when one cannot source red palm oil.

These are used in marinades, sauces and dressings. Although I love the sweeter flavor of **apple cider vinegar**, you can easily swap it for **red or white wine vinegar**. Do not confuse white wine vinegar with distilled white vinegar, which is more assertive in its sharpness. **Balsamic vinegar** is especially wonderful in the **Hibiscus & Scotch Bonnet Balsamic Dressing** paired with the **Tomato & Strawberry Salad** (see page 170). Although I use a thick and aged balsamic vinegar with a good balance of smooth viscosity, sweetness, acidity and depth of flavor, feel free to play around with what you like and what you can get your hands on.

SEASONING & SPICES

When I say "season to perfection," this is an opportunity to taste and decide what your dish needs—a little more cayenne, a pinch or more of salt or black pepper. As the master of your palate and plate, you have the power to decide and perfect your dish. I love spices, as you will learn in this book, and to take some dishes even further with sensory delights, some recipes call for an extra shower of fragrant spices, freshly ground black pepper or grains of paradise, or some spiced butter or oil as a finishing touch.

SALT

I cannot overstate the importance of salt as a basic ingredient. It is essential to add flavor and balance to your meal. It is also very useful to extract moisture from vegetables, such as onions, to allow them to cook for longer and for the better. The problematic salt is that which is hidden in processed food, rather than the salt which you sprinkle on your food. The amount of salt you use can be very subjective and so, when I say a pinch of salt, I mean a three-finger pinch, while a generous pinch of salt means a five-finger pinch. But my fingers may be smaller or larger than yours, so getting used to what a pinch means to you is important. I use **fine sea salt** as well as **sea salt flakes** or crystals in my

home cooking. I have created some exciting, flavored salt blends, such as **Hibiscus Salt** (see page 266) to season popcorn, chocolate, fish and roasts like **Harissa Leg of Lamb with Hibiscus & Cumin Salt** (see page 132) or for finishing salads. It is worth noting that ½ teaspoon fine sea salt equals 1 teaspoon sea salt flakes. If you have been asked to stay away from salt for medical reasons, please follow the advice of your medical practitioner.

BLACK PEPPER

I adore black pepper and my recipes often call specifically for freshly ground black pepper. Once ground, black pepper loses a lot of its natural oils and flavor, and for this reason I always keep a small batch of good-quality black peppercorns to use whole in brews, such as my **Kenyan Masala Chai** (see page 32), in homemade spice blends or to pour into my pepper grinder for daily use.

BERBERE SPICE

This captivating spice blend is an important characteristic of Ethiopian and Eritrean cooking, used in stews, like the famous bubbling lava that is **Berbere Chicken Stew** (see page 86), the region's most famous chicken stew. With a mix of dried red chilies and a host of fragrant spices, Berbere spice is wonderful added to just about anything from tomato sauces for pasta, to meatballs, vegetable roasts and stewed lentils or legumes. I always have a jarful, which I reach for at least once a week.

CURRY SPICES

Three types of curry spice blends feature in this book. Sweet and heady **garam masala**, which I most often use in East African- and South African-inspired recipes, fragrant **Caribbean-style curry spice** with allspice (pimento), which is most commonly used in Nigerian and West African curries, and **Smoky African Curry Spice** (see page 268)—my special blend, which combines the headiness and fragrance of

both curries with a bewitchingly smoky aroma and flavor from added paprika and the wonderful grains of selim.

CALABASH NUTMEG

Calabash nutmeg is an interesting African variety of nutmeg. Larger than the more widely known nutmeg, it has a smooth outer layer which reveals a coarse bean-like pod inside. It is woody and aromatic and is a major component in Nigerian pepper soup. I would advise against using regular nutmeg as a substitute in your **Pepper Soup Spice Blend** (see page 271).

FENNEL SEED & ANISEED

Fennel is one of my favorite spices. Aromatic and wonderful, it can be used in place of aniseed, which is commonly used in West African cooking. While fennel seeds are greenish and long, aniseed is small and dark, and also much spicier in flavor. They are both wonderful in fish marinades and are essential spices in some of the spice blends in this book.

GRAINS OF PARADISE

This is a most indulgent alternative to black pepper. Pungent, aromatic, citrusy with hints of pepper and cardamom, grains of paradise are most closely related to alligator pepper, a coarse pod that houses similar pungent and peppery grains. It is commonly used in West African soups and stews, and is an important ingredient in traditional celebratory foods such as **Spiced Peanut Dip** (see page 40). In the UK, I buy what is sold as grains of paradise in place of alligator peppers, with a strong suspicion that the two are often confused for one another. I often use grains of paradise crushed as I would black pepper, in soups, stews and as a finishing pepper for its much more aromatic and flavorful characteristics. You can simply pour it in a pepper grinder for daily use.

GRAINS OF SELIM / SELIM PEPPER

This is one of my favorite spices: a long, dark, smoked pod with its mysteriously musky flavor

and aroma. It is known by many names—in my mother's Ibo/Igbo dialect in Nigeria, it is called *uda*, while in other parts of Africa it is known as Senegal or Kani pepper or Ethiopian pepper. In this book it is the magic ingredient in **Smoky Tomato & Date Jam** (see page 257) and in several soups and stews. Lightly smash it and drop into soups and stews, or place the pods in a bouquet garni and remove before serving. The pods can also be crushed or ground to a powder.

NIGERIAN PEPPER SOUP SPICE

This is one of the most popular spice blends in Nigerian soups, yet many do not know what it is made of. Many of us grow up only ever seeing this aromatic spice blend poured into a broth to make a soothing drinking soup. When I started writing about food, my mother and I went around the markets speaking to the women who sell and grind the individual spices that make up this blend. Since then, I have only ever ground my own. See **Pepper Soup Spice Blend** on page 271 for a simple recipe to get you started.

RAS EL HANOUT

Ras el hanout means "head of the shop" in Arabic. This spice mix is revered in North African cooking as the combination of the best of the spice merchant's collection. The majority of these spices traveled from India, Persia and other parts of Africa to Morocco. No one mix is the same, making this one of the best spice blends to tinker with to create your own amazing version. Although it is readily available in shops, I prefer to blend my own at home—a fragrant and floral, peppery and sweet blend with dried roses, lavender, allspice, aniseed and more (see page 269). This version, inspired by the blends found in Fez, is described by celebrated Moroccan chef Fatema Hal as an "Imperial blend" in her cookbook *Les Saveurs et Les Gestes*. Ready-made Ras el hanout is also easily available in stores and spice merchants. Use either or both types of blend interchangeably.

Paprika is one of the most used ingredients in this book. I love it. It is made from dried and ground red peppers of several varieties, and adds warmth and a depth of flavor. **Smoked paprika** is stronger tasting and imparts a rich flavor and smoky aroma to stews, roasts and marinades. I add it to jollof as it mimics the smoky flavors I love in the traditional jollof which is cooked over firewood or coals. Use it sparingly, as too much will leave a bitter taste in your dish. **Sweet paprika** is often labeled simply as paprika.

A host of other spices, including earthy **coriander**, warming **cumin**, piney and fruity **cardamom**, fragrant and sweet **cinnamon**, **cloves**, **nutmeg** and more, are essential to many recipes in this book.

This wonderful West African blend of ground peanuts and spices imparts a warming and deeply aromatic flavor to everything from roasts and grills to salads and stews. You can find my recipe on page 272.

GRAINS & PULSES

Attiéké is a popular staple in the Ivory Coast and its neighboring countries in West Africa. Couscous-like in texture, it is fermented, grated and steamed cassava (yucca). Popularly served with a fresh and chunky tomato, onion and chili salad or sauce called moyo, a kind of **Sauce Piment** (see page 259), attiéké is often sold precooked, and the locals steam it further on the stove top or in the microwave. In **African Grain Salad** (see page 164), I use garri—unfermented dried and ground cassava—and sometimes use nutty fonio instead.

Although often called peas, **black-eyed peas** are actually beans, and are one of the most popular staple foods across Africa. Having traveled across the continent through slavery, they remain an important link between Africa and its diaspora. I often use dry legumes in slow-cooked recipes, as I prefer the taste and texture. I also keep a supply of black-eyed bean flour, gram flour (a mix of lentil and chickpea flour) and canned or jarred legumes for quick bakes, dips and salads. I often substitute black-eyed beans for chickpeas, especially in recipes like **Bean Tarts** *Moin Moin* (see page 56) and **Àkàrà** (see page 44).

Fonio, as it is called in Senegal, is also known as *acha* in northern Nigeria and is one of the most important and enduring heritage grains in West Africa. It is commonly found in Nigeria, Mali, Senegal, Burkina Faso and Guinea. Western explorers ignorantly called it "hungry rice," when in fact it is a sustainable produce that grows well under difficult conditions or drought, providing sustenance, especially during periods of food scarcity in between harvests. Africans are proud of this product and are increasingly producing and exporting this fine grain. It can be steamed like attiéké and used as a gluten-free alternative to couscous. The mellow and nutty, fast-growing and drought-resistant minuscule grains have also been found in the tombs of pharaohs in Egypt, proving they have been considered precious for thousands of years—in this life and the next.

Rice is an important ingredient and a staple in much of African cooking. Different regions grow a variety of wonderful local grains, yet the most used rices are imported long-grain, basmati and jasmine rice. Although I have used these three types in this book, I urge you to explore more heritage grains, if possible, as hopefully this will boost the economies of the countries producing them as demand increases. See leratofoods.com for updates on my discoveries.

A heritage grain native to the Horn of Africa, **teff** is a grass species and one of the earliest domesticated plants in the area. These mildly nutty, tiny seeds are ground and cooked as a porridge or patiently fermented and cooked like a pancake to become injera. The distinctively spongy and sour bread is a popular conduit for almost all meals in the area.

CHILIES

If proverbs are the palm oil with which words are eaten, chilies are the fires that keep the memories of the feast alive in our mouths and in our hearts.

There are many kinds of chilies and, in this book, I stick to just a handful with varying flavors and degrees of heat. Always stemmed but seldom deseeded, unless otherwise stated, leave the chilies with seeds and membranes attached if you want more intensity and heat. To temper the heat, use a spoon or the edge of a knife to scrape off the seeds and the attached membrane, which holds all the fire. If you are trying to discover your heat tolerance, don't be afraid to build layers of heat slowly by starting with a little less chili, tasting, then adding more.

For less heat, pierce the chili and drop it into your soup or stew to release some of its heat, then remove halfway through cooking or just before serving. Mince the cooked chili or grind with oil and serve alongside your meals or give it a rinse and use it in homemade chili oil.

There are so many ways to use chilies. Play around and discover your favorites—mix and match different varieties for nuanced flavors.

DRIED CHILIES

These are a great store-cupboard ingredient. You can grind them to make your own chili flakes and powder, like in **Berbere Spice Blend** (see page 273). Remove the seeds if a recipe calls for it, to remove their bitter taste, or reduce the amount if there are far too many. Toast the chilies for a few minutes to release their aromatic oils before grinding to a powder. To blend dried chilies for marinades or sauces, rehydrate them first by soaking in a bowl filled with hot water. Leave to soak for 20–30 minutes until softened. Drain and blend as needed.

I have used a variety of dried chilies in the spice blends in the book for their nuanced flavors and heat, while using some others for standout hot sauces. Feel free to swap chilies around or use your preferred mild, medium or hot varieties.

Kashmiri—Mild and smoky, with a deep vibrant red color, these chilies are popularly used in South Asian recipes and impart a lovely, deep color and warmth to any dish.

Guajillo—Mexican dried chilies, they can be mild to medium and have a brick red hue and a fruity, berry-like flavor.

New Mexico Chilies—On the mild scale with earthy and subtle sweet flavors.

Cayenne—Hot and smoky chili peppers used in the **Blackened Red Pepper Sauce** (see page 52).

FRESH CHILIES

African Bird's Eye—or "pili pili" (which means pepper pepper in Swahili) as they are called in East and Central Africa—are slim and pointed chilies that will truly bring fire to any dish. They are either long or short. Swap 1 scotch bonnet for 1 long bird's eye chili.

Finger or Indian chilies are bigger, hot and tart, typically used green in curries, marinades and salads. This is my favorite chili for samosa, jams and chutneys. You can use this as a hotter choice when a recipe calls for green chilies.

Jalapeños can range from warm to hot. They can be used as a milder choice when green chilies are called for. Similar nondescript varieties of red and green chilies are sold just as "chilies" in supermarkets.

Scotch bonnet peppers are a wonderful hot chili pepper with a distinctive sweet and aromatic flavor. Cherry shaped, they come in fully ripened red, fruity yellow and tart green varieties. I especially love the yellow or orange-hued scotch bonnets, as they impart a fruity flavor to stews and marinades.

Similar in flavor to scotch bonnets, **habaneros** are larger and less wrinkly. You may have bought habanero labeled as scotch bonnet and vice versa more often than you think! Although both chilies are interchangeable, I suggest being conscious of the size of the chili and how it may affect your desired heat level.

HERBS & EDIBLE FLOWERS

African basil is also known as clove basil and is wildly fragrant with distinctively jagged edges. The herb is native to regions across Africa and the African diaspora, including Haiti and Jamaica. It is also used in Gujarati, Sri Lankan and Thai cooking. In Nigeria it is called *scent leaf*; in Hawaii it is called wild basil. In recipes that call for African basil or scented leaves, you can use Thai basil or basil instead.

In this book, soft herbs such as the peppery **cilantro**, fragrant **parsley**, **basil** and woodsy **dill** are also commonly used in fritters, for sauces and salads, and as a garnish. Stronger herbs like **thyme**, **bay** and **rosemary** are used to add incredible flavor to a variety of recipes.

Although glossy and aromatic **curry leaves** are synonymous with South Asian and Southeast Asian cooking, my first experience of curry leaves was plucking them from the garden for Mum's stews. To use them in your cooking, lightly fry to flavor oil, blend into marinades, throw into stews, or temper in oil and whole spices and pour over curries or chutneys like the **Coconut, Ginger & Tamarind Chutney** (see page 258).

Dried edible roses are wonderful and fragrant in spice blends, such as **Imperial Ras el Hanout** (see page 269), and are beautiful scattered over heady lamb dishes, chocolate cakes and fragrant puddings, like **Sinful Bread Pudding** (see page 238).

Hibiscus is a flowering plant with many varieties common in tropical and subtropical regions. It is closely related to the okra plant. The petals fall off, leaving behind the calyx (often called flowers), which are harvested, dried and mostly used in tisanes. Across Africa it is celebrated for being rich in antioxidants and vitamin C. It is also known as Jamaican sorrel and used in *agua de Jamaica* served across Mexico. Quite a few recipes in this book call for dried red hibiscus, which I grew up drinking as a refreshing brewed cold drink before eventually creating savory recipes and desserts with the slightly tart reddish/crimson calyxes. Some recipes call for the whole dried hibiscus and some call for ground dried hibiscus (it is possible to make your own, by grinding the whole calyxes to a fine powder using a coffee grinder). Hibiscus can be bought as dried whole calyxes, ready-ground or as a loose-leaf tea.

Makrut or **Thai lime leaves** are wonderfully aromatic leaves of the makrut lime fruit, a variety of lime with a rough-textured knobbly skin, native to tropical Southeast Asia and southern China. It was brought over to Africa and is now popularly used in Madagascar, Mauritius and surrounding island nations. The leaves are a dark, vibrant green and strong scented. They are sliced and used in soups and stews or blended into curries. In this book, I grind the leaves to create the aromatic **Paradise Spice** (see page 270), a fragrant blend that will transport you to paradise. Makrut lime leaves can be bought fresh or frozen, dried or as a ground powder. See **Cook's Tips** on page 274 for more.

Saffron is a wonderful spice with crimson hay-like threads and a carotenoid pigment responsible for the golden yellow tone it imparts to food. Famously called the most expensive spice in the world (by weight), this is a store-cupboard must-have in my home and is essential in quite a few fragrant recipes in this book. Be discerning in sourcing saffron, as an increasing number of merchants dye threads or corn silks with turmeric and red dyes, flooding the food market with these. Real saffron should be a deep dark red, smell floral, and hold much of its color even when soaked.

FRUITS & VEGETABLES

Garden eggs/eggplants/West African aubergines (also known as **Thai eggplants**) are much smaller than the large purple eggplants we are used to in North African and Middle Eastern cooking. They are more egglike in shape, hence the name "eggplants." They can be white, cream, reddish or green in color, sometimes eaten raw, roasted, boiled or steamed and added to sauces like my **Grandma's Garden Egg & Sautéed Tomatoes** (see page 82).

A variety of **greens** from **spinach**, **taro leaves**, **amaranth**, **pumpkin leaves** and more are used in African cooking. Although I adore amaranth, especially the red-hued variety, I have better access to spinach, **Swiss** and **rainbow chard**, and **kale** at home in the UK. Feel free to swap greens around and cook with whatever is most accessible to you.

Groundnuts, also known as **peanuts**, are an essential ingredient in a lot of West African recipes. Not only enjoyed boiled or roasted as a snack, they are often roasted and used in soups, stews and spice rubs, such as **My Decadent Peanut Stew** (see page 78) or the famous **Sizzling Suya** (see page 116). In this book, whole peanuts (ready roasted or roasted at home) and natural peanut butter are interchangeable in several recipes. You can stock up on both or make your own peanut butter at home. One of my favorite desserts, **Candied Peanut Butter Chocolate Cake** (see page 228), celebrates peanuts in three different layers. Although the strong flavor and aroma of roasted peanuts are wonderful and unique, you can replace them with milder almonds, cashews or your favorite nuts, and swap peanut butter for almond butter or even sesame seed paste (tahini) in marinades and sauces.

Unwaxed **lemons** and **limes** are used across the book to enliven marinades and sauces. Although limes are more tart in flavor, they can be used interchangeably with a mix of other citrus, such as oranges and clementines. I often include the zest as well, since therein lies most of the wonderful flavor in the oils. To extract as much juice as possible from a lemon or lime, press down on the fruit with your palm and roll against a chopping board before juicing. Although considered safe to eat, you can remove the wax from citrus fruits by pouring hot water over the fruit, then using a vegetable brush to clean it under running water. Dry it with a cloth before use.

Okra/okro is predominantly grown in West Africa, Ethiopia and South Asia, with its pods eaten in various cuisines around the world. The sweet and grassy pods of the mallow family are known for their mucilaginous texture. Okra can be fried, boiled or roasted. In soups and stews, cut it into chunks and cook for a minimal amount of time for minimal slime. You could also cover the pods in vinegar and soak them for 30 minutes before using. Rinse, then cook as the recipe requires. For maximum slime, grate before adding to your soup or stew.

I have a strong preference for **Romano peppers** or long peppers. In West Africa, a similar variety known as *tatashe* tends to be slightly warmer in heat and shorter in length. This is the pepper that gives jollof its appealing rouge hue. **Red bell peppers** are a suitable alternative.

Plantains are a staple in my diet, at our cookery classes and across the African continent (see pages 277–80 for **How to Cook Plantains**). A member of the banana family, plantain has a starchy nature that makes it difficult to digest without cooking. They develop over time from green, starchy and unripe, to yellow, sweet, soft and ripe, before slowly turning black, softer and much sweeter.

Tamarind is a wonderful fruit enjoyed for its sweet and sour flavor. It is an important ingredient in several recipes in this book. It is used across Africa in a variety of ways—in soups and stews and in chutneys. I use tamarind paste, which is thick, dark and easy to add to dishes, but you can also buy tamarind as a block which needs to be diluted in hot water and strained for any seeds. My recipes call for the paste but watch out for pastes with added ingredients, such as vinegar and salt, and adjust your seasoning with this in mind.

Originally from Asia, **ginger** and **garlic** are common ingredients in many African stews, sauces and marinades. Dried ginger is a major export of Nigeria. Recipes in this book call for fresh garlic and ginger, as well as dried garlic and ginger granules. If using organic ginger, I do not bother peeling the skin but if you prefer to peel, simply use the curved side of the spoon to scrape the skin off without wasting too much of the ginger.

A relative of ginger, **turmeric** is an important root spice in curries. Its vivid yellow hue is responsible for the golden color of my **South African Yellow Rice** (see page 212) and many more recipes in this book. Native to the Asian subcontinent, it is now also predominantly grown in Polynesia and across Africa.

Yam is a long tuber common in West African cooking. Its bark is dark, rough and fibrous, while the white or cream flesh is similar to a potato. Like cassava, it is often boiled, fried or roasted, and is served as an accompaniment to stews and soups like *Egusi* (see page 74) or added to thicken soups. When buying yam in West Africa, we would typically ask for the ends to be cut open and for the yams to be cut in half, to inspect the white flesh for any signs of rotting. Kindly ask your grocer to do this before taking a large tuber home. Although we would not call it *fufu*, in this book, **"Pounded" Yam** (see page 74) serves as an example of *fufu*—a pounded or cooked mash or dough made from cooked cassava or cassava flour, maize meal, plantains and more.

Cassava or manioc is commonly known as yucca in South America. Like other produce, such as chilies and cacao, it was introduced to Africa by Portuguese explorers, and the manioc plant has since become a major food source across the continent. It looks like a slim sweet potato, with dark brown bark and fibrous white flesh. It is often boiled, fried, roasted or processed into a flour and used as one of the many varieties of *fufu*, a pounded or cooked mash served alongside soups and stews.

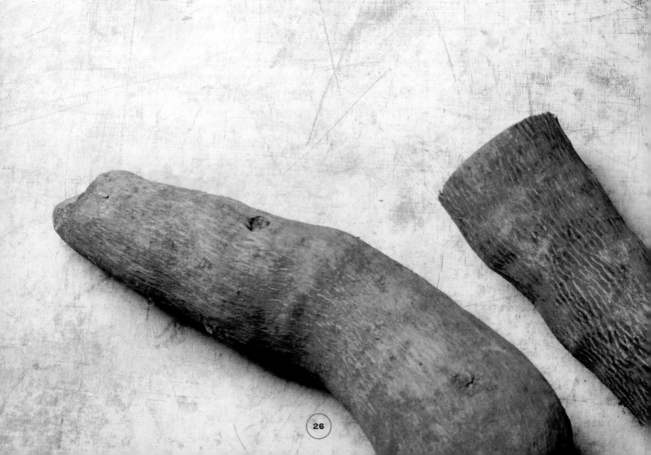

OTHER STORE-CUPBOARD INGREDIENTS

Baobab is one of the most extraordinary trees in the world. Native to Madagascar and mainland Africa, it has large, hollow trunks and leaves like crowns. It is also known as the Tree of Life. One of the oldest trees in the world, it provides shelter and food. Its zesty, berry-like fruits are readily available across Africa, while the dried powder form is sold all over the world. When dried, it can be kept for longer, sprinkled into soups and stews, brewed in teas and used in desserts and dressings, such as in my **Serengeti Salad** on page 168.

Coconut cream is a thick substance from the flesh of coconuts, and it contains more fat than **coconut milk**. Growing up in Nigeria, when it was time for coconut rice, several small coconuts would be cracked open, with the water set aside and the white meat cut out of the shell. The meat would be grated and mixed with the coconut water and extra water before being squeezed to extract as much coconut goodness as possible. Then the liquid would be set aside for the milk and thicker cream to separate. Now I just stock up on a good-quality unsweetened coconut cream and milk. Look at the back of the can or pack to see the percentage of coconut. The higher, the more delicious.

In the UK, **cornflour** is the starchy and finely milled flour known as cornstarch in many other parts of the world. It is great for thickening sauces and is used to help develop a crispier texture when frying.

In West African cooking, **crayfish** lend their pungent and briny flavor to many dishes. Crayfish are distinctively smaller than prawns and the clawed crayfish known in other lands. They can be reddish, brown or golden in color, and are usually salted and sundried or smoked. Dried shrimps are a good alternative. You could also dry prawns or shrimps in the oven until crisp, leave them to cool and blitz in a spice grinder or food processor.

Dates are sold fresh, dried, or in **molasses** or **date-syrup** form. I use all of these in my recipes. I love the rich, caramel flavor of date syrup, while fresh or rehydrated dates add a moist texture to cakes and banana bread. If using dried dates, rehydrate them by soaking in hot water for a few minutes, then drain and use as described in the recipe. Although dates have a much stronger flavor than honey, you can use honey as an alternative in baking and desserts.

Egusi, also called agushi in Ghana, are melon seeds from the gourd family. These are peeled, dried, crushed and used to thicken stews and soups. They are cream-colored versions of pumpkin seeds. In some parts of Nigeria, ground sesame seeds or sesame seed paste (tahini) is sometimes used as a richer and more luxurious alternative to egusi.

Africa produces some of the best **fair-trade teas**, **coffee** and **chocolate** in the world. Coffee was famously discovered on the continent by an Ethiopian goat herder called Kaldi. There is an increasing variety of great-quality fair-trade or fairly traded teas, coffee and chocolate, many sourced to support and encourage greater earnings for farmers and producers who are often exploited by international markets. I grew up with a mother who is obsessed with tea and this inspired my fascination. I even have a kettle with different temperature settings for various types of tea! For **Kenyan Masala Chai** (see page 32), I love to use a Kenyan black tea which produces a deep red and full-bodied liquor. Boiling loose-leaf tea for chai is the most brutal way I treat tea leaves, otherwise they are steeped in hot water for just a few minutes before straining and serving. The climate and rich soil in the East African highlands produce wonderful teas with varying flavor profiles, from chocolatey to floral.

Chocolate is an important ingredient at my feasts, a bittersweet treat and a topic that inspires a lot of great conversation and opportunity for learning. The largest supply of cocoa in the world comes from West Africa. Although an increasing number of small-scale producers and chocolatiers are working with farmers to supply the best-quality cocoa at fairer prices, there is still a long way to go.

Cocoa is mostly produced for the demanding export market and sadly not really affordable to those who produce it.

I adore **harissa** paste in almost everything, from fish stews to marinades and dips. I find store-bought brands in the West to be much milder than harissa from North Africa, so I make my own at home with a mix of milder dried chilies and hotter dried or roasted chilies. Hibiscus and harissa are a wonderful combination and I hope you enjoy it not only with fish, as seen in my **Slow-Roasted Salmon** dish on page 139, but also in your favorite roasts and dips. Find my recipes for **Red Harissa** and a verdant variation with green chilies and herbs on page 260.

Maize meal or cornmeal is a coarsely ground variety of corn used across Africa. It is also called cornflour outside the UK and is used for stiff doughs and porridges, especially loved in East and Central Africa. This is what is used for the popular *mealie pap* in South Africa, *posho* in Uganda, *nsima/nshima* in Malawi and Zambia respectively, and *ugali* in Kenya and Tanzania. See how to cook with maize meal in **Cheesy Maize Meal Cakes "Mealies"** (see page 202).

Moringa is an enduring tree popular in Africa and the Asian subcontinent. Its leaves and seeds are thought to be highly medicinal and are used in soups and stews as well as tisanes. The green leaves are commonly dried and found in a variety of delicacies. While it's becoming quite fashionable now, it has always been a readily available ingredient with the trees dotted around many homes. If you have access to the leaves, enjoy them in soups and stews, otherwise you can find the powder and use it to sprinkle into sauces, dressings and drinks.

Preserved lemons are a staple in North African cooking and are now widely available outside the region. Pickled in salt, these lemons are wonderful in salads, roasts and stews. With less intense zest and more depth of flavor than fresh lemons, they are uniquely fragrant. I like to use the entire fruit but be mindful of the salt when cooking—you can rinse them before use.

Beneseed, also known as **sesame seeds**, are a great staple in Africa and a brilliant export crop enjoyed across the world in various forms, from paste (tahini) and seeds used in breads, to Japanese *furikake* seasoning and the much-loved Chinese black sesame paste, enjoyed as a pudding or for breakfast. The nutty paste of ground sesame seeds commonly sold as **tahini** is a versatile store-cupboard favorite that I keep handy. The paste is used to make sesame cookies, also known as bene cookies, not only in Nigeria but across the pond as African culture traveled with its people to the United States and the diaspora. I love using the paste as a nut-free alternative and to enrich dressings, such as in **Black-Eyed Pea Salad** (see page 165), or in sauces such as the **Fish in Sesame Sauce** (see page 156).

I love to use **rose water** and **orange blossom water** in syrups for pancakes, ice cream, desserts, drinks and savory dishes, inspired by my love for North African cooking.

The **stock** I use most often is a low-salt vegan bouillon, as I find it easiest when cooking for a variety of diets, but I will sometimes use homemade beef or chicken stock for specific recipes that call for them. To make vegetable stock, I blend sautéed or roasted carrots, onions and garlic to a puree and keep it in the freezer to use as and when it is needed. I try to use the best-quality stock available as it makes such a big difference to the flavor of the finished dish.

Vanilla is thought to be the second most expensive spice in the world, and Madagascar and neighboring Comoros produce some of the best-quality vanilla beans in the world. Its flowers are human-pollinated and the closest in flavor notes to its native plant is a variety in Mexico, which is pollinated by bees. Vanilla from Madagascar is also known as bourbon vanilla, for its rich and smoky sweet flavor and aroma. Uganda also produces wonderfully creamy vanilla beans with a more mellow flavor profile than the bourbon vanilla. If you can't get hold of a vanilla pod, the seeds of 1 pod equals 1 tablespoon of vanilla paste.

Drinks, Dips & Sharing Plates

Kenyan Masala Chai

SERVES 4

I adore chai, which means tea in Hindi, a derivative of the Chinese word for tea, *cha*. This recipe is inspired by the wonderful pots of spiced tea I enjoyed in Kenya. Kenyan masala chai enjoyed across East Africa is a joyous brew of black tea, spices and aromatics. A legacy of the deeply embedded relationship between Indian and East African foods, as a result of the trade winds that blew across the Indian Ocean and into Africa. The whiff of warming ginger and spices brewing is enough to set one at ease, ready for a relaxing teatime. While I love strong teas sweetened with honey instead of sugar, this recipe allows you to temper the strength of the tea and spices, tailoring its sweetness to your liking.

2 tbsp Kenyan fair-trade black loose-leaf tea
2-inch piece of ginger, slightly smashed
2 cinnamon sticks
1 tsp black peppercorns
6 green cardamom pods
4 cloves
750ml milk

TO SERVE
Light brown sugar or your favorite sweetener

YOU WILL NEED
Small fine mesh strainer

1. Place the tea, ginger and whole spices in a saucepan with 750ml water and bring to a rolling boil. Reduce the heat and simmer for 10 minutes, until the tea and spices are wonderfully fragrant and the water slightly reduced.

2. Pour in the milk and bring back to a boil. Reduce the heat ever so slightly to maintain a steady but strong simmer for up to 10 minutes, stirring occasionally. Keep a close eye as your chai will boil over in the blink of an eye. Keep stirring to prevent the froth from rising. You can remove the pan from the heat as soon as it threatens to erupt, then swiftly return to the heat to continue simmering. As the chai simmers, a skin will form on the top. This is normal and will be strained with the solids.

3. Taste to check the strength and lighten with a splash of milk if it is too strong, or boil for a few more minutes if it is too weak. Strain into another pan or heatproof jug, discarding the solids.

4. Serve immediately with sugar or your sweetener of choice and the perfect companion of **Black Pepper & Vanilla Chai Shortbread** (see page 250).

Bisaap
Spiced Hibiscus & Ginger

MAKES ABOUT 2 LITERS

My first memory of *bisaap* was in Benin, a francophone country neighboring Nigeria where I spent my early teens. Kids and adults alike would rush to the lady holding a bucket sitting on top of a tightly wrapped cloth resting on her head as she called out, "*Bisaap! Bisaap!*" She would gracefully lower her bucket and distribute crimson-colored frozen blocks of hibiscus juice wrapped in cellophane. We would each buy a bag or two and rinse it with water before biting off the tip to quench our thirst with elated desperation. It was always so refreshing, with a little heat lingering on the lips and at the back of the tongue from the generous amount of warming ginger. Zesty and a little tart, hibiscus is a cross between cranberry and pomegranates; it was like nothing I had ever tasted and I fell in love instantly! My version is naturally sweetened with pineapple and apples, fragrant and warming with spices and ginger.

100g dried hibiscus
100g piece of ginger, roughly chopped
1 pineapple, peeled, cored and cut into small chunks
3 sweet apples, cored and cut into small chunks
6 clementines or 3 sweet oranges, peeled, segmented and deseeded
6 cloves
2 cinnamon sticks
1 star anise

TO SERVE
1 orange, 1 lemon and 1 lime, thinly sliced
Light brown sugar or your favorite sweetener (optional)
Champagne or rum (optional)

YOU WILL NEED
A fine mesh strainer or cheesecloth

1. Place the dried hibiscus in a colander and rinse briefly under cold running water to remove any debris (be careful not to rinse for too long or it will lose its wonderful crimson hue). Drain and set aside.

2. Place all the remaining ingredients in a large pot and pour in 2 liters water. Bring to a boil, then reduce the heat and simmer steadily for 25 minutes.

3. Add the hibiscus and simmer for a further 10 minutes.

4. Remove from the heat and leave to steep for up to 30 minutes or until cool.

5. Using a fine mesh strainer or cheesecloth, strain the liquid into a large bowl. Discard the spices but pick the chunks of ginger, pineapple, clementine and apple from the strainer and place them in a food processor. Blend to a puree, then pour this through a clean strainer and squeeze out all the wonderful juice. Add this to the hibiscus drink and discard the pulp.

6. Place the citrus slices in a jug, pour in the juice and chill in the fridge before serving. Sweeten, if you like, or serve with a dash of rum or top with champagne, as I do at dinner parties, Christmas and New Year!

Variation
For a warm drink or tea, reheat in a saucepan over a medium heat.

Golden Chermoula & Yogurt Dip

SERVES 4–6 AS SHARING PLATES

500g Greek yogurt
1 fat garlic clove, peeled and
    crushed
4–6 tbsp **Golden Chermoula**
    (see page 261)
Extra-virgin olive oil, to drizzle
20g fresh dill, leaves picked (mint
    or flat-leaf parsley leaves are
    excellent substitutes)
Dried edible rose petals, to garnish

Creamy yogurt is the perfect conduit for herbaceous and wonderfully spiced chermoula. Serve this with your favorite roasts or grills, or enjoy as a dip alongside various recipes in this book, such as **Smoky Eggplants & Sautéed Tomatoes** (see page 42), **Kefta with Spiced Butter** (see page 128) or the **Harissa Leg of Lamb with Hibiscus & Cumin Salt** (see page 132). Substitute Greek yogurt for coconut yogurt, or your preferred dairy-free yogurt.

1. Place the yogurt and garlic in a bowl. Season to taste with sea salt flakes and black pepper and whisk to combine.

2. Spoon the yogurt onto a shallow bowl or deep plate and flatten slightly. Spoon the chermoula onto the yogurt and press in with a spoon to make "wells." Drizzle with oil and scatter over the dill and dried rose petals.

3. Serve right away or store tightly covered in the fridge if serving later.

Hibiscus & Pomegranate "Chapman"

MAKES ABOUT 1 LITER

Chapman is a classic drink of my childhood. My friends and I always felt so grown up drinking these at Ikoyi Club, a country club in Lagos, where it famously originates. Technically a nonalcoholic punch with the distinct mix of flavored soda, pomegranate-bursting grenadine and Angostura bitters, the original version is rumored to have been a concoction created by a bartender at Ikoyi Club as a special request for his favorite customer who happened to be called Chapman. Although there are other contradictory tales of its origins, the legacy lives on and I am thrilled to share it with you. I have included two distinctive recipes, one with my own homemade fruit soda and hibiscus syrup mix, and a version closer to the classic, which uses sparkling juice and grenadine for its distinctive rouge tint. Cheers!

500ml soda water
125ml fresh pomegranate juice
   (1 medium pomegranate)
125ml fresh orange juice
   (2 oranges)
125ml fresh lemon juice
A few dashes Angostura bitters
1 lemon, sliced
1 lime, sliced
¼ cucumber, sliced

TO SERVE
125ml **Hibiscus Syrup** (see page
   267) or grenadine syrup
Crushed ice
Seeds of 1 pomegranate
A few small sprigs of mint

1. Pour the soda water and fruit juices into a large jug and mix. Add the Angostura bitters, tasting after a few dashes. Reserve a slice of the lemon, lime and cucumber for each glass, then place the rest in the jug. Store in the fridge until chilled and ready to serve.

2. Divide the **Hibiscus Syrup** evenly between the glasses. Add a small amount of ice (we don't want this marvelous concoction watered down), a slice of lemon, lime, cucumber and a teaspoon of pomegranate seeds to each glass and top with the chilled juice. Finish with a sprig of mint. Mix your cocktail before drinking.

Variation
To make an **Original-style Chapman**, you'll need 500ml sparkling orange juice, 500ml sparkling lemon-lime juice, a few dashes of Angostura bitters, 125ml grenadine syrup, 1 lemon, sliced, 1 lime, sliced, ¼ cucumber, sliced, and some crushed ice. Mix as above. Divide the grenadine between the glasses. Divide the citrus and cucumber between the jug and the glasses and chill in the fridge before serving. Serve as above, or mix all the ingredients in the jug before serving.

Lerato's Tip
If the syrup is too thick, heat for 15 seconds in the microwave to loosen or in a saucepan with a little water added. Leave to come up to room temperature before using. To minimize diluting your drink, you can also freeze soda or juice into ice cubes instead of adding ice.

Twice-Cooked Yam & Cassava Chips

WITH CHILI AND LIME SALT

Golden and crispy on the outside, yet fluffy and tender inside, these chips originate from a recipe I have adapted from Tauntie Justine's twice-fried yam chips. *Tauntie* (which means auntie) was the family cook of our friends the d'Almeidas in the Republic of Benin, with whom we lived while in my early teens. She ruled the kitchen like a gendarmerie (drill sergeant). I remember her firm yet high-pitched call to eat, *"Viens manger, les enfants!"* Instead of splashing water into the cooking oil like Tauntie Justine bravely did, my twice-cooked yam and cassava chips are first blanched in warm oil, then fried at a higher temperature for that tender interior and golden crisp finish. I love serving the chips with a lip-puckering chili and lime salt, inspired by the vibrant Kenyan and Tanzanian *muhogo* (Swahili for the fried cassava chips popularly sold in the street markets). Fresh out of the hot oil, the chips are typically served with chili salt and a dash of lime squeezed on top. My chili and lime salt is an explosion of flavors, perfect not only for the yam and cassava chips but as a condiment, too.

250g puna yam
250g cassava (yucca)
Vegetable oil, for frying

FOR THE CHILI AND LIME SALT
1 tbsp sea salt flakes
½ tsp chili powder or cayenne
    pepper
Zest of 1 lime
¼ tsp ground turmeric

1. To prepare the chili and lime salt, crush the sea salt flakes with a mortar and pestle, then mix in a small bowl with the chili powder, lime zest and turmeric. Leave to sit until ready to serve. The fragrant oils from the lime zest will infuse into the salt flakes.

2. Half fill two large bowls with cold water to soak the yams and cassava immediately after peeling. This helps to prevent oxidization, which would cause the tubers to turn brown. From the center of the yam tuber, cut 1-inch discs weighing around 250 grams in total. The end of the tuber can be bitter, and the slimmer tips are usually less starchy. Carefully score and peel the dark bark. Cut into thick chips and swiftly drop into one of the bowls of water. Rinse thoroughly, rubbing with your palms until the slippery starchy feel is no more. Rinse again, fill the bowl with fresh water and leave to soak while you prepare the cassava.

3. Cut the ends off the cassava, then cut the tuber into 3 or 4 chip-length chunks, as this will be easier to tackle. Score the length of each piece and peel off the dark bark and the second layer of skin using your thumb and knife simultaneously. Cut each piece in half and carefully carve out the fibrous center. Cut your desired portion into 1-inch-thick chips and rinse thoroughly in the second bowl of cold water. Refill the bowl with clean water and leave to soak.

4. Half fill a large, heavy-based saucepan with oil and heat to 300°F (see page 275). Line two baking trays with kitchen paper and set aside.

5. Drain the yam chips and pat dry. Use a large, slotted spoon to lower a few chips at a time into the warm oil and cook in small batches to avoid overcrowding. At this temperature, the chips will blanch and become tender, rather than fry. Cook for 6–7 minutes, until softened but not browned. Using a slotted spoon, transfer the chips onto one of the prepared trays to drain. Repeat until all the yam chips are blanched.

6. Raise the temperature of the oil to 350°F (see page 275). Lower the blanched chips into the oil and fry for 5 minutes, or until wonderfully golden brown and crisp. Using a slotted spoon, transfer to the second prepared tray. Repeat to fry the remaining batches.

7. Fry the cassava as above.

8. Serve the freshly fried chips with the **Chili and Lime Salt** in a dipping bowl and a teaspoon for sprinkling.

Baby Eggplants

WITH SPICED PEANUT DIP

SERVES 6-8

Usher in good fortune with this spiced peanut dip. This joyous food of our ancestors is a traditional delicacy of the Igbo/Ibo tribe and is enjoyed across Nigeria at celebratory events. At many Nigerian weddings you'll find the elders dipping raw garden eggs (small eggplants, also known as Thai eggplants) into bowls of spiced peanut butter as they chant prayers for prosperity and fertility. You could also roast the eggplants, as I do, for a wonderful buttery texture. I use grains of paradise here, similar to the peppery seeds of *osé oji*, or alligator pepper, which is a unique West African spice (see page 20).

FOR THE EGGPLANTS

8-10 baby eggplants, sliced open crossways (but not all the way through), leaving stalks attached
1 tsp paprika
3 tbsp peanut, olive or vegetable oil

FOR THE SPICED PEANUT DIP

350g unsalted roasted peanuts, or 275g crunchy or smooth peanut butter
3 garlic cloves, peeled
1-inch piece of ginger, peeled and roughly chopped
2-4 tbsp peanut, olive or vegetable oil
1 tsp sea salt flakes, crushed, or ½ tsp fine sea salt
1 tsp paprika
A good grating of nutmeg, or ¼ tsp ground nutmeg
2-3 tsp freshly ground grains of paradise or black pepper
½-2 tsp chili flakes (to taste)

TO SERVE

Smoked salt or **Smoky Selim Salt** (see page 266), to taste
Small handful of scented leaves (e.g., African clove basil, Thai basil, or flat-leaf parsley), torn
50g roasted peanuts, chopped

1. Preheat the oven to 425°F and line a baking tray with baking parchment.

2. To make the spiced peanut dip, combine the peanuts, garlic and ginger in a food processor. Blend for 1 minute, then scrape down the sides. Add a little of the oil and blend again for another minute. Repeat this process up to 5 times, until the nuts are your desired texture (crumbly, chunky or creamy). Season with the salt, paprika and nutmeg, then add the grains of paradise and chili flakes, a teaspoon at a time. Taste and add more, if you like, until it is wonderful.

3. Season the insides of the eggplants with sea salt flakes, black pepper and the paprika. Arrange on the prepared tray and stuff some spiced peanut dip inside each one. Keep the remaining dip to serve alongside.

4. Drizzle the oil over the eggplants and bake for 15-20 minutes, until tender.

5. Sprinkle with a little smoked salt and serve on a platter with the remaining spiced peanut dip in a bowl alongside. Scatter over the torn scented leaves and chopped roasted peanuts to serve.

Lerato's Tip

For allergy sufferers, this recipe can be made with sesame seed paste (tahini) instead of peanuts. Store the dip in an airtight container and refrigerate for up to 5 days. Or omit the garlic and ginger and store topped up with oil in a sterilized jar for up to a month. The dip will separate, so use a clean spoon to stir before serving. Add tablespoonfuls to hummus or use in **My Decadent Peanut Stew** (see page 78).

Zaalouk
Smoky Eggplants & Sautéed Tomatoes

SERVES 4–6 AS SHARING PLATES

I was lucky to meet a Dada in Marrakech who inspired this recipe. The Dadas, typically of sub-Saharan origin, are descendants of respected cooks of noble families in Morocco. They are known to hold the many secrets of traditional Moroccan cooking and Dada Fatiya taught me a method of peeling alternate vertical stripes from the skin of the eggplant before finely chopping it and frying it over a high heat. This is a technique I have since adopted and adapted for achieving smoky eggplants without grilling. Removing just a little of the skin allows the salad to retain a bit of bite, but you can leave the skin on or peel it entirely. Call it a salad or a dip, *zaalouk* can be chunky or smooth, and I love the flexibility this dish affords you. While I like a lot of tomatoes in my *zaalouk*, feel free to play around with your preferred ratio of eggplants to tomatoes.

125ml olive oil

2–3 large eggplants, peeled (see introduction) and cut into small cubes

4 garlic cloves, peeled and crushed

2 heaped tsp paprika

2 tsp ground cumin

½–1 tsp chili flakes

800g vine-ripened tomatoes, roughly chopped

3–4 tbsp lemon juice

TO SERVE

2–4 tbsp **Golden Chermoula** (see page 261) or a small handful of fresh cilantro or parsley leaves

1. Drizzle 4 tablespoons of the oil in a large heavy-based sauté or frying pan, for which you have a lid, and place over a medium–high heat. Once shimmering, add the eggplants and a generous pinch of fine sea salt. Sauté for 10 minutes, stirring often, until they have released their moisture and are golden brown.

2. Stir in the garlic, spices and chili flakes until fragrant. Remove from the heat, tip into a bowl and set aside.

3. Using the same pan, drizzle in the remaining oil and, once shimmering, add the tomatoes, scraping any spices stuck to the bottom of the pan. Cover with a lid and cook for 15–20 minutes over a medium heat, stirring frequently. Add some water if it looks dry, a tablespoon at a time.

4. Once the tomatoes have broken down, return the eggplants to the pan and season with a generous pinch of fine sea salt and black pepper. Cover and simmer for 10 minutes, stirring frequently.

5. Remove the lid and continue to cook until the liquid is absorbed, stirring frequently. Reduce the heat, if necessary, to prevent burning. (I love chunky *zaalouk*, but if you prefer a puree, mash the veggies using the back of a wooden spoon.) Stir in the lemon juice to taste and remove the pan from the heat.

6. Top with **Golden Chermoula** or scatter over fresh herbs, such as cilantro and parsley. Serve as a salad or as a dip with bread and crudités.

Lerato's Tip

You can grill the eggplants instead of frying. Cut each in half lengthways, brush with oil and grill skin-side up for 15 minutes, until the skin is scorched and the flesh is tender. Scoop out the flesh and discard the charred skin.

Ghanaian Eto
Smashed Plantains & Peanuts

WITH AVOCADO

SERVES 2-4

My friend Angie gushed about a much-loved dish she enjoyed as a child. Her grandma *Nana* would prepare a spicy plantain mash with peanut butter and boiled eggs. "No one can make *eto* like my grandma," she would say. There are several versions of this celebratory dish, most usually with mashed yams, plantains and even roasted *cocoyam* (taro). The ingredients are typically mashed in a clay pot known as *asanka* or *apotoyewa* by the Akan people, or *kaaa* by the Ga people of Ghana. In my version, the smoked paprika imparts a wonderful smokiness that replaces the traditionally used palm oil and salted smoked or dried fish. I'll whisper one of Angela's grandma Nana's secrets before you begin: use yellow, just-ripened plantains for the perfect texture and level of sweetness. Who are we to argue with an African grandma?

4 large ripe plantains, peeled (see page 277) and cut into chunks
4 free-range eggs
4 tbsp sustainable palm oil, plus extra for drizzling
1 small red onion, peeled and sliced
2 garlic cloves, peeled and crushed
½–1 scotch bonnet pepper, stemmed and roughly chopped
50g roasted peanuts, or 2 heaped tbsp crunchy peanut butter
1 tsp smoked paprika
1 tsp sea salt flakes or ½ tsp fine sea salt

TO SERVE
2 tbsp roasted peanuts, chopped
1 mild red chili, stemmed and finely sliced (optional)
Smoked salt or **Smoky Selim Salt** (see page 266), to taste
1 small avocado, peeled, destoned and sliced

Lerato's Tip
Peanuts can be replaced with cashews, almonds or sesame paste (tahini).

1. Place the plantains in a saucepan, cover with water and bring to a boil. Cook for 15–20 minutes until completely tender, adding the eggs partway through the cooking time (cook them for 6–8 minutes for soft boiled or 10–12 minutes for hard boiled). Use a slotted spoon to transfer the eggs into a bowl of cold water, then carefully drain the plantains. Return them to the pan and cover with a lid to keep warm.

2. Meanwhile, pour the oil into a small saucepan over a medium heat. Once it is sizzling, add the red onion and a pinch of sea salt and fry for 7–10 minutes, stirring occasionally, until softened. Remove them from the pan with a slotted spoon and set aside. Reserve the oil.

3. Place half the fried onion in a mortar or a small food processor with the garlic and scotch bonnet and grind to a puree. Add the roasted peanuts or peanut butter, smoked paprika and salt and grind to a coarse puree.

4. Place the puree in a large bowl. Add the plantains and mash everything together with 2–3 tablespoons of the red oil from the pan. Taste and season to perfection.

5. Transfer to a warm shallow bowl and use the back of a spoon to make "wells." Drizzle some of the cooking oil over and spoon the remaining fried onions on top.

6. Peel and halve the eggs and place on the mash. Scatter over the peanuts and chili, if you like a little more heat, and finish with a pinch of smoked salt on the egg yolks. Serve with the avocado slices alongside.

Àkàrà
Bean Fritters
WITH GINGER & SPRING ONIONS

SERVES 4

I adore *àkàrà*. These sumptuous, deep-fried fritters are enjoyed across West Africa and the diaspora. A true triumph for the humble black-eyed pea, they are known as *koose* in Northern regions and *acarajé* by custodians of West African culture in Brazil. I remember joyous mornings feasting on the classic duo of steaming hot *àkàrà* and Nigerian "pap"—a creamy custard made with fermented corn. In my version, ginger and spring onions add a little warmth and bite to the fritters. *Àkàrà* is wonderful served plain, stuffed in a baguette (as you'll find them in Dakar, Senegal), or stuffed with chunks of spiced prawns and peppers, as enjoyed in Salvador de Bahia, Brazil.

200g dried black-eyed peas, unpeeled or peeled (see page 274)
½ medium red onion, peeled and roughly chopped
½–1 scotch bonnet pepper, or 2–3 red chilies, stemmed and roughly chopped
1 red Romano or bell pepper, stemmed, deseeded and roughly chopped
1-inch piece of ginger, peeled and roughly chopped
2 tsp smoked paprika
¾ tsp fine sea salt
1 large free-range egg, beaten
5 spring onions, trimmed and sliced
Vegetable oil, for frying

1. Soak the beans for 8 hours or overnight in a large bowl filled with water.

2. Place the beans in a colander, drain, then rinse under running water. Tip into a food processor with the onion, scotch bonnet or chilies, red pepper and ginger and blend until smooth and thick. Pour in up to 60ml water to loosen the batter.

3. Pour into a bowl and add the smoked paprika, salt and egg and whisk vigorously for a few minutes. Gently fold in the spring onions.

4. Fill a nonstick frying pan with oil to a depth of about 2 inches and heat it to 350°F (see page 275). Scoop a heaped tablespoonful of batter and use a second tablespoon to help lower it into the oil, or use an ice cream scoop for ease. Repeat until you have a few fritters in the pan, being careful not to overcrowd them. Fry in batches for 3–4 minutes, turning occasionally, until golden and crisp.

5. Drain on kitchen paper and serve hot or at room temperature with **Sauce Piment** (see page 259).

Variation
Chickpeas or lentils are a great alternative to beans here. I always keep black-eyed pea, chickpea or gram flour handy for fritters, steamed puddings or for thickening sauces. For bean fritters, mix 200g bean or gram flour with 200–250ml water until thick and smooth, and blend with the remaining ingredients as above. If adding grated or finely chopped vegetables, be aware of the additional liquid content and fry them in very little oil for 3–5 minutes on each side.

Salmon & Green Pea Samosas

MAKES ABOUT 24

Freshly cooked, steaming hot samosas, or fondly called *sambusa* in East Africa, are utterly irresistible. When in Kenya, where beef samosas are quite popular and often made with a homemade pastry that comes out satisfyingly crisp, I kindly ask for a steady supply for breakfast, lunch and dinner! In Nigeria, samosas are part of the "small chops" platters of delectable snacks served at parties. For this recipe, I wanted a lighter and sweeter samosa. Fragrant fennel marries perfectly with the salmon and sweet green peas. Although I use spring roll wrappers, you can easily swap with filo pastry, doubling each sheet if need be.

2 tsp plain flour
1 500g pack 10-inch, square frozen
    spring roll wrappers, defrosted
Vegetable oil, for frying

FOR THE FILLING
1 medium potato, peeled and cut
    into ½-inch cubes
2 tbsp vegetable oil
1 tbsp unsalted butter
½ tsp cumin seeds, lightly crushed
½ tsp fennel seeds, lightly crushed
½ white onion, peeled and diced
2 fat garlic cloves, peeled and
    crushed
2-inch piece of ginger, peeled and
    grated
2 green chilies, stemmed and finely
    chopped
½ tsp ground turmeric
½ tsp ground cumin
1½ tsp garam masala
260g salmon fillets, skin removed,
    cut into small chunks
1 tbsp fresh lemon juice
120g peas, defrosted if frozen
10g fresh mint leaves, finely
    chopped

1. Bring a saucepan of salted water to a boil. Add the potato and cook for 5 minutes, until just tender. Drain and set aside.

2. Heat the oil and butter in a large sauté pan, for which you have a lid. Add the cumin and fennel seeds and, once fragrant, stir in the onion. Sprinkle over a pinch of fine sea salt and fry over a medium heat, stirring occasionally, until soft and golden. Add the garlic, ginger, chilies and ground spices and cook for 1 minute, stirring frequently.

3. Add the salmon chunks to the pan and mix thoroughly to coat in all the wonderful spices and aromatics. Season with a generous pinch of fine sea salt and some freshly ground grains of paradise or black pepper. Pour in the lemon juice and 90ml water, cover with a lid and cook over a low heat for 8–10 minutes, or until just cooked through.

4. Remove the lid and use a fork to break down the fish into shredded pieces. Add the potatoes and peas, stir to combine and cook uncovered to remove any excess liquid (you need a dry mixture). Remove from the heat and set aside to cool.

5. Fold in the mint leaves and season to perfection, if needed.

6. In a small bowl, mix the flour with 1–2 tablespoons water to create a thick but spreadable glue, which you will use to seal the samosas.

7. Prepare a clean and dry "workstation" for rolling the samosas.

8. Unwrap the spring rolls and delicately remove one wrapper, covering the rest with a clean kitchen towel to prevent drying out. Place the wrap on a flat surface and fold the top down in half to form a rectangle. Take the bottom left corner and fold up to form a triangle, with the remaining wrapper to the right. Now take the top left corner and fold over to the right to form another triangle. What remains of the wrap will look like a square.

9. Use your fingers or a teaspoon to spread a little flour paste onto the unfolded edge of the wrap. Lift up the top layer of wrap and fold over the triangle and press to seal. Spread a little paste onto the remaining unfolded half and fold up and press to seal. You will now have a triangular pouch. Fill the opening with a tablespoon of the filling, then spread some flour paste around the inner edge before sealing tightly. Repeat until all the filling is used up.

10. Preheat the oven to 280°F and line a tray with baking parchment or kitchen paper.

11. Pour about 1½ inch oil into a deep, heavy-based pan set over a medium heat (it should be 325°F—see page 275). Fry the samosas in batches for 4–5 minutes, turning over halfway through, until golden brown and crispy. Remove with a slotted spoon and drain on the prepared tray. Keep the fried batch warm in the oven while you finish frying the rest.

12. Leave to cool slightly before devouring, as they will be piping hot. Serve with **Coconut, Ginger & Tamarind Chutney** (see page 258). (See photo on page 48.)

Lerato's Tip

Make sure the filling is dry and completely cooled before filling the wrappers. Use mushrooms, such as chanterelles, instead of salmon, and a nondairy spread, instead of butter, for a vegan alternative. After cooking the aromatics and spices, add the mushrooms and sauté over a high heat to brown and cook through. Use two forks to shred the mushrooms into finer pieces and continue with the recipe.

Nigerian Meat Pies

MAKES ABOUT 10

Nigerian meat pies are unbelievably moreish. When I was taught to bake them as a child, we practiced with cute little pies and they were the most wonderful pouches of delight—perfect for sharing at picnics or for an African-inspired afternoon tea. Although typically baked with margarine because of its low melting point for a lovely flaky crust, I happily make mine with softened butter, kept cold until needed. I glaze my pies twice, allowing them to rest in the fridge between glazes for a lovely golden finish.

FOR THE DOUGH
500g plain flour
2 tsp baking powder
1 tsp fine sea salt
250g unsalted butter, cut into small cubes, chilled
2 large free-range eggs, whisked and chilled
60ml cold water

FOR THE FILLING
1 tbsp vegetable oil
1 medium white onion, peeled and diced
2 garlic cloves, peeled and finely grated
1 tsp grated fresh ginger
1 tsp thyme
1 tsp curry powder
350g beef mince
250ml strong beef stock
1 large or 2 medium potatoes (about 250g), peeled and diced
2 medium carrots, scrubbed and diced
2 tbsp plain flour
1 tsp fine sea salt
½ tsp freshly ground black pepper

FOR THE GLAZE
1 free-range egg yolk, beaten with 1 tsp water

1. To prepare the dough by hand, sift the flour, baking powder and salt into a large mixing bowl. Add the cubes of butter and use a table knife to cut the butter into the dough. Very gently rub the butter into the flour using your fingertips, lifting the mixture as you do, allowing it to fall back into the bowl, until it transforms into a breadcrumb-like texture. Create a well in the center and pour in the whisked egg. Use the knife to cut the egg in, adding 2 tablespoons of cold water at a time, until the dough starts to come together. Using your fingers, gently mix the dough until stiff and smooth.

   If using a food processor, sift the flour, baking powder and salt into your processor. Add the butter and whizz on a medium setting until a breadcrumb-like texture. Add the eggs and whizz for about 5 seconds, then slowly add water, 2 tablespoons at a time, until well combined and smooth.

2. Lightly dust a clean and dry work surface with flour, tip the dough onto it and gently and very briefly knead until smooth. Flatten the dough and place in a bowl. Cover tightly and chill in the fridge for at least an hour before using.

3. Meanwhile, to make the filling, heat the oil in a large frying pan over a medium heat. Add the onion and a pinch of fine sea salt and cook for 10 minutes, until golden. Add the garlic and ginger and fry for up to 1 minute, until fragrant, then stir in the thyme and curry powder.

4. Add the beef mince and cook for 5 minutes, until lightly browned, stirring constantly and pressing with the back of a spoon to break up into smaller pieces.

5. Pour in the stock and bring to a simmer. Add the potatoes and carrots, reduce the heat to medium-low, cover with a lid and simmer for 2 minutes, until the vegetables are almost cooked but still with a little bite.

6. Remove the lid and increase the heat to medium to cook off some liquid, without overcooking the potatoes and carrots. There should be a small amount of liquid left in the pan to create a moist filling.

7. Mix the flour with 2 tablespoons of water in a small bowl, then stir into the pan. Season with the sea salt and black pepper and simmer over a low heat for 2 minutes, until the filling is thickened. Check and adjust the seasoning, if needed, then remove from the heat and leave to cool completely.

8. Preheat the oven to 400°F and line a baking tray with baking parchment.

9. Roll the dough into a log and divide into 3 equal portions. Lightly flour a work surface. Flatten and roll each portion into a ¼-inch-thick disc. Using a small bowl about 5 inches wide and a small knife, cut out discs and place them on the prepared baking tray. Reroll any excess to make more. Repeat with all portions of dough.

10. Divide the filling between the discs, covering one half of the circle and leaving enough space to crimp the edges. Use your finger to wet the edges with a little water and carefully fold the dough in half to cover the filling. Lightly press to seal the pies, and finally, crimp with a fork.

11. Add a small pinch of fine sea salt to the beaten egg, then brush the surface of each pie. (If possible, place the baking tray in the fridge to chill for 10 minutes, then brush the pies with a second coating of egg wash before baking.)

12. Pierce each pie with a fork and place the tray in the middle of the oven to bake for 25–30 minutes, or until golden brown.

13. Serve warm or at room temperature. (See photo on page 49.)

Ewa Agoyin Black-Eyed Pea Mash
WITH BLACKENED RED PEPPER SAUCE

This is "street food" that affectionately became "home food" to me—black-eyed peas cooked until exceedingly tender, then mashed and served with burnt onions and a vivid and spicy pepper sauce with accompanying glowing red oil. I would recommend frying the onions almost to the point of burning for a crispy sweet finish to this dish. Although there was a complete ban on what my mother called "outside food," while at my father's, I yearned to wake up to the alluring calls of the Agoyin women, who chanted, *"Ewa Agoyin! Ewa Agoyin!* Come and buy, *Ewa Agoyin!"* as they circled around the houses. In Yoruba language, *ewa* simply means beans, while *Agoyin* refers to the Egun tribe of people who settled in Badagry (the infamous slave-trade hub) from neighboring Republic of Benin and Togo. I would rush down the steps in my pajamas, grabbing two wide plates as I ran outside. The Agoyin women would dish the beans into the center of the plate before elegantly using the back of the spoon to press it down, creating wells. The sauce would be spooned on top with extra helpings of spiced palm oil spread all over, dripping down and around the sides of the beans. As loyal customers, the kind women would often give us *jara* (meaning extra in Yoruba). I would cover the dish with the second plate and head back into the house to tuck into heaven. In this evolution of my childhood classic, the contrast in texture between the mashed and creamy whole beans with the earthy peppery notes of fresh parsley brings the dish together beautifully.

SERVES 4–6 AS SHARING PLATES

FOR THE MASHED BEANS

300g dried black-eyed peas (or
    your favorite beans or chickpeas),
    rinsed
1 small brown onion, peeled and cut
    into wedges
1 bay leaf
1 garlic clove, peeled
¾ tsp fine sea salt
20g fresh flat-leaf parsley, leaves
    finely chopped

**FOR THE BLACKENED RED
    PEPPER SAUCE**

2 red or brown onions, 1 roughly
    chopped and 1 sliced
4 garlic cloves, peeled
2 red Romano peppers, stemmed,
    deseeded and roughly chopped
3-inch piece of ginger, peeled and
    chopped
200ml coconut or vegetable oil,
    plus more to cover
4 sprigs of thyme
100g dried cayenne chilies, soaked
    and stemmed, or chili flakes
2 tsp aniseed
50g ground crayfish or dried
    shrimp (optional)
½ tsp fine sea salt
1 tsp freshly ground black pepper

Lerato's Tip

Keep the remaining sauce in a
sterilized jar topped with at least
½ inch of oil. Refrigerate and use
within a month or freeze in a
container for up to 3 months.

---

1. Place the beans in a large flameproof casserole with 1.25 liters water and bring to a boil over a medium-high heat. Skim off any foam; tuck in the onion wedges, bay leaf and garlic; and season with the salt. Cover with a lid slightly ajar, reduce the heat to medium and cook for 50–60 minutes, until meltingly soft. Check after 25 minutes and add another 250ml water, if necessary.

2. Meanwhile, to make the sauce, combine the chopped onion, all the garlic, peppers and ginger in a blender. Pulse to break down then blend to a textured puree. If needed, loosen with a little oil.

3. Place a wide sauté pan, for which you have a lid, over a medium heat and add the oil. Add the sliced onion to the pan and fry for 10–15 minutes, or until starting to crisp. Gently pour in the pepper puree, add the thyme, cover and cook for 10 minutes.

4. Stir in all the remaining sauce ingredients, lower the heat, cover and cook for about 30 minutes, stirring frequently to prevent burning. The color will deepen from a deep rouge to reddish-black as the sauce thickens. As it dries, top up with more oil, enough to float above the sauce. This is important in order to fry the chilies properly. When the sauce is blackened and wonderful, take it off the heat and leave to cool. Once cool, remove the thyme and season to perfection.

5. Remove a little less than half of the beans from the saucepan and set aside in a bowl. If there is a lot of liquid left in the pot, cook most of it off, leaving just a little to mash into the beans. Discard the bay leaf and remove and reserve the garlic clove. Mash the beans as smoothly or coarsely as you desire. Season to perfection and set aside.

6. Mash the reserved garlic in a small bowl and mix with the chopped parsley and some of the red oil from the sauce. Pour into the unmashed beans, stir and season to perfection.

7. Spoon the mashed beans into a shallow bowl. Use the back of a spoon to create "wells." Spoon some blackened pepper sauce into the wells and top with the unmashed beans. Finally, drizzle the glistening red oil all over.

8. Serve with soft bread rolls, **Fried** or **Baked Plantains** (see page 278) for a hearty meal, or with a rainbow of crudités for sharing.

Wara/Wagashi
Fried Halloumi

**WITH CHERRY TOMATOES &
RED PEPPER SAUCE**

SERVES 4

2 225g blocks of halloumi or firm/
extra-firm tofu (*dairy wara or
soya wara*)
5 tbsp cornstarch or gluten-free
flour
1 tsp smoked paprika
¾ tsp garlic granules
¼ tsp fine sea salt for halloumi or
¾ tsp fine sea salt (for tofu)
½ tsp freshly ground black pepper
3–4 tbsp vegetable oil, peanut or
olive oil
Handful of fresh basil leaves, sliced

FOR THE RED PEPPER SAUCE
2 red Romano peppers, stemmed,
deseeded and roughly chopped
2 mild red chilies, stemmed,
deseeded and roughly chopped
4 garlic cloves, peeled
1-inch piece of ginger, peeled and
roughly chopped
75ml vegetable oil
1 large brown onion, peeled and
thinly sliced
1 tsp smoked paprika
1–2 tsp chili flakes
4 sprigs of thyme
1 tsp freshly ground black pepper
10 cherry tomatoes, halved (mixed
colors, if available)

This most interesting dish is inspired by *wara (wagashi*
in Ghana), a delicacy I was introduced to by my
neighbors in Abuja, the capital of Nigeria. One version
is made with tofu and the other is a dairy version made
with something akin to Greek halloumi. Often tossed
into stews or soups or enjoyed as a delightful snack, in
my recipe a light dusting of flour and spices before
frying gives the halloumi a lovely crust. The mellow
cheesy flavor and texture works beautifully with the
spicy red pepper sauce and sweet tomatoes.

1. To make the red pepper sauce, place the Romano
peppers, chilies, garlic and ginger in a food processor
and pulse to a coarse puree.

2. Place a frying or sauté pan over a medium heat and
pour in the vegetable oil. Add the onion and fry for 5–7
minutes, stirring frequently to prevent burning, until it
starts to take on a bit of color. Pour in the pepper
puree, stir and leave to cook for 5 minutes. Add the
smoked paprika, chili flakes, thyme sprigs and black
pepper and cook for another 5 minutes. Stir in the
cherry tomatoes and cook uncovered for 8–10
minutes. Pick out the thyme stalk and discard. If
cooking with tofu, season well with fine sea salt; if
cooking with halloumi, season lightly.

3. Meanwhile, if cooking with tofu, wrap it in a clean cloth
and place in a colander in the sink with something
heavy on top. Leave to drain for 30 minutes to remove
excess moisture. If using halloumi, simply drain. Slice
the tofu or halloumi into ½-inch-thick slabs.

4. Place the flour, spices, salt and black pepper in a bowl
and mix well to combine. Toss the tofu or halloumi in
the flour, coating on all sides.

5. Place a frying pan over a high heat. Drizzle 3 tablespoons
of the oil into the pan and swirl to coat the base.
Once hot, cook the tofu or halloumi in batches for
1–2 minutes on each side, until golden brown. Remove
from the heat and transfer to a plate. Heat a little
more oil and repeat until all the slices are cooked.

6. Transfer the sauce to a warm platter and spread out.
Place the fried halloumi or tofu on top and scatter
over the sliced basil. Serve immediately on its own
or with bread, such as **My East African Chapati**
(see page 196) or **Medina Bread** (see page 194),
to soak up the wonderful sauce.

Moin Moin
Bean Tarts

**WITH PAN-ROASTED TOMATOES &
PEPPERS OR MUSHROOMS &
CARAMELIZED ONIONS**

SERVES 4-6

FOR THE BEAN TART

200g black-eyed peas, peeled (see
    page 274) or unpeeled
½ brown onion, peeled and
    chopped
1 red Romano pepper or bell
    pepper, stemmed, deseeded and
    roughly chopped
½ scotch bonnet pepper or
    habanero chili, stemmed and
    roughly chopped
300ml warm stock
1 tsp smoked paprika
90ml vegetable oil
1 large free-range egg (optional)

FOR THE PUREE

1 400g jar or can black-eyed peas
    or chickpeas (drained weight
    230-250g)
1 fat garlic clove, peeled and
    crushed
2 tbsp vegetable oil
1 tsp paprika

YOU WILL NEED

A 9-inch cake tin or a 11 × 8-inch
    baking tin

This is one of my favorite recipes. A reincarnation of
moin moin—a bean pudding popular in Nigeria typically
steamed in verdant banana-like leaves. These tarts are
plant-based and so adaptable I couldn't pick just one
topping. I first concocted this recipe for my African
Afternoon Tea pop-ups and it has been a favorite at my
teas and picnics ever since. Enjoy either or both tarts
for lunch or host your own African-inspired tea with
muffin-sized versions of these sumptuous tarts.

1. Soak the beans for 8 hours or overnight in a large bowl
    filled with water.

2. Preheat the oven to 400°F and place a rack in the
    middle of the oven and another just below. Line the
    base of the tin with baking parchment and brush the
    sides with oil.

3. Drain and rinse the beans then tip into a blender with
    the remaining bean tart ingredients, except the oil
    and egg. Pulse to crush the beans, then blend until
    smooth and creamy. Pour into a bowl and whisk in the
    oil and egg until well combined and fluffy. Season with
    ½ teaspoon fine sea salt and mix once more.

4. Pour the bean puree into the prepared tin, cover
    tightly with foil and place on the middle rack. Fill a
    second tray with water and place on the lower rack.
    This will create steam that will keep the bean tart
    moist. Bake for 50 minutes, then remove the foil and
    bake for another 10 minutes, until a skewer or small
    knife comes out somewhat clean. Remove from the
    oven and set aside to cool in its tin.

5. Drain the black-eyed peas or chickpeas and rinse.
    Place in a saucepan, cover with water and bring to a
    boil, to warm and soften the beans even further.
    Simmer for 5 minutes, then drain, saving 60ml of the
    cooking liquid. Tip the beans into a food processor
    with the garlic and oil, and blend to a puree until fluffy
    and smooth, adding a little of the reserved cooking
    liquid to loosen, if necessary. Season with the paprika,
    fine sea salt and black pepper, and set aside.

6. Remove the bean tart from the baking dish, turning it
    upside down on to a wide plate and gently peeling off
    the baking parchment. Spoon the puree onto the tart
    and spread to cover the surface.

7. Finish with your choice of topping—see options
    opposite. (See photo on pages 58-9.)

PAN-ROASTED TOMATOES & PEPPERS

2 tbsp vegetable or olive oil
1 red Romano or bell pepper,
    stemmed and thinly sliced
300g cherry tomatoes, halved
¼ tsp cayenne pepper
2 garlic cloves, peeled and crushed
1 tbsp balsamic vinegar, plus 1 tsp
    for drizzling (thick if possible)
Small handful of scented leaves
    (e.g., African clove basil, Thai basil
    or flat-leaf parsley), torn

1. Place the oil in a sauté or frying pan over a medium-high heat. Once piping hot, add the pepper and cook for 1–2 minutes, until softened. Add the tomatoes and sprinkle the cayenne over the top. Stir in the garlic, toss and cook for 1–2 minutes, until the tomatoes begin to blister and break down. Season with a pinch of fine sea salt and freshly ground black pepper or grains of paradise. Drizzle over the balsamic vinegar, stir to combine and remove the pan from the heat.

2. Arrange the peppers and tomatoes on top of the puree and pour over any luscious cooking liquid or oil remaining in the pan. Scatter over the scented leaves and drizzle with a little more balsamic vinegar. Cut into your desired portion and serve warm or cold.

MUSHROOMS & CARAMELIZED ONIONS

4 tbsp vegetable or olive oil
1 large red onion, peeled and thinly
    sliced
300g mix of chestnut mushrooms
    and chanterelles, thinly sliced
2 garlic cloves, peeled and crushed
1 tsp paprika
¼ tsp chili flakes
Sprinkling of fresh thyme leaves

1. Heat half the oil in a large sauté or frying pan over a medium heat. Once hot, add the onion with a pinch of fine sea salt and fry for 10 minutes, stirring occasionally, until translucent. Add 1–2 tablespoons of water to keep the onions moist and to prevent burning as you continue to cook for another 15–20 minutes, until the onions begin to break down and turn golden. Reduce the heat, if they start to brown too quickly, then increase the heat to medium and continue to cook for a final 10–15 minutes, scraping the bottom of the pan and stirring occasionally until the onions are a deep golden color and wonderfully caramelized. Remove the onions from the pan and set aside.

2. Place the remaining oil in the same pan and increase the heat to medium–high. Once piping hot, add the sliced mushrooms and sauté for 8–10 minutes, stirring occasionally, but not too frequently to allow the mushrooms to brown properly, creating a wonderful rich flavor.

3. Once the mushrooms are thoroughly browned, return the caramelized onion to the pan, reduce the heat to medium and add the garlic, paprika and chili flakes. Stir until fragrant. Season to perfection with fine sea salt and freshly ground black pepper or grains of paradise, scatter over the thyme leaves and remove from the heat.

4. Spoon the caramelized onion and mushroom onto the tart topped with the puree, cut into your desired portion and serve warm or cold.

Plantain & Prawn Cakes

MAKES ABOUT 14

I have adored plantains since childhood. Although they are abundant across Africa and in the tropics, on the English Sussex coast where I live, only three shops sell them in limited quantities. For fear of not being able to find any, I often end up buying more than I need, leaving a few to turn from my preferred just-ripened yellow to black. These overripe plantains are perfect for pancakes and fritters such as these. Perhaps an unusual harmonious balance with the sweet plantains, and the chunky prawns remain delicate and juicy for a moreish treat.

1 large very ripe plantain (yellow with black patches), peeled (see page 277) and cut into chunks
100g plain flour
50g cornstarch
2 red or green chilies, stemmed, deseeded (optional) and roughly chopped
4 spring onions, trimmed and roughly chopped
4 garlic cloves, peeled and crushed
1-inch piece of ginger, peeled and finely chopped
400g raw king prawns, peeled and deveined
1 medium free-range egg, beaten
2 tbsp finely chopped cilantro
¾ tsp fine sea salt
Vegetable oil, for frying

1. Place the plantain in a wide bowl and mash to a puree with a fork. Set aside.

2. Mix the flours in a small bowl and set aside.

3. Place the chilies and spring onions in a food processor with the garlic and ginger. Pulse until well combined. Add the prawns and pulse a few times, making sure there are still juicy chunks that will create the most amazing fritters. Tip into the bowl of plantain.

4. Fold in the egg and cilantro. Season with the fine sea salt, then fold in the flours until fully incorporated. Your mixture should be sticky and moist. If runny, add a generous pinch more flour to correct it.

5. Fill a nonstick frying pan with oil to a depth of ½ inch and set over a medium heat. Test the oil is hot enough by dropping in a little of the batter. It should sizzle steadily and brown immediately. Scoop a heaped tablespoon of batter and use a second tablespoon to help lower it into the oil. Press lightly to flatten the batter. Repeat until you have about 3 or 4 cakes in the pan, taking care not to overcrowd them. Fry for 3–4 minutes, turning halfway, until a deep golden color and crisp all over. Remove with a slotted spoon and drain on kitchen paper. Cover the cooked fritters with baking parchment and a clean kitchen towel to keep them warm. Continue until all the fritters are cooked.

6. Serve with my favorite concoction of harissa swirled in yogurt or some **Smoky Tomato & Date Jam** (see page 257). With its refreshing tang and tingling heat from the lime and chili, **Kachumbari with Hibiscus Pickled Onion** (see page 160) is a wonderful accompaniment for a more substantial yet light lunch.

Lerato's Tip

If using frozen prawns, defrost them in the fridge a few hours before cooking or place in a bowl filled with enough cold water to cover all the prawns. Leave for 15–20 minutes to defrost, then drain and pat dry.

Crispy Coconut Squid & Prawns

SERVES 4–6 AS SHARING PLATES

This recipe is inspired by the wonderful selection of tropical fruits and seafood you find while exploring East Africa and especially the Zanzibar archipelago. Prawns and squid are cooked in creamy coconut batter, and seasoned with aromatic and fragrant makrut lime leaves, ginger and curry. When in Tanzania you mustn't miss the buzzing Forodhani Gardens in Stone Town, Zanzibar, where you can find the best bounty of the sea from an impressive variety of fresh fish and seafood grilled to order, cooked in curries, or deep fried in batter.

250g raw squid, cut into ¼-inch rings
250g raw king prawns, peeled and deveined
Juice of 1 lemon
4 garlic cloves, peeled and grated
2-inch piece of ginger, peeled and grated
2 green chilies, stemmed and finely diced
1 bunch of spring onions, trimmed and finely sliced
2 tsp mild curry powder
2 tsp **Paradise Spice** (see page 270), plus ½ tsp to serve
2 tsp freshly ground grains of paradise or black pepper
Generous pinch of sea salt flakes
500ml vegetable oil, for frying

FOR THE BATTER
160g unsweetened desiccated coconut
120g cornstarch
300ml coconut milk
1½ tsp sea salt flakes

1. Place the squid, prawns, lemon juice, garlic, ginger, chilies, spring onions, spices and salt in a large bowl. Mix thoroughly, cover and leave in the fridge to marinate for up to 2 hours.

2. Remove the squid and prawns from the fridge and bring to room temperature. Meanwhile, heat the oil in a large, deep pan to 350°F (see page 275) and line a tray with kitchen paper.

3. Carefully strain any liquid that may have settled in the marinade.

4. Combine the desiccated coconut and cornstarch in a wide bowl. Add the coconut milk and whisk until the batter is thick and well combined. Set aside for 10 minutes.

5. Season the batter with the salt, add the prawns, squid and aromatics from the marinade and mix to coat well.

6. Once the oil is hot enough, use a tablespoon to scoop a good mix of batter-coated prawns and squid into the hot oil. Fry for 3–4 minutes in batches to avoid overcrowding, turning halfway through cooking until golden and crispy. Remove from the oil with a slotted spoon and leave to drain in a single layer, on the prepared tray. Continue until all the fritters are cooked.

7. Sprinkle crushed sea salt flakes and the remaining ½ teaspoon of **Paradise Spice** over the top for a fragrant finish. Serve with **Coconut, Ginger & Tamarind Chutney** (see page 258).

Plantain Shakshuka

SERVES 4-6

Vegetable oil, for frying

FOR THE PLANTAIN
1 large plantain, peeled (see page 277) and cut into ¾-inch chunks
¼ tsp paprika

FOR THE SHAKSHUKA
4 tbsp olive oil
1 white onion, peeled and roughly chopped
2 bell peppers (red and yellow), stemmed, deseeded and cut into ½-inch slices
¾ tsp fine sea salt
4 garlic cloves, peeled and crushed
2 tbsp **Red Harissa** (see page 260)
1 tbsp tomato puree
3 tsp cumin seeds, toasted and crushed, or 1½ tsp ground cumin
2 tsp paprika
½ tsp ground turmeric
½ tsp chili flakes (optional)
800g vine-ripened tomatoes, or 2 400g cans plum tomatoes
8 medium free-range eggs, 2 beaten

TO SERVE
1 small bunch of fresh cilantro, torn

Lerato's Tip

Serve with feta crumbled on top or with slices of avocado. You can replace the eggs with chunks of roasted zucchini, eggplant or silken tofu and cook as above.

Shakshuka is Tunisia's gift to the world. A one-pot dish of eggs on top of a lava of tomatoes and peppers, this moreish legacy traveled across North Africa, to Israel and the Middle East. My plantain shakshuka was created by chance when I threw in some leftover plantains. Unsurprisingly, the result was a stunning marriage of North and West African flavors. This is sure to become one of your brunch-time favorites.

1. Heat ¾ inch of oil in a shallow frying pan to 375°F (see page 275). Use a slotted spoon to lower the plantain chunks into the hot oil. Cook in batches for a few minutes, turning frequently to ensure browning on all sides. Remove and drain on kitchen paper. Sprinkle with a pinch of fine sea salt and the paprika while the plantain is still hot, and toss to coat well.

2. To prepare the shakshuka, pour the olive oil into a 10-inch sauté pan, for which you have a lid, and set over a medium heat. Add the onion and peppers, season with the salt and cook for 5 minutes until softened.

3. Add the garlic, Red Harissa and tomato puree and cook for 3 minutes, stirring frequently, then stir in the dry spices, and the chili flakes if your harissa isn't hot enough. Tip in the tomatoes, cover and simmer for 15–20 minutes, until thickened and sweetened, stirring occasionally and breaking down the tomatoes with a wooden spoon.

4. Scoop half of the sauce into a bowl, then spread the remaining sauce out evenly in the pan. Scatter half of the plantain chunks over the top, then pour the 2 beaten eggs over the top to cover the plantain and sauce. Cover and cook for 2 minutes.

5. Pour the reserved sauce over the layer of eggs and gently spread out evenly. Scatter over the remaining plantain. Crack the remaining eggs, one at a time, into a bowl. Use the back of the spoon to make 6 "wells" in the sauce. Pour an egg in each one, cover the pan and cook for a final 10 minutes over a medium-low heat, or until the eggs are cooked as you like them. If you have an ovenproof pan, you can also finish the shakshuka in an oven preheated to 400°F for 5 minutes.

6. Scatter over the chopped cilantro and serve with **Red Harissa** (see page 260) and toasted slices of baguette or **Medina Bread** (see page 194).

Tagine Maadnous
Tunisian Tagine

This delightful tagine is far from the Berber *(Imazighen)* style braise you might be accustomed to. I was first told of this frittata-style dish by a Tunisian whom I met in London, on one of the many random yet wonderfully explorative and informative conversations I hold with complete strangers. *Maadnous* means parsley in Arabic and, as the name suggests, this dish is typically heavy with those herbaceous greens, as well as having eggs, meat, cheese, vegetables and spices baked within. Instead of chicken or mince, as is commonly used in Tunisia, I have added Merguez, a slim, spiced North African sausage. And instead of the cute little cheese triangles, also enjoyed by the locals and which I thoroughly enjoyed in my lunchbox as a child, I use a semi-soft and aged Swiss Gruyère, with a sweet and nutty character. A golden Parmigiano-Reggiano is grated on top, for a nutty and fruity finish. You can use mince and harissa if you can't find Merguez. Bake until perfectly set and leave to rest for a few minutes before cutting into triangles, squares or whatever your heart desires.

SERVES 6-8

Butter, for greasing

2 medium potatoes, peeled and
    diced

2 tbsp olive or vegetable oil

450g Merguez sausages (about
    6-8 sausages), skin removed

1 large brown onion, peeled and
    diced

3 garlic cloves, peeled and crushed

2 red chilies, stemmed and finely
    chopped

4 spring onions, trimmed and sliced

2 tsp Ras el hanout

1 tsp ground cumin

½ tsp ground turmeric

1 tsp dried thyme

½ tsp cayenne pepper (optional)

60g fresh flat-leaf parsley, roughly
    chopped

20g fresh cilantro, roughly
    chopped

20g chives, finely chopped

8 large free-range eggs

¾ tsp fine sea salt

125g Gruyère or mild semi-soft
    cheese, cut into small chunks
    (e.g., Fontina, Gouda, Emmental,
    or mozzarella)

50g Parmigiano-Reggiano, grated

YOU WILL NEED

A 13 × 9-inch glass or ceramic
    baking dish or a 11-inch nonstick
    ovenproof shallow casserole or
    pan

1. Preheat the oven to 400°F and grease the baking dish with butter.

2. Place the potatoes in a saucepan and bring to a boil. Cook uncovered for 5 minutes, until just tender. Drain and set aside.

3. Heat the oil in a pan over a medium-high heat and add the sausage meat. Cook for 8-10 minutes, stirring frequently and breaking the meat up, until browned all over and cooked through. Use a slotted spoon to remove the sausage meat and set aside.

4. Reduce the heat to medium and add the onion and season with a pinch of fine sea salt. Cook for 8 minutes, until softened, then add the garlic, chilies, spring onions and dried spices. Cook for 3 minutes, stirring frequently, then return the sausage meat to the pan with the potatoes and mix well to coat in the wonderful spices. Stir in the fresh herbs and cook for 1 minute, then remove from the heat and season with freshly ground black pepper.

5. Whisk the eggs in a large bowl with the sea salt, until light and fluffy. Add the sausage, potato and herb mix, and fold in the chunks of cheese, until well combined.

6. Grease the baking dish or, if using the same pan, wipe it clean then grease all over with butter. Pour the mixture into your prepared pan or baking dish and place in the middle of the oven to bake for 20 minutes.

7. Remove from the oven and scatter the grated cheese over the top. Continue to bake for 5-10 minutes, until set, golden and the cheese is melted. Insert a skewer into the center to check it is cooked through.

8. Leave to cool before serving with **Medina Bread** (see page 194) and a side of **Red Harissa** (see page 260).

Variation

For a vegan version, mushrooms or vegan sausages and silken tofu are excellent substitutes for Merguez and eggs. Brown the mushrooms in oil before mixing with the other ingredients as above. Crumble 450g silken tofu into a food processor with 60ml plant-based milk and 2 heaped tablespoons cornstarch. Blend until smooth. Mix into the bowl with the mushrooms, potatoes, spices and herbs and season with salt and pepper. Grease the baking dish with oil and bake for up to 40 minutes, until well set.

My Golden Ugandan Rolex

SERVES 4 OR 2 GREEDY GOBS LIKE MYSELF

Vegetable oil, for frying

2 garlic cloves, peeled and crushed

1 green finger chili, stemmed and finely chopped (or 2 milder jalapeños)

5 multicolored cherry tomatoes (about 80g), cut into wedges, or 1 medium tomato, deseeded and roughly chopped

30g baby spinach leaves, chopped

2 spring onions, trimmed and chopped

4 large free-range eggs

¼ tsp ground turmeric

2 chapati (see **My East African Chapati** on page 196) or flatbreads

TO SERVE

Smoky Tomato & Date Jam (see page 257), to taste

4 rashers dry-cured streaky smoked bacon, fried until crisp, then torn (optional)

40g fresh cilantro or baby spinach leaves

¼ small red cabbage, shredded

1–2 carrots, scrubbed and julienned

Unless you have been enthralled by this wonder while walking the streets of Kampala, you might be forgiven for assuming this is a recipe for a luxury timepiece. *Ugandan Rolex* is a malapropism of "rolled eggs," a melodic corruption most likely to have occurred as the street sellers would call out to the passing crowds. Across Uganda there are many variations, some with minced meat, chicken or cheese. You simply cannot go wrong, whatever you choose to embellish your Golden Ugandan Rolex with.

1. Place a 10-inch nonstick frying pan over a medium heat and add 1 tablespoon of oil. Add the garlic and chili and cook for 30 seconds, until fragrant. Add the tomatoes and cook for 2–3 minutes, tossing now and again. Stir in the spinach and leave to wilt for 1 minute, then take the pan off the heat. Tip everything into a bowl, add the spring onions, season with just a little pinch of fine sea salt and toss well.

2. Crack two of the eggs into a mug or bowl and whisk lightly. Add half the turmeric, a pinch of fine sea salt and half the spinach, chili and tomato mix. Stir to combine.

3. Wipe the pan clean and place over a medium-high heat. Drizzle in 2 teaspoons of oil and brush or swirl to coat the base and up the sides a bit. Give the eggs one more mix then pour into the pan, quickly and briefly swirling around as it sizzles to make sure the entire surface is covered. Leave undisturbed for 10 seconds, then swirl the pan once more so any excess runny liquid fills the gaps. Reduce the heat to medium and cook for 30 seconds, until it is mostly cooked with a little raw egg on top. Loosen the sides and bottom with a spatula, then place a chapati on top of the egg and press down for 10 seconds to "glue" them together. Continue to cook for about 1 minute, or until the eggs are beautifully golden, then flip and cook the chapati for 30 seconds. Transfer to a plate lined with kitchen paper. Repeat to make the second roll.

4. To assemble each roll, spread ½ tablespoon or more of **Smoky Tomato & Date Jam** on the egg side of the roll, top with half the bacon, if using, then half the cilantro leaves or baby spinach, shredded cabbage and carrots. Roll up tightly and wrap in baking parchment pretending to be a Ugandan newspaper. Twist the ends and leave the wrap to rest and seal for a few minutes before cutting in half and devouring.

Sumptuous
Stews & Soups

Aromatic & Soothing Chicken Pepper Soup

SERVES 6

½ red Romano or bell pepper, deseeded and roughly chopped

1 large red onion, peeled and roughly chopped

4 garlic cloves, peeled and roughly chopped

1-inch piece of ginger, peeled and roughly chopped

2 tbsp ground dried shrimp or crayfish

1 yellow scotch bonnet pepper, stemmed and deseeded, or pierced and left whole (optional)

2 tbsp vegetable oil

1.2kg skinless and boneless chicken thighs, cut into bite-sized pieces

6 sprigs of thyme

2 tbsp **Pepper Soup Spice Blend** (see page 271)

2 lemongrass stalks, tough outer layer removed and stalks bashed

1.2 liters strong chicken stock

1-inch yams, peeled and cut into 1-inch chunks (or taro/coco yams, cassava/yucca or sweet potatoes)

3 makrut lime leaves

Small handful of scented leaves (African basil, Thai basil or flat-leaf parsley)

Palm oil or **Red Oil** (see page 262), to serve

I think of this soup as a "broth of life." Refreshingly spicy, aromatic and soothing, my version includes a wonderful **Pepper Soup Spice Blend** (see page 271), as well as lemongrass, just like my mum would make it. Although typically cooked with bone-in chicken, which produces a delicious stock, I prefer to use boneless chicken and a strong stock to make it easier to devour. Growing up, my mother would prepare pepper soup whenever we were under the weather and it worked like magic. To this day, when I call her complaining about an ailment, she responds with, "Have you made pepper soup?" It truly is our magic elixir.

1. Place the red pepper, onion, garlic, ginger, ground dried shrimp or crayfish and scotch bonnet, if not using whole, in a blender with a splash of water and blitz to a puree.

2. Heat the oil in a large pot set over a medium-high heat. Add the chicken and cook for 5 minutes, stirring occasionally, as it begins to brown a little.

3. Pour in the aromatic puree, add the thyme and the **Pepper Soup Spice Blend** and season with 1 teaspoon fine sea salt. Tuck the lemongrass into the pot and pour in 600ml of the chicken stock. Add the scotch bonnet if using whole, bring to a strong simmer and cook for 5 minutes. Turn down the heat to medium, cover with a lid and simmer steadily for 20 minutes.

4. Tuck the small pieces of yam and the makrut lime leaves into the pot, pour in the remaining chicken stock and season again with ½ teaspoon fine sea salt if needed. Bring to a steady simmer and cook uncovered for 15 minutes, or until the yams are tender and the chicken is cooked through. Push the thyme sprigs, lemongrass and makrut lime leaves aside.

5. Scatter over the scented leaves to infuse the hot soup and serve hot or at room temperature with a drizzle of palm or **Red Oil** in each bowlful.

Variation
Other tubers like taro and cassava, as well as their leaves, are used in various soups across Africa. White potatoes would cook in a similar amount of time as the yams, but sweet potatoes will cook a bit quicker (about 10 minutes). You can use the same recipe to make fish pepper soup, substituting a firm white fish for the chicken and cooked for less time.

Pumpkin Pepper Soup

**WITH PLANTAIN CHIPS
& TOASTED SEEDS**

SERVES 4–6

3 tbsp olive oil

1 large brown onion, peeled and roughly chopped

3 garlic cloves, peeled and finely chopped

2-inch piece of ginger, peeled and grated

1 medium red Romano or bell pepper, stemmed, deseeded and sliced

2 carrots, scrubbed and finely chopped

1 celery stick, trimmed and finely chopped

½–1 scotch bonnet pepper, stemmed and chopped, or pierced and left whole, or 2–4 red chilies, stemmed and finely chopped

1 tsp fennel seeds, toasted and ground

2 tbsp **Pepper Soup Spice Blend** (see page 271)

2–3 makrut lime leaves, ribs removed and leaves finely sliced, or 1 tsp **Paradise Spice** (see page 270)

6 sprigs of thyme

1 medium or 2 small pumpkins or squash (about 900g–1kg), peeled and cut into 1-inch chunks

1.25 liters hot vegetable or chicken stock

60g plantain chips, shop-bought or homemade (see page 280)

4 tbsp toasted pumpkin seeds

50ml **Scotch Bonnet & Turmeric Oil** (see page 262) (optional for more heat)

This comforting soup has been a staple at my supper clubs for quite some time. I wanted to create a dish that was both familiar and surprising. Creamy pumpkins or squash accompany the bewitchingly comforting West African pepper soup spices or fragrant saffron and North African Ras el hanout. Both variations are dressed with crumbled sweet plantain chips and toasted pumpkin seeds for a satisfying crunch.

1. Heat the oil in a large heavy-based saucepan over a medium heat. Once hot and shimmering, add the onion and a pinch of fine sea salt and cook for 10 minutes, stirring frequently, until softened and golden but not dark. Add the garlic, ginger, red pepper, carrot, celery and scotch bonnet or chilies, if not using whole. Reduce the heat to medium-low, cover with a lid and cook for 10 minutes, until the vegetables are tender. Add a splash of water if needed to prevent sticking.

2. Stir in the fennel seeds, the **Pepper Soup Spice Blend**, lime leaves or **Paradise Spice** and thyme sprigs. Add the pumpkin or squash and pour in 1 liter of the hot stock. Bring to a boil, add the scotch bonnet at this stage if using whole, then reduce the heat to a simmer, cover with a lid and cook for 20 minutes, until tender.

3. Discard the thyme sprig and remove the scotch bonnet if left whole. Remove from the heat and blend until smooth with a stick blender, or leave to cool before tipping into a jug blender and blitzing until smooth.

4. Pour the soup back into the pot, if necessary, and, if it is too thick, add the remaining 250ml stock. Season to perfection with fine sea salt and gently reheat.

5. Serve each bowlful topped with crumbled plantain chips and toasted pumpkin seeds. For more tingling heat, drizzle with **Scotch Bonnet & Turmeric Oil**. Now tuck into your warm hug in a bowl!

Variation

To make a **North African Spiced Pepper Soup with Saffron**, replace the scotch bonnet with 2 red chilies, stemmed (deseeded for milder heat), and replace the **Pepper Soup Spice Bend** with 1–2 tablespoons **Ras el hanout**. Swap the lime leaves with a small handful of fresh cilantro and add a pinch of saffron.

Mothered Oxtail Stew

WITH SCOTCH BONNET & PIMENTO

SERVES 4

1.5kg oxtail, cut into small chunks
(by your kind butcher)
2–3 heaped tbsp plain flour
60ml vegetable oil
2 red Romano or bell peppers,
stemmed, deseeded and sliced
2 brown onions, peeled and sliced
4 medium carrots, scrubbed and
cut into round chunks
2-inch piece of ginger, peeled and
grated
4 garlic cloves, peeled and crushed
1 tsp ground allspice (pimento)
2 tsp paprika
2 tbsp tomato puree
250ml good-quality fruity red wine
2 400g cans whole plum or
chopped tomatoes
6 sprigs of thyme
2 bay leaves
500ml beef stock, plus extra
1–2 scotch bonnet peppers (yellow
if possible), stemmed, pierced
and left whole
Handful of fresh parsley, chopped

Lerato's Tip

To cook in the oven, preheat to
350°F and, after step 5, cover with
a lid and transfer to the oven for
3 hours, or until perfectly tender.
Stir halfway through and leave
uncovered to thicken for the final
30 minutes.

Mothered oxtail stew is pure love in a pot. This recipe is inspired by my friend Nicola's childhood memories of her mum tending to her stew for hours in Malawi. A mothered dish, it gives back as much love as you show it. This method of cooking is reminiscent of *potjiekos* (pronounced poy-kee-kos), which is enjoyed across southern Africa, from South Africa to Namibia. Those dishes typically include meat on the bone, vegetables and spices simmered in three-legged, cast-iron cauldrons set atop an open flame. Here the allspice and scotch bonnet create a fragrant and spicy sauce that is satisfying and comforting.

1. Place the oxtail in a large bowl. Pat dry and lightly dust with flour and season with sea salt and black pepper.

2. Place a large heavy-based flameproof casserole over a medium-high heat. Add enough oil to coat the base and, once hot, fry the oxtail in batches until brown on all sides. Remove the meat with a slotted spoon and set aside.

3. Reduce the heat to medium and add the peppers and onions. Sauté for 7–10 minutes, stirring frequently, until softened and starting to take on a little color. Stir in half of the carrots and all the ginger and garlic. Add the spices, tomato puree and 2 tablespoons of water and cook for 3 minutes.

4. Put the oxtail pieces back in the pan and stir to coat. Season with 1 teaspoon fine sea salt and ½ teaspoon freshly ground grains of paradise or black pepper, cover with a lid and cook for 5 minutes, stirring occasionally to avoid sticking.

5. Pour in the wine to deglaze the pan, then stir in the tomatoes, herbs and the stock. Throw in as many scotch bonnets as your heart desires and increase the heat to medium-high to bring to a strong simmer.

6. Reduce the heat to low, cover and simmer gently for 3–4 hours, until the meat is luxuriously tender and the sauce dark, thick and unctuous. Stir occasionally and add a little splash of stock, if needed. Add the remaining carrots and cook uncovered for 10 minutes.

7. Leave to cool slightly. Skim any excess oil floating on the surface. Season to perfection and serve scattered with fresh parsley alongside a steaming bowl of rice or **Vanilla Mashed Potatoes** (see page 191) and **Braised Greens with Sweet Red Peppers** (see page 172).

Egusi
Mum's Melon Seed Soup

WITH POUNDED YAM

SERVES 4

Pounded yam and *egusi*! What a classic Nigerian feast. One of my fondest childhood memories of my mum's cooking and one of the first recipes she taught me before I fled the nest was *egusi*. Although relatively dry, *egusi* is technically a soup. Much loved by various tribes across West Africa, it is named after its key ingredient, melon seeds from the gourd family. The seeds are ground and added to the broth to thicken it and eventually form clumps when ready. They are creamy colored and similar to green pumpkin seeds, with a slight bitterness when raw and an aromatic and sweet flavor once cooked. Known as *plasas* in Sierra Leone and fondly called *palaver sauce* in Ghana, one can see how this stew/soup may be cause for much debate. Among many other variations, some tribes include tomatoes, while green-loving tribes like ours love to add bitter leaves and spinach. Although I never saw my mother wield the giant pestle traditionally used to pound yam in an equally giant wooden mortar, I have tried it on several occasions to satisfy my curiosity. It is hard work and requires the synchronicity of athletes. My pounded yam requires no pounding at all, as your trusted cake mixer or food processor does all the hard work of whipping the cooked tuber into a deliciously soft cloud.

1 brown onion, peeled and roughly chopped

2 red Romano peppers, stemmed, deseeded and roughly chopped

1 scotch bonnet pepper (yellow if possible), stemmed and roughly chopped, or pierced and left whole

60ml vegetable oil

8 bone-in chicken thighs and drumsticks (about 800–850g)

3 tbsp ground dried shrimp or crayfish

500ml strong chicken or beef stock

125ml sustainable palm oil or **Red Oil** (see page 262)

3 pods of selim pepper, ground

200g egusi seeds (or pumpkin seeds)

200g smoked fish (soft and boneless), cut into pieces

400g spinach, sliced into shreds

FOR THE "POUNDED" YAM
650g white puna yam (African yam)

YOU WILL NEED
A mixer with paddle attachment

1. Place the onion, Romano pepper and scotch bonnet, if not leaving whole, in a blender with a splash of water and blitz to a puree. Set aside for later.

2. Pour the vegetable oil into a large flameproof casserole and set over a medium heat; the oil should coat the bottom of the pan. Pat the chicken dry and, once the oil is hot, place the chicken in the pan and brown in batches for 4–5 minutes undisturbed on each side.

3. Return all the browned chicken to the pan and season with ½ teaspoon fine sea salt. Add 1 tablespoon of the ground dried shrimp or crayfish, pour in 125ml of the strong stock, cover with a lid and simmer for 20 minutes, until cooked through. Carefully pour the contents of the pan into a heatproof bowl and set aside.

4. Set the same pan over a medium heat and pour in the palm oil or **Red Oil**. Once hot, add the onion and pepper puree. Cover and cook for 10–15 minutes, stirring frequently to prevent sticking. Once the puree is thick and slightly reduced, stir in the remaining ground dried shrimp or crayfish and the ground selim pepper. Return the chicken to the pan and the scotch bonnet if using whole and carefully pour in any of the chicken's cooking liquid. Cover with a lid and cook for

15 minutes, pouring in a splash of stock to keep the sauce moist.

5. Meanwhile, prepare the yam by half filling a large bowl with water and cutting ¾-inch discs from the center of the tuber. Carefully score and peel the dark bark. Cut the yam into medium-sized chunks and drop into the bowl of water to prevent them oxidizing and turning brown. Rinse thoroughly, rubbing the chunks between your palms until the slippery starchy feel is no more. Place the yams in a large saucepan and fill with water. Bring to a boil, cover with a lid and cook for 15–20 minutes, depending on the thickness and age of the yam, until soft and falling apart.

6. Meanwhile, blend the egusi seeds with a little water until smooth and thick. Pour into the pan with the chicken, stir to combine and cook for 5 minutes. Tuck the pieces of smoked fish into the sauce and pour in 150–300ml of the stock, depending on how thick your sauce is. Cover with a lid and cook for 10 minutes, stirring occasionally to prevent burning.

7. Remove the scotch bonnet if whole and set aside for those who love more heat. Stir the spinach into the pan and check the seasoning. Cover with a lid and cook for a final 3–5 minutes to soften the greens. Remove from the heat and leave to sit for 5 minutes as it continues to bubble in residual heat.

8. For the "pounded" yam, remove the yam from the heat and use a slotted spoon to transfer into the large bowl of a freestanding mixer. Reserve the cooking water. Using the paddle attachment on low speed, beat the yam chunks to break them up for 20 seconds, then increase to a high speed and beat for another 20 seconds, until they begin to form a smooth dough. Scrape down the sides and the paddle and add a few small splashes of the cooking water to soften the dough. Beat once again for 20 seconds, until the dough is soft and fluffy, being careful not to add too much water or overbeat, as the dough could lose its elasticity.

9. Lightly wet your clean hands and mold the fluffy yam dough into small individual portions. Serve immediately with the *egusi* and dig in. (See photo on pages 76-7.)

Variation

For a plant-based version of this sumptuous stew, soak 60g dried shiitake mushrooms in 450ml hot vegetable stock. Thickly slice 1kg mushrooms and brown in oil over a medium-high heat until golden. Season with fine sea salt. Drain the soaked mushrooms and chop, saving the stock. Add the browned and rehydrated mushrooms to the cooked pepper puree and continue as above using the reserved mushroom-soaking liquid as stock. If using wild spinach, kale or sturdier greens, blanch in hot water for 5–10 minutes to soften before adding to the pan.

My Decadent Peanut Stew

This is one of the most-requested dishes at our cookery classes—creamy with the help of the peanuts or peanut butter and smoky from the paprika and the magical pods of selim peppers. Peanut stew is a popular delicacy across Africa, especially in the western region. In some areas it is cooked as a thick stew, while in others it is a runny soup. In francophone Benin, where I spent a considerable amount of time as a teenager, it is called *sauce d'arachide* and in Senegal, Mali and Gambia it is popularly known as *maafe*. Blending the peanuts and aromatics into a paste makes it easier for you to add the peanuts into the dish. I much prefer a coarser texture, but you can blitz yours as smoothly as you desire. I love to spread some of the peanut paste over the chicken before grilling or roasting and tucking it back into the stew to finish cooking. When cooking a plant-based version, you can either brush the paste over the vegetables, roast until tender and serve alongside the stew, or cook the vegetables in the stew. Potatoes, squashes, spinach and chickpeas are all wonderful additions to a decadent plant-based peanut stew.

SERVES 4–6

250g roasted unsalted peanuts
2 brown onions, peeled, 1 chopped
  and 1 sliced
4 garlic cloves, peeled
3 pods of selim peppers, smashed
1–2 scotch bonnet peppers,
  stemmed and roughly chopped,
  or pierced and left whole
300–500ml chicken or vegetable
  stock
1kg bone-in chicken thighs and legs
2½ tsp paprika
1 tsp chili flakes
2–3 tbsp peanut or vegetable oil
6 sprigs of thyme, leaves picked, or
  1 tsp dried
2-inch piece of ginger, peeled and
  grated
1 red Romano or bell pepper,
  stemmed, deseeded and sliced
1 tbsp tomato puree
1 400g can plum tomatoes

TO SERVE
40g fresh cilantro, chopped
1 red chili, stemmed and finely
  sliced

Lerato's Tip

See page 274 for roasting nuts at
home. You can substitute 150g
natural and unsweetened smooth
or crunchy peanut butter for the
220g roasted peanuts. Substitute
smoked paprika for paprika if you
are out of selim peppers.

1. Preheat the grill to high.

2. Place 220g of the peanuts in a food processor with the chopped onion, 2 garlic cloves, the selim peppers and as many "scotchies" as your heart desires, if not leaving whole. Blend to a coarse puree, adding a small splash of water to loosen. Scrape into a bowl, then pour 300ml of the stock into the processor and blend to extract any remaining puree. Set both aside for later.

3. Cut two or three diagonal slashes into the skin on each piece of chicken and spread 3 tablespoons of the peanut puree on top and all over. Sprinkle over 1½ teaspoons of the paprika and ½ teaspoon of the chili flakes. Season with freshly ground black pepper and fine sea salt. Drizzle over 1 tablespoon of the oil and brush to coat all sides. Arrange the chicken skin-side up on a grilling tray and place under the grill to char for 5–7 minutes on each side. Set aside.

4. Place a large, heavy-based saucepan over a medium heat. Add 1 tablespoon of the oil and, when hot, add the sliced onion and a pinch of fine sea salt. Cover with a lid and cook for 10 minutes, stirring occasionally, until translucent. Remove the lid and continue to cook for 15 minutes, until the onions become dark golden. Add a tablespoon of water to prevent burning, if necessary.

5. Crush the remaining garlic cloves and add to the pan. Stir in the thyme and ginger, add the red pepper and tomato puree and cook for 5 minutes. Stir in the remaining paprika and chili flakes and pour in the tomatoes, breaking them up with a wooden spoon. Cover and cook for 5 minutes. Finally, add the remaining peanut puree, cover with a lid slightly ajar and cook for 10 minutes, stirring occasionally.

6. Pour in the stock from the food processor, stir and bring to a strong simmer. Tuck the grilled chicken into the sauce, as well as the scotch bonnets, if using whole. Season with salt and grains of paradise or black pepper. Cover and simmer for 20 minutes, stirring frequently to prevent sticking, until the chicken is cooked through and the sauce is decadent, thick and creamy. You can add a little more stock if the sauce is too thick. Taste and season to perfection.

7. Chop the remaining peanuts and scatter over the stew with the cilantro and sliced chili for a little more kick of heat. Serve with rice or a side of vegetables and greens.

Roasted Chicken in Stew

SERVES 4-6

This one-pot is supremely easy and a joy to cook. The whole chicken is covered in butter and spices, part roasted atop a bed of vegetables, then cooked in a deeply aromatic and rich tomato stew, keeping it moist and a dream to devour. Growing up in Lagos, I was quite the picky child and the offer of bread and stew, or rice and stew, was always a guaranteed way to feed me. Now, I enjoy this with a steaming bowl of rice and plantains, but when I want to appease my inner child, a bowl of stew with a hunk of bread is all I could wish for.

FOR THE ROAST CHICKEN

2 medium carrots, scrubbed, halved lengthways and cut into chunks
1 large red onion, peeled and quartered
1 whole free-range chicken (about 1.5kg)
2 tbsp unsalted butter, softened
1 tbsp sea salt flakes
2 tsp freshly ground black pepper
2 tsp smoked paprika
1 tsp garlic granules
1 tsp dried thyme
1 tsp cayenne powder (optional)

FOR THE STEW

800g vine-ripened tomatoes, or 2 400g cans plum tomatoes
1 large onion, peeled and diced
1 Romano pepper, stemmed, deseeded and sliced
1 scotch bonnet pepper, stemmed and deseeded (optional)
4 large garlic cloves, peeled
2 tbsp grated fresh ginger
2 tsp curry powder
60ml vegetable oil
6 sprigs of thyme or 1 tsp dried
400ml chicken stock
Handful of fresh parsley, chopped

Lerato's Tip

Cooking this dish with thighs and drumsticks is also great, especially if you are short on time. Adjust the cooking time as required.

1. Preheat the oven to 400°F. You will need a large and heavy-based flameproof casserole or shallow oven-friendly pot (about 11–12 inches wide) with enough space to fit a whole chicken comfortably.

2. Place the carrots and quartered onion into the pot. Tie the legs of the chicken together, then rest the bird on top of the vegetables. Rub the softened butter over the chicken, then poke tiny holes all over using a skewer to render the fat for extra crispy skin.

3. In a small bowl, mix the sea salt, freshly ground black pepper, smoked paprika, garlic granules, thyme and cayenne pepper, if using. Dust the spice mixture generously over the surface and inside the cavity of the bird. Transfer the casserole to the oven and roast uncovered for 45 minutes.

4. Meanwhile, to make the stew, place the tomatoes, diced onion, pepper, scotch bonnet, if using, garlic, ginger and curry powder in a food processor and blend to a puree.

5. Carefully remove the casserole from the oven, place over a medium heat and pour in the oil. Add the puree and stir around the chicken, carefully avoiding the breast. Add the thyme and cook for 10 minutes.

6. Pour in the chicken stock, season with 1 teaspoon sea salt flakes and ½ teaspoon freshly ground black pepper and bring to a boil. Once bubbling, carefully return to the oven uncovered for another 45 minutes.

7. Once cooked, with skin darkened and crispy, remove the casserole from the oven and let the chicken rest in the stew for 15 minutes before serving. Either serve the entire dish at the table, scattered with chopped herbs, or carefully remove the chicken, place on a serving platter and pull apart, removing the bones, and serve alongside the stew with rice, pasta or bread.

Grandma's Garden Egg & Sautéed Tomatoes

WITH SMOKY SALTED PEANUTS

**SERVES 4 AS A MAIN
OR 6 AS SHARING PLATES**

1 red Romano or bell pepper, halved
and deseeded

12 garden eggs/Thai eggplants,
trimmed and halved, or 2–3
medium eggplants, cut into large
chunks

45ml vegetable oil

1 large red onion, peeled, halved
and sliced

3 garlic cloves, peeled and crushed

2 pods of selim pepper, lightly
smashed (or 2 black cardamom
pods)

800g vine-ripened tomatoes,
roughly chopped, or 2 400g cans
plum tomatoes

1 scotch bonnet pepper or
habanero chili, stemmed and
finely sliced, or pierced and left
whole

1 tsp smoked paprika

1–2 tbsp dried ground shrimps or
crayfish (optional)

5g scented leaves (such as African
clove basil, Thai basil or flat-leaf
parsley), roughly chopped

TO SERVE

Red Oil (see page 262) or
sustainable palm oil

50g roasted peanuts, chopped

Smoked salt or **Smoky Selim Salt**
(see page 266)

Grandma Theresa, who I am named after, was a phenomenal cook. I relish the stories my mum shares with me since her passing when I was a young teen. Grandma and Papa, as we called them, were not big meat eaters and this sumptuous stew was one of their favorite dishes. These eggplants, which are small, round, white, green or orange versions of purple eggplants, are popular in West African cooking. Once cooked, they are smashed and served as a creamy accompaniment to a rich tomato sauce. Although the skins shrivel, you can leave them unpeeled. I love to finish this dish with peanuts and a sprinkle of smoked salt. I think Grandma and Papa would have loved this.

1. Preheat the oven to 400°F and line a large roasting tray with baking parchment.

2. Place the pepper cut-side down in the roasting tray and cook in the oven for 30–35 minutes, until the skin is shriveled and lightly blistered. Set aside to cool.

3. Meanwhile, place the eggplants in a large pot of salted water and bring to a boil. Cook for 10–15 minutes, until softened with the skins shriveling. Drain and set aside.

4. Heat the oil in a large sauté pan over a medium heat. Add the onion with a pinch of fine sea salt and cook for 5 minutes, until softened. Stir in the garlic and cook for about 1 minute, until fragrant.

5. Roughly chop the roasted pepper and tip into the pan with the onions. Add the selim peppers, tomatoes and scotch bonnet or habanero, cover with a lid and cook for 20 minutes, until the tomatoes break down, stirring occasionally to prevent sticking. Add a small splash of water if it looks dry. Fish out the selim peppers and the scotch bonnet, if left whole, and save for another recipe.

6. Stir in the smoked paprika, ground shrimp or crayfish, if using, and add the eggplants, mashing them into the tomatoes, until the sauce is as coarse or smooth as you like. Cook uncovered for 5 minutes.

7. Season to perfection and scatter over the scented leaves. Spoon the stew into bowls with a teaspoon of lovely smoky-flavored **Red Oil** drizzled on top. Scatter over the roasted peanuts with a few pinches of smoked salt and serve with boiled or roasted yam, like my grandma and grandpa did, or enjoy with steaming hot potatoes.

Plantain & Coconut Curry

WITH RED KIDNEY BEANS

SERVES 4–6

I created this smoky, sweet curry during the pandemic, inspired by a chat with my good friend Mboni. We met over 18 years ago at university in London. While sharing stories of our favorite foods growing up, she told me of her mum's fervent cravings while pregnant with Mboni's younger sister for *ndizi na nyama*, an indulgent green banana and beef curry. It was a recipe passed on from her *bibi* (Swahili for grandma). Mama Mboni would reserve some of the coconut milk to drizzle on top of the finished dish. In my version, the sweet curry is also smoky and fragrant with allspice, paprika and the bewitching smoky selim peppers, known as *uda* in my mother's Ibo tribe in Nigeria. Prepare to be enchanted.

FOR THE PUREE

4 garlic cloves, peeled and crushed
1-inch piece of ginger, peeled and grated
1 400g can tomatoes (plum, chopped or cherry)
1 red bell pepper, stemmed and deseeded
½–1 scotch bonnet pepper or 1 bird's eye chili, stemmed and chopped, or pierced and left whole (optional)

FOR THE CURRY

3 tbsp vegetable oil
1 large brown onion, peeled and diced
1 red bell pepper, deseeded and sliced
2 tbsp **Smoky African Curry Spice** (see page 268), or 1½ tbsp Caribbean-style curry powder and 1 tsp smoked paprika
6 sprigs of thyme
2 large ripe plantains (firm and yellow), peeled (see page 277) and cut into ¾- to 1-inch chunks, or 4 green bananas (about 500g in total)
2 400g cans red kidney beans (drained weight 400–500g)
300ml stock (vegetable or chicken)
1 400ml can unsweetened coconut milk, shaken
Handful of fresh cilantro or flat-leaf parsley, roughly chopped, to serve
1 mild red chili, thinly sliced, to serve

1. To make the puree, place the garlic, ginger and tomatoes in a food processor with the red pepper and the scotch bonnet or red chili, if using, and not leaving whole, and blitz until smooth.

2. Pour the oil into a wide casserole, for which you have a lid, and set over a medium heat. Once shimmering, add the onion and red pepper with a pinch of fine sea salt. Fry for 5 minutes, until softened, then pour the puree into the pan. Cover partially with the lid to avoid the sauce spattering and cook for 10 minutes, stirring occasionally until thickened.

3. Stir in the **Smoky African Curry Spice** or curry powder and paprika, add the scotch bonnet or chili, if using whole, and the thyme. Continue to cook for 5 minutes.

4. When the sauce is darker, thicker and wonderfully fragrant, add the plantains and drained kidney beans. Pour in the stock and most of the coconut milk, saving 4 tablespoons for later. Season with ¾ teaspoon fine salt and ½ teaspoon freshly ground black pepper, bring up to a boil, then reduce the heat, cover with a lid and simmer for 10 minutes.

5. Remove the lid and check the seasoning. Continue to cook with the lid off, for another 10 minutes, until the plantain is tender and the sauce is sumptuous and thick. If unripe and green, the plantain may need up to 30 minutes to cook properly.

6. Just before serving, drizzle the remaining coconut milk over the top and scatter with chopped cilantro or parsley and thinly sliced fresh chilies, and serve with a steaming bowl of rice or lentils.

Berbere Chicken Stew

Doro wat, or *wot* as it is locally called, is a great introduction to the foods of Ethiopia and Eritrea. Perhaps the most famous of all stews from the Horn of Africa, this is not an everyday meal but is reserved for special celebrations such as Easter or Christmas. It can take a whole day of preparation, from the meticulous cleaning of the chicken, to cooking down the copious amount of onions in spiced butter *Niter Kibbeh* (see page 264), before the revelation of a deeply aromatic lava reddened with the wondrous **Berbere Spice Blend** (see page 273). *Doro wat* is traditionally served with boiled eggs, slashed to soak up the oils from the sauce as they rest on top, and **injera**, the much loved spongy bread made from local heritage grains known as teff. Try my **Quick Injera** (see page 203) or source the real deal from an Ethiopian or Eritrean store.

FOR THE STEW

4–5 large red onions (about
　1.25–1.5kg), peeled and diced

2 tbsp vegetable oil

3 tbsp **Ethiopian Spiced Clarified
　Butter** (see page 264), ghee or
　vegetable oil

8 garlic cloves, peeled and crushed

2-inch piece of ginger, peeled and
　grated

3 tbsp **Berbere Spice Blend**
　(see page 273)

2 tbsp tomato puree

500ml chicken stock

1 tsp **Ethiopian Finishing Spice**
　(see page 270) or fragrant curry
　powder

6 free-range eggs, boiled and
　peeled

FOR THE CHICKEN

12 chicken thighs, bone in and
　skinless (about 1.2kg total weight)

Juice of 3 lemons

4 garlic cloves, peeled and crushed

1-inch piece of ginger, peeled and
　grated

Vegetable oil, to drizzle

TO SERVE

Quick Injera (see page 203)
　or steaming hot rice

1. Place a large, heavy-based flameproof casserole over a medium heat. Add the onions and cook uncovered for 15–20 minutes, stirring occasionally, until the mixture is dry. Add the oil and 2 tablespoons of the **Spiced Clarified Butter**, stirring to prevent sticking. Regulate the heat between medium and medium-low to prevent burning and cook for 30–40 minutes, until the onions become golden and jammy. (This may take longer, depending on how wet your onions are.)

2. Meanwhile, place the chicken in a large bowl. Pour over the lemon juice and rub into the chicken. Cover and set aside in the fridge for 20 minutes.

3. Preheat the oven to 425°F and oil a roasting tray. Remove the chicken from the fridge and discard the lemon juice. Add ½ teaspoon fine sea salt, the garlic, ginger and a drizzle of oil to the chicken and massage thoroughly. Place on the prepared tray and roast for 20 minutes.

4. Add the remaining **Spiced Clarified Butter** to the onions and stir in the garlic and ginger. Cook for about 1 minute, until fragrant. Add 2 tablespoons of the **Berbere Spice Blend**, stir and taste before adding more to your heart's content. Stir in the tomato puree and cook for 3 minutes.

5. Tuck the roasted chicken into the pan with the onions, pour in 300ml of the stock and bring to a strong simmer. Season with 1 teaspoon fine sea salt, reduce the heat to medium-low, cover and simmer for 30 minutes, adding a little more stock, if needed, until the sauce is thick and the chicken cooked through.

6. Stir in the **Ethiopian Finishing Spice**, taste and season to perfection. Add the eggs (you can cut incisions in the eggs if you want the sauce to seep in; I prefer to leave my eggs whole, slicing in half to serve) and simmer uncovered for another 5 minutes.

7. Remove from the heat and leave the sauce to settle slightly before serving with a bowl of steaming rice, or for an Ethiopian/Eritrean feast, line a large warm plate with injera and top with some of the stew including eggs and pulled-apart chicken. Serve with greens such as **Braised Greens with Sweet Red Peppers** (see page 172), **Spiced Butter Lentils** (see page 213) and cottage cheese, similar to Ethiopian *ayib*. (See photo on pages 84–5.)

Cape Malay Chicken Curry

SERVES 4-6

3 tbsp coconut oil

1 large brown onion, peeled and diced

10 curry leaves (optional)

2 green or red chilies, stemmed and finely chopped

4 garlic cloves, peeled and crushed

2-inch piece of ginger, peeled and grated

1 cinnamon stick or 1 tsp ground cinnamon

½ tsp ground turmeric

6 cardamom pods, seeds crushed

1 tsp cumin seeds, toasted and ground

1 tsp fennel seeds, toasted and ground

2 medium ripe tomatoes, diced

2 tbsp garam masala

3 medium potatoes, peeled and cut into small chunks

700g boneless chicken thighs, skin removed and cut into small chunks

250ml chicken or vegetable stock

3 tbsp smooth apricot jam

1 400ml can coconut milk

Fresh cilantro, finely chopped, to serve

Bring the spirit of vibrant *bo-kaap*, one of the legacies of the Cape Malays of South Africa, into your home with this sweet and glorious curry. In the early 17th century, Javanese, Southeast Asian and East African slaves were brought into South Africa to work on the farms in and around Cape Town. These groups of people settled to become Cape Malays and their culture and food have become an important part of South Africa's celebrated rainbow cuisine.

1. Melt the coconut oil in a heavy-based flameproof casserole set over a medium heat. Add the onion and a pinch of fine sea salt and fry until it turns golden brown.

2. Add the curry leaves, if using, and the chilies. Stir in the garlic, ginger and all the dried spices, apart from the garam masala, and cook for a few seconds, adding a tablespoon or more of water, if needed, to unravel any stickiness.

3. Tip in the tomatoes, stir to mingle with the aromatics, cover with a lid and cook for about 5 minutes, to let the tomatoes break down.

4. Add the garam masala, potatoes and chicken, stir to coat well, then cover with a lid and cook for 5 minutes, as the chicken takes on the rich dark color and flavors of the spice paste.

5. Gently pour in the stock, stir well, then cover and cook for 10 minutes.

6. Add the apricot jam to sweeten and the coconut milk to thicken the curry, season with 1 teaspoon fine sea salt or to taste, stir well and cook uncovered for another 15 minutes, or until the chicken is cooked through, the potatoes are soft and the sauce is invitingly creamy.

7. Serve with **South African Yellow Rice** (see page 212) and **Smoky Tomato & Date Jam** (see page 257).

Variation

With this deeply aromatic and rich curry base, you can add your favorite proteins or vegetables. Add tougher veggies at the same time as the potatoes and softer veggies for the final 5–15 minutes, depending on the type. Butternut squash, eggplants, sweet potatoes and cauliflower would all make wonderful plant-based alternatives. Simple curry powder can be used instead of garam masala.

Poulet Yassa
Grilled Chicken in Caramelized Onion & Lemon Sauce

Escape to Senegal with *Poulet Yassa,* a dish that is pure sunshine on a plate. I love serving and teaching this recipe. It is one of the most popular dishes at my feasts and cookery classes, and is especially easy to cook, with readily available ingredients. It truly teaches us to trust the process, trust the ingredients and trust your instincts when cooking. I usually encourage my cooks to taste the raw sauce at the very beginning (before adding the chicken) and then taste it again after cooking, as this dish is full of surprises as it transforms from lip-puckering tartness, to sweet, spicy, zingy and balanced. I love using a combination of sweeter lemons and tart limes. Your *yassa* can be as mild or as fiery as you wish. Finely mince the scotch bonnet for lots of heat or pierce the chili and tuck it into the sauce to release its warming and fragrant oils for less heat. You can also omit the scotch bonnet entirely or swap it for other chilies (see my notes about cooking with chilies on page 22) and play around with it in different ways. But that tingling heat is a big part of the rousing West African experience. Trust me! (See pages 176–7 for a plant-based variation of this dish.)

SERVES 4-6

1kg chicken legs and thighs, bone in
    and skin on
1 tsp fine sea salt
3 tbsp peanut or neutral vegetable
    oil, plus more for brushing

FOR THE MARINADE
1 medium brown onion, peeled and
    roughly chopped
4 garlic cloves, peeled
Handful of fresh flat-leaf parsley
1 tsp cayenne pepper
Zest and juice of 1 lemon
2 tsp Dijon mustard

FOR THE SAUCE
3 tbsp peanut or vegetable oil
3 medium brown onions, peeled,
    halved and sliced (just under
    ½ inch thick)
1 red Romano or bell pepper,
    deseeded and sliced (just under
    ½ inch thick)
2 garlic cloves, peeled and grated
Juice of 4 limes or 2 lemons,
    or a combination of both
2 tbsp Dijon mustard
300ml chicken stock
6 sprigs of thyme or 1 tsp dried
1 bay leaf
1 scotch bonnet pepper, pierced
    and left whole
½ tsp fine sea salt
½ tsp freshly ground black pepper

TO SERVE
Honey, if needed
Handful of parsley, leaves plucked

1. Cut a few slashes diagonally across the chicken skin, season with the fine sea salt and massage it into the chicken. Place in a wide bowl.

2. Combine the marinade ingredients in a food processor and blend to a smooth paste. Tip the paste onto the chicken, add 2 tablespoons of the oil and massage thoroughly, carefully tucking some of the marinade under the skin and into the slashes. Cover and refrigerate for 2 hours, or overnight for a more flavorful marinade and to tenderize tougher poultry.

3. Remove the chicken from the fridge 30 minutes before cooking to allow it to come up to room temperature. Preheat the grill to medium-high.

4. Drizzle the chicken with the remaining oil. Toss well and arrange in one layer on an oiled grilling tray or rack with thighs skin-side up. Reserve any marinade left in the bowl. Grill each side for 10 minutes, until browned with a nice char on the skin. Set aside to finish cooking in the sauce.

5. Meanwhile, to make the sauce, heat the oil in a wide saucepan and add the onions and any leftover marinade. Sprinkle with a pinch of fine sea salt, cover with a lid and cook over a medium heat for 10 minutes, stirring often, until the onions are translucent. Remove the lid and continue cooking uncovered for another 15–20 minutes, until the onions begin to brown and eventually caramelize in their natural sugars. Add a splash of water, if needed, to prevent burning.

6. Add the pepper and cook for 5 minutes. Stir in the garlic until fragrant. Pour in the lime or lemon juice and add the Dijon mustard, chicken stock, thyme, bay leaf and scotch bonnet. Season with the sea salt and freshly ground pepper and bring to a simmer.

7. Tuck the chicken, skin-side up, into the sauce. Cover and simmer for 20 minutes, or until the sauce is reduced and the chicken is cooked through.

8. Taste to check the seasoning. If you find the sauce too tart, scoop out 2 tablespoons of sauce into a small bowl and add ½ teaspoon of honey, mix well then pour back into your sauce. Gently stir and taste again. Repeat with another ½ teaspoon of honey, if needed.

9. Scatter with parsley and serve with simple sides, such as rice, steamed couscous, fonio or creamy mashed potatoes and green beans. (See photo on page 89.)

Mrouzia
Celebration Lamb Tagine
WITH RAISINS, HONEY & ALMONDS

Mrouzia is one of the most indulgent tagines in Morocco. This lavishly sweet dish is traditionally prepared with the meat covered in suet and cooked confit-style. Spices such as ginger and Ras el hanout are added for an intensely flavored dish, thickened and sweetened with honey, dried fruits and almonds. In some parts of Morocco, molasses made from raisins is added instead of the whole fruits. This is a favorite dish to celebrate the "Big Sacrifice," known as *Eid al-Fitr* in Islam, a celebration marking the end of Ramadan. It is a time for prayer and fasting, family and charity, especially sharing with others. In the old days, the confit-style of cooking and the honey served to preserve the large amount of slaughtered meat that would be cooked and shared among family, friends and neighbors. Now with modern electricity, it is unnecessary to cook with as much fat. I prefer to add the dried fruits and honey at the last stage of cooking, and finish with toasted almonds and dried roses for a magnificent feast.

**SERVES 4 AS A MAIN OR
8 AS SHARING PLATES**

1kg lamb shanks (about 4), trimmed
  (you could also use neck or lamb
  shoulder chops)
2 tbsp unsalted butter or ghee
3 tbsp vegetable oil
2 brown onions, peeled and finely
  chopped
4 garlic cloves, peeled and crushed
1-inch piece of ginger, peeled and
  finely grated
A good pinch of saffron strands
750ml lamb, chicken or vegetable
  stock
1 cinnamon stick
100g raisins
100g dried apricots, finely chopped
3 tbsp honey
1½ tsp ground cinnamon
2 tsp **Imperial Ras el Hanout
  Spice Blend** (see page 269 or
  store-bought)

FOR THE MARINADE
1½ tbsp **Imperial Ras el Hanout**
  (see page 269 or store-bought)
½ tsp ground turmeric
1 tsp fine sea salt
1 tsp freshly ground black pepper

TO FINISH
50–100g flaked almonds
Dried edible rose petals

1. Combine the marinade spices, sea salt and pepper in a large bowl and add a little water to form a thick paste. Add the lamb pieces and coat all sides. Cover and leave to marinate in the fridge for 4 hours or overnight, if possible.

2. Set a large, heavy-based flameproof pan or casserole over a medium-high heat, add the butter or ghee and the oil. Brown the lamb in small batches until golden on all sides. Remove with a slotted spoon and set aside.

3. Reduce the heat to medium, add the onions to the pan and cook for 5 minutes until softened. Stir in the garlic and ginger until fragrant. Return the meat to the pan and cook in the aromatics for 5 minutes, stirring occasionally to prevent sticking.

4. Crumble the saffron into the pan and carefully pour in half of the stock into the side of the saucepan, avoiding the top of the meat, and bring to a strong simmer. Reduce the heat, add the cinnamon stick, cover with a lid and simmer steadily for 2½ hours, or until the meat is luxuriously tender. Top up with a little more stock or water, if necessary, to keep the sauce moist.

5. Once the meat is tender, add the raisins and apricots along with a little more stock or hot water. Drizzle in the honey and add the ground cinnamon and Ras el hanout. Stir to combine and bring to a strong simmer once again. Reduce the heat, cover with a lid and simmer for a final 20–30 minutes, until the raisins are plump and the sauce is thick and reduced. If necessary, remove the lid and simmer for a few minutes to thicken the sauce.

6. Meanwhile, preheat the oven to 350°F.

7. Spread the almonds onto a baking tray and toast for 3–4 minutes, turning halfway, until light golden. Remove from the baking tray and set aside.

8. Once the sauce is reduced, take the casserole off the heat. Taste and season to perfection. Arrange the meat in a warm shallow dish, spoon the wonderful sauce with the plump raisins over and around the meat, and scatter over the toasted almonds and dried rose petals. Serve with **Roasted Pepper Salad** (see page 179) and **African Grain Salad** (see page 164). (See photo on page 93.)

Juicy Berbere Meatballs in Tomato Sauce

SERVES 4-6

FOR THE MEATBALLS
500g minced beef
1 small red onion, peeled and diced
2 fat garlic cloves, peeled and crushed
1 large free-range egg, beaten
1½ tsp **Berbere Spice Blend** (see page 273)
20g fresh flat-leaf parsley, leaves picked and finely chopped
1 tsp dried oregano
4 tbsp panko breadcrumbs
1 tsp fine sea salt
2 tbsp vegetable or olive oil
1 tbsp **Ethiopian Spiced Clarified Butter** (see page 264)

FOR THE TOMATO SAUCE
1 tbsp vegetable or olive oil
3 tbsp **Ethiopian Spiced Clarified Butter** (see page 264)
1 large red onion, peeled and diced
3 fat garlic cloves, peeled and grated
2 tbsp **Berbere Spice Blend** (see page 273)
1 tbsp tomato puree
2 tsp dried oregano
1 700g jar passata or 2 400g cans whole or chopped tomatoes

Lerato's Tip

This mince makes great burger patties, and is wonderful made with turkey, lamb or a mix of cooked lentils and red kidney beans for a plant-based alternative.

I simply adore this recipe and cook it at least once a week. Once you have prepared a tub of the deeply aromatic **Berbere Spice Blend** (see page 273), you will be inspired to use it in several dishes, as I do. The Ethiopian/Eritrean spice blend is added to the meatballs as well as the tomato sauce, which could easily become your new favorite pasta sauce.

1. Combine all the meatball ingredients in a bowl, except the oil and **Spiced Clarified Butter**, and reserve some parsley for garnishing later. Mix thoroughly with your hands to distribute all the different flavors and textures evenly. Wet or oil your hands to prevent the mixture sticking, then scoop a heaped tablespoonful of mince into your palm and roll into a ball about 1 inch in diameter. Repeat until you have about 20 meatballs.

2. Heat the oil and **Spiced Clarified Butter** in a wide saucepan or frying pan set over a medium heat. Fry the meatballs in 2 or 3 batches for 5 minutes, turning a few times until browned all over. The aim is not to cook them fully at this stage. Remove from the pan and set aside.

3. Discard any charred bits from the pan and place the pan back over a medium heat to make the sauce. Add the oil and 2 tablespoons of the **Spiced Clarified Butter** and, when melted, add the onion and fry for 5 minutes, until softened. Stir in the garlic for about 30 seconds, until fragrant, then add the **Berbere Spice Blend**, tomato puree and oregano, stirring the puree into the aromatics. Cover with a lid and cook for 2–3 minutes over a medium-low heat, stirring frequently.

4. Pour in the passata or canned tomatoes and cook over a medium heat for 10 minutes, until thickened. If using whole tomatoes, you may need to cook for longer, and use a wooden spoon to break them up.

5. Season the sauce with ¼ teaspoon fine sea salt, add the meatballs and reduce the heat to medium-low. Cover with a lid and simmer for 20 minutes, stirring occasionally, until the meatballs are cooked through, and the tomatoes are sweet.

6. Stir in the remaining **Spiced Clarified Butter** and simmer for 1 minute for a bewitchingly fragrant and sumptuous sauce. Sprinkle with the reserved parsley and serve with spaghetti or your favorite pasta, injera (see page 203), or a garlic and herb flatbread to mop up the wonderful sauce.

Slow-Cooked & Sweet Beef Stew

When Nigerians say, "This is the best thing since rice and stew!" this is the kind of stew we are referring to. Rich, dark, slow-cooked and just wonderful. "Sweet stew," as we like to call it, but not because there is an addition of sugar or sweetener. The pick of ingredients matters a great deal, like choosing the very best tomatoes—for me that means fresh, vine-ripened cherry or plum tomatoes at peak ripeness, or the best-quality passata or jarred or canned tomatoes you can find. A quality broth or stock, store-bought or homemade, is also important, and cooking the beef shin patiently to break down its connecting tissues adds a wonderful flavor and unctuousness to the stew. My mother loved to cook stews with fragrant curry leaves, which she grew around the house, and I have continued this tradition.

SERVES 4

1kg vine-ripened tomatoes, or
    800g passata, or 2 400g cans
    plum or chopped tomatoes
1 Romano or bell pepper, stemmed,
    deseeded and roughly chopped
1 large brown onion, peeled and
    roughly chopped
1 scotch bonnet pepper, stemmed
    and roughly chopped, or pierced
    and left whole
4 tbsp vegetable, peanut or olive oil
5 curry leaves (optional)
1 medium red onion, peeled and
    finely chopped
1 tsp curry powder
2 tsp paprika
1 tsp dried thyme
1 tsp dried oregano
1 tbsp tomato puree
1kg beef shin, cut into small chunks
300–500ml beef or chicken stock

1. Place the tomatoes, pepper, onion and scotch bonnet, if not using whole, into a blender and blitz to a puree. Set aside.

2. Heat the oil in a large, heavy-based saucepan over a medium heat. Add the curry leaves, if using, and fry until fragrant, then fish them out to use later. Stir the red onion into the pan with a generous pinch of fine sea salt and fry, stirring occasionally, for 10 minutes, until golden.

3. Add the curry powder, paprika, dried herbs and tomato puree and cook for 2 minutes, stirring continuously, until fragrant.

4. Add the beef and mix well to coat in the aromatics. Cook for 10–15 minutes, stirring occasionally, and scraping the bottom as the beef browns on all sides.

5. Gently pour in the blended tomato and pepper puree and bring to a simmer. Cover with a lid and cook for 25 minutes if made with fresh or canned tomatoes, or 10–15 minutes if using passata, stirring occasionally, until reduced and rich in color.

6. Pour in 300ml of the stock, season with 1 teaspoon fine sea salt and some freshly ground black pepper, and stir to incorporate any puree stuck to the bottom of the pan. Add the scotch bonnet, if using whole, and bring up to a strong simmer. Reduce the heat, cover with a lid and simmer for 1–1½ hours, stirring occasionally to prevent sticking, until thick and glossy, with the beef tender. If necessary, add a little more stock as the stew thickens. Once cooked, remove the scotch bonnet if left whole, mince and serve on the side.

7. Serve your sweet stew with rice and **Fried** or **Roasted Plantain** (see page 278) for a wholesome and heart-warming Nigerian-inspired meal.

Variations
If using a stewing cut of beef with little or no fat, the beef will need less time to cook. If your tomatoes aren't the best quality, finely grate one or two carrots into the sauce for a sweeter flavor. For a vegetable-based stew with eggplants, sweet potatoes or cauliflower, once the puree is cooked, from step 6, add the vegetables with just enough stock, cover and cook until tender.

Roasts, Grills & Cooking with Fire

Ras el Hanout Rainbow Roast

WITH CHERMOULA

SERVES 4

1 large red onion, peeled and cut
  into small wedges
1 plantain, peeled (see page 277),
  cut in half lengthways, then cut
  into 1-inch chunks
1 red pepper, stemmed, deseeded
  and cut into 1-inch chunks
1 yellow pepper, stemmed, deseeded
  and cut into 1-inch chunks
1 zucchini, trimmed, cut in half
  lengthways, then cut into 1-inch
  chunks
1 eggplant, trimmed, cut in half
  lengthways, then cut into 1-inch
  chunks
1 400g can chickpeas, drained and
  rinsed (230–250g drained weight)
4 tbsp extra-virgin avocado or olive
  oil
2 tsp cumin seeds, lightly crushed
2 tsp coriander seeds, lightly crushed
2 tbsp Ras el hanout
2 garlic cloves, peeled
250g good-quality halloumi, or
  300g tofu, drained and cut into
  about 8 slices

FOR THE CHERMOULA

1 garlic clove, peeled
20g fresh cilantro, leaves and stalks
  roughly chopped
20g fresh flat-leaf parsley leaves
1 tsp ground cumin
1 tsp paprika
½ tsp ground turmeric
½ tsp chili flakes
1–2 tbsp fresh lemon juice
60ml extra-virgin olive oil

I love recipes that are easy to put together without sacrificing flavor, and this vibrant roast is the gift that keeps on giving. Add your favorite or leftover vegetables, cautiously layering them according to individual rigor—harder vegetables, such as spuds and cauliflower, going in first, with softer eggplants and zucchini added later. Both halloumi and tofu take beautifully to the floral and heady Ras el hanout, but you could add any of your favorite proteins. You can also grill them separately for a nice char, then add them to your roast afterwards. I love a combination of my floral and sweet **Imperial Ras el Hanout** (see page 269) and the smokier headier version, which includes cumin and coriander. I could go on and on to show you how the versatility of this dish knows no bounds. The proof will be in the eating.

1. Preheat the oven to 400°F.

2. Place all the vegetables and the chickpeas in a roasting tray (you may need two) and drizzle with the oil. Mix the cumin and coriander seeds together, then scatter 2½ teaspoons over the vegetables, saving the rest for later. Sprinkle over the Ras el hanout and season with fine sea salt and freshly ground black pepper. Finely grate the garlic cloves over the vegetables and toss everything together. Roast in the oven for 30–35 minutes.

3. Meanwhile, prepare the chermoula dressing. Place the garlic clove in a food processor with the herbs, spices and chili flakes. Drizzle in the lemon juice and oil with a few tablespoons of water and whizz until you have a runny dressing. Season well, then brush some onto the halloumi or tofu. Leave to marinate while the vegetables roast. Tip the dressing into a small bowl.

4. Remove the tray from the oven, scatter the halloumi or tofu over the top and sprinkle with the remaining 1½ teaspoons of cumin and coriander seeds. Return to the oven and roast for a final 15 minutes, until the vegetables are tender and browned and the halloumi or tofu lightly golden.

5. Drizzle some of the chermoula over the vegetables and serve on its own or with couscous, fonio or **African Grain Salad** (see page 164).

Suya Roasted Cauliflower

SERVES 4

1 large head of cauliflower (about 800g), leaves and stalk removed
300g cherry tomatoes, halved
1 red Romano or bell pepper, stemmed, deseeded and roughly chopped
½ small red onion, peeled and halved
1 tbsp peanut or vegetable oil, plus more for drizzling

FOR THE SPICED PEANUT PUREE
180g blanched peanuts, or 100g natural and unsweetened peanut butter
½ small red onion, peeled and roughly chopped
4 garlic cloves, peeled and roughly chopped
2-inch piece of ginger, peeled and roughly chopped
2 tbsp **Suya Spice Blend** (see page 272)
1 tsp smoked paprika

TO SERVE
Small handful of fresh cilantro, chopped
1 tsp **Suya Spice Blend** (see page 272)

Lerato's Tip

Although I love roasting a whole cauliflower, you could also break the cauliflower into florets or cut it into steaks and spread them with the puree before roasting uncovered for 30–40 minutes.

The humble cauliflower is transformed into the star with luxuriously spiced peanut puree and fragrant suya spices. I created this dish for my plant-based cookery class to impress and it delivers every time!

1. To make the spiced peanut puree, place a flameproof casserole over a medium heat and pour in the peanuts. Swirl the nuts around a few times, using a wooden spoon to avoid burning. Roast until golden, then remove from the pan to cool. Reserve 2 tablespoons (about 30g) of the roasted peanuts and place the rest in a food processor with the other puree ingredients. Add 60ml water and blend, scraping down the sides now and again. Add more water, a tablespoon at a time, to loosen the paste, if needed, until spreadable but with some texture. Season with ½ teaspoon fine sea salt and reserve 2 heaped tablespoons of the puree for later.

2. Preheat the oven to 425°F.

3. Carve a triangle into the stalk of the cauliflower and place the cauliflower in the casserole. Spread the puree onto the whole surface, covering it in a thick coating. Turn the cauliflower over, season the cavity and spoon some puree inside. Place the cauliflower flat-side down and tuck the cherry tomatoes, red pepper and onion around the cauliflower. Brush or drizzle all the vegetables, including the cauliflower, with the oil and pour 60ml water around the sides. Cover with a lid and roast in the middle of the oven for 30 minutes, then remove the lid and roast for another 30 minutes, until beautifully dark and golden, and you can pierce a knife into the cauliflower with little resistance. Set aside while you prepare the sauce.

4. Place the roasted pepper, cherry tomatoes and onion in a food processor with the reserved peanut puree and blend until smooth. Drizzle with a little oil and season with a pinch of fine sea salt and black pepper.

5. Spoon the tomato and spiced peanut puree onto a warm serving plate and place the cauliflower on top. Chop the reserved roasted peanuts, scatter them over the top with the chopped cilantro and sprinkle over the **Suya Spice Blend**. Serve as a main dish or an accompaniment to your favorite salad, roast or grains.

Coconut & Peanut Suya Roast Chicken

SERVES 4-6

Coconuts and peanuts are widely used ingredients across Africa. I have often found their combination very tempting, yet a little too indulgent when used in equally large quantities, so I choose to pair them in moderation. In this very adaptable one-pan recipe, the balance of luxuriously creamy coconut and heady roasted peanuts combines with the fragrant suya spices for a match made in heaven. For a vegetarian or vegan roast, replace the chicken with halloumi or tofu and throw in a selection of your favorite vegetables and legumes.

3 red onions, peeled, 1 roughly chopped and 1 cut into wedges

1-inch piece of ginger, peeled and roughly chopped

4 garlic cloves, peeled and roughly chopped

½–1 scotch bonnet pepper or 3–4 chilies, stemmed and roughly chopped

2 bell peppers (1 yellow and 1 red), stemmed, deseeded and cut into 1-inch chunks

60ml coconut cream

6 tbsp **Suya Spice Blend** (see page 272)

2 tbsp coconut or vegetable oil

8 chicken thighs, skin on and bone in

6 sprigs of thyme or ¾ tsp dried thyme

2 tbsp unsweetened desiccated coconut

1. Tip the roughly chopped onion, ginger, garlic and scotch bonnet or chilies into a blender and blitz until smooth, adding a splash of water to loosen the paste, if needed.

2. Place the paste in a large dish or bowl, add the onion wedges, peppers, coconut cream and season with 1 teaspoon fine sea salt. Stir in 4 tablespoons of the **Suya Spice Blend**, drizzle in 1 tablespoon of the oil then add the chicken, coating all sides thoroughly. Cover and leave to marinate in the fridge for 1–3 hours, or overnight, if you have time to do so.

3. Preheat the oven to 400°F and remove the chicken from the fridge to come up to room temperature.

4. Tip the chicken along with the vegetables and any remaining marinade into a roasting tray, drizzle with the remaining oil and arrange the chicken skin-side up in a single layer. Tuck the fresh thyme underneath or sprinkle with the dried thyme and roast for 30 minutes.

5. Meanwhile, mix the remaining **Suya Spice Blend** with the desiccated coconut and a generous pinch of sea salt flakes. Remove tray from the oven, sprinkle with the spiced coconut and return to the oven to roast for a final 15 minutes, until cooked through, golden and crispy, with a little char on the onions.

Variation

For summer barbecues or indoor grills, cut the onions into larger wedges and halve the peppers. Shake off any excess marinade and brush with oil before placing the chicken on a sizzling hot grill or barbecue. Grill until cooked through with a lovely char.

Harissa Yogurt Poussins

WITH RAS EL HANOUT BUTTER

SERVES 4–8

4 whole poussins, about 400g each
3 tbsp **Ras el Hanout Butter** (see page 263), melted

FOR THE MARINADE
125g natural yogurt
Juice of 1 lemon
2 tbsp olive oil
4 tbsp **Red Harissa** (see page 260 or shop-bought)
3 fat garlic cloves, peeled and grated
2 tsp fennel seeds, toasted and crushed
1 tsp ground turmeric
1½ tsp fine sea salt

When not spatchcocking, my ideal roast chicken involves finding the smallest possible bird, for maximum flavor and speed of cooking. The marinade is a great balance of tanginess and warmth from the yogurt, citrus and harissa, with a light anise flavor from the fennel seeds, which I adore. This is a wonderful roast you could also throw on a barbecue or grill.

1. Mix all the marinade ingredients together and divide between the poussins, slathering all over and including the cavity. Cover and refrigerate for 2 hours, or overnight, if possible.

2. Preheat the oven to 400°F and remove the birds from the fridge to come to room temperature.

3. Place the poussins on a large roasting tray, leaving a bit of space between them. Roast for 45–50 minutes, until golden, slightly charred and cooked through, brushing after 30 minutes with half the **Ras el Hanout Butter**.

4. Carefully lift the poussins onto a warm serving dish, brush with the remaining spiced butter and leave to rest before tucking in with **Saffron Potatoes & Peas** (see page 186) and **Herb Salad with Hibiscus & Pomegranates** (see page 162).

Under the Mango Trees

KODO VILLAGE, NIGER STATE, NIGERIA

A sweet breeze brushed over my face, replacing the scorch in the air with a comforting tropical aroma that heightened my senses so deeply I could taste it. It was a sweltering day in April, at about 100°F. Hot and humid, as harmattan (the dusty wind from the Sahara Desert) had retreated, signaling the end of the dry season, allowing for sunshine and humidity before the arrival of the monsoon between June and October, which is known as the rainy season.

With my mother as my accomplice, we had set off to find gold in the form of shea butter. I had heard it was being produced by women from a cooperative in Niger State in the Northern region of Nigeria. After a great day learning about each step in the production of this highly prized nut butter, we bought a few containers, enough to last me a year on my return to England. I struggled to keep awake on the 12-mile journey back to Minna, the capital, as we drove past the thick bushes with food hawkers and farmers dotted on either side of the road.

The towns and villages in Niger State are jeweled with fresh fruits and vegetables. The proximity to other farming states, like Kano, Kaduna and temperate Jos Plateau, known for its strawberries and some of the country's best tomatoes, makes it a great place for fresh pickings of plump tomatoes, peppers, green beans, garden eggs and their cousins the purple eggplants, a wide variety of spinach and other leafy greens, carrots, herbs and more.

"Mangoes! Look! Mangoes!" my mother said. I woke up to the familiar sweetness in the air. We had been waiting for the mango season and had been pining for them for so long that I thought I must have eaten some in a dream. I confess that some of my commitment was down to the fact that I had a deadline looming for my mango-themed cookery column that week. But this was no dream. We had found a group of women selling baskets and buckets of mangoes of different shapes and sizes under a thick bush of mango trees. I beamed with excitement, enchanted by this seemingly ordinary but rather extraordinary sight. It was wonderful being in the birthplace of these delightful fruits.

How enterprising of these women to set up shop there. These mangoes had far fewer air miles than those in our local supermarket in England! Some of the fruits were unripe with green, sturdy flesh, others were ripe with a bright blush of reddish-orange. They were beautiful, deeply fragrant and all too tempting. The women looked at me, perplexed, as I poked and prodded the mangoes, testing for the soft push of ripened, juicy flesh. Over the years I have come to understand that window shopping and touching in African markets is not advised for fear of awakening the wrath of the seller.

There is a strong suspicion of people investigating their goods, and the only way to quench it is to buy lots of what you are poking and prodding.

This time I was not worried because at the other end of the mango bushes, my mother haggled away. As she is exceptionally good at it and because most of my market trips have been with her, I never truly perfected the art of "pricing" (haggling) until I traveled to Morocco and was forced to do it for myself. That is another tale to tell. However, I show a lot of teeth in England when it comes to getting the best deals, so I must have picked up a few tips from Mum.

The women traders were calm, a demeanor that I learned is natural among the northerners. Even though they were all selling mangoes, there was no sense of rivalry, and my mum went back and forth between the women, haggling for more of these sweet fruits. The woman who finally sold to my mother accompanied her to the car. She accepted the money and untied a bit of her waist-tied wrapper. She tucked the money into the fabric and tied it back up again. Growing up I always wondered how much money the market women could amass in their wrappers.

The woman chuckled while my mother jokingly smacked her back. She must have given my mother a hard time while haggling. It was time to go home, now that our sweet mangoes filled up the trunk of the car alongside the golden shea butter. Oh, how excited I was, like a kid in a candy store. Under the mango trees, I had been completely consumed by the wonders of nature, the rich pickings that surrounded us and the

endless possibilities of food once we open ourselves to them.

The journey back to Minna was spent concocting mango recipes, while my mother savagely devoured fresh mangoes. Aha, I thought! How about a mango and moringa fool and a mango and scotch bonnet marinade for a chargrilled roast? With her mouth full and remembering that she would be my guinea pig for testing these recipes, Mum nodded and smiled. "Mmmm, great ideas, my daughter."

Mango & Lime Piri Piri Chicken

SERVES 4–6

I adore this recipe with Mozambican-inspired "piri piri"—the famous tangy chili marinade, sauce or dip enjoyed across the world. This recipe is a summer classic in my home and at my feasts, immediately transporting you to an African tropical coast. I use sweeter scotch bonnets instead of the traditional and more assertive African bird's eye, called *pili pili* in East Africa. You could mix several different chilies for a beautifully nuanced flavor and varying heat. The sweeter the mangoes, the sweeter your marinade, so "pluck" wisely.

1 1.5kg chicken, jointed into 8
pieces, or a mix of thighs and
drumsticks

FOR THE MARINADE
Juice of 2 limes
2 tsp fine sea salt
2 garlic cloves, peeled and finely
grated

FOR THE MANGO & LIME PIRI PIRI
Zest of 1 lime and juice of 2 limes
3 medium ripe mangoes, peeled
and destoned
2 scotch bonnet peppers (red and
yellow), or bird's eye chilies,
stemmed and roughly chopped
3 garlic cloves, peeled
½ red bell pepper, stemmed and
deseeded
2-inch piece of ginger, peeled and
roughly chopped
½ medium brown onion, peeled and
roughly chopped
90ml vegetable oil
1 tbsp **Smoky African Curry Spice**
(see page 268) or 1 tsp ground
allspice plus 2 tsp smoked
paprika
1 tsp dried thyme
1 tsp dried oregano
2 tbsp red wine vinegar

TO SERVE
Handful of fresh cilantro, chopped
2 limes, cut into wedges

1. To make the marinade, mix the lime juice, salt and garlic in a large bowl. Add the chicken and massage into every nook to coat well. Set aside.

2. Combine all the ingredients for the **Mango & Lime Piri Piri**, except the thyme, oregano and vinegar, in a blender and blitz to a smooth paste. Add a little more oil if the paste is too thick. Sprinkle in the thyme and oregano and mix thoroughly.

3. Spoon enough of the paste into the bowl to coat the chicken heavily, leaving a good amount to one side for a sauce. Cover and leave in the fridge for 2 hours or overnight.

4. Place the remaining piri piri in a small saucepan with the red wine vinegar and cook over a medium-low heat for 10 minutes. Taste and season until you fall in love with it. You can store the sauce in a sterilized jar in the fridge and use within a month.

5. Remove the chicken from the fridge to come up to room temperature and preheat the oven to 400°F.

6. Place the chicken on a roasting tray and slide into the middle of the oven to roast for 30 minutes, brushing with the piri piri sauce halfway through.

7. Preheat the grill to high.

8. Carefully transfer the chicken from the oven to under the grill for a final 10 minutes, turning halfway for a deliciously smoky char all over.

9. Brush the chicken with a few tablespoons more of the piri piri sauce, scatter some cilantro over the top and serve with the remaining sauce and lime wedges.

Kuku Paka
East African Succulent Coconut Grilled Chicken

Kuku paka is one of my favorite Swahili delicacies that combines the African, Indian and Arabic flavor nuances dominant in the region. In my recipe, which I developed over a few years, the chicken is poached in a luxuriously creamy and aromatic spiced coconut broth to ensure maximum moistness, before coating in a sweet layer of coconut and tamarind and grilling for that traditional char that is a staple with this dish. The sauce is finished with fruity and sour tamarind, then reduced to a beautifully thick consistency and made even more decadent with a final drizzle of coconut cream. This recipe is so indulgent, it will have you coming back for more.

2 tbsp coconut or vegetable oil

1 brown onion, peeled and diced

4 garlic cloves, peeled and crushed

2-inch piece of ginger, peeled and grated

3–4 finger chilies, stemmed and finely chopped

4 black cardamom pods, or 2–3 pods of selim peppers, smashed

¼ tsp ground turmeric

1 tbsp garam masala or curry powder

1 tsp cayenne pepper

2 medium tomatoes, roughly chopped

40g fresh cilantro, finely chopped

1 400g can unsweetened coconut milk

1kg chicken legs, or a mix of thighs and drumsticks, bone in and skin on

1–2 tsp tamarind paste, or 1 tbsp lime juice plus 1 tsp light brown sugar

60g coconut cream (or solids from chilled and unshaken full-fat coconut milk)

FOR THE GRILLED CHICKEN

1 tsp garam masala or curry powder

3 garlic cloves, peeled and crushed

2–3 tsp tamarind paste (see page 25)

1 tsp cayenne pepper

3 tbsp unsweetened desiccated coconut

½ tsp fine sea salt

2 tbsp coconut oil, melted, or vegetable oil

TO SERVE

4 tbsp coconut flakes, toasted

1 red chili, stemmed and thinly sliced

2 limes, cut into wedges

Lerato's Tip

Taste the sauce after adding each teaspoon of tamarind paste, as a little goes a long way.

1. Heat the oil in a wide flameproof casserole set over a medium heat. Add the onion and sauté for 10 minutes, until softened. Add the garlic and cook until fragrant, then stir in the ginger and chilies, along with the smashed pods and dried spices. Cook for 3 minutes, adding a tablespoon or two of water if the pan becomes dry.

2. Add the tomatoes and a little less than half the cilantro. Stir to combine, cover with a lid and leave to simmer for 10 minutes, stirring occasionally to prevent burning, until the tomatoes are broken down. Pour in the coconut milk and stir to unravel any delicious crust at the bottom.

3. Score the chicken by cutting several deep slashes diagonally across the skin. Tuck the chicken into the creamy coconut sauce and season with ½ teaspoon fine sea salt. Cover with a lid and simmer over a medium-low heat for 25 minutes.

4. Meanwhile, combine all the ingredients for the grilled chicken in a bowl, except for 1 tablespoon of the oil, and mix to a thick paste. Loosen slightly with a few teaspoons of water, if needed.

5. Preheat the grill to high and prepare a large grilling tray by brushing with oil.

6. Use tongs or a slotted spoon to remove the chicken pieces from the sauce, draining the sauce back into the saucepan, and transfer the chicken to the grilling tray. Rub or brush the grilled chicken paste onto all sides of the legs and arrange in one layer. Brush with the reserved oil and place under the grill to cook for 5–7 minutes on each side, brushing with more oil when you turn them, until golden and with a good char.

7. Meanwhile, to finish the sauce, fish out the spice pods and discard. If you like a smooth sauce, leave to cool slightly, then use a stick blender to blend until smooth. Add the tamarind or lime juice and sugar, return to a medium-low heat and simmer for up to 10 minutes, stirring occasionally, until the sauce has reduced and thickened. Stir in the coconut cream, taste and season to perfection. Remove from the heat and return the chicken to the pan to soak up the wonderful sauce.

8. Scatter over the toasted coconut flakes, chili and remaining cilantro. Serve right away with rice or **My East African Chapati** (see page 196) and a squeeze of fresh lime. (See photo on page 114.)

Sizzling Suya

Suya is a deliciously etched memory of my childhood. A much-loved street food with thin strips of meat heavily spiced in an aromatic blend of peanuts, ginger, chili and more, it is grilled on an open fire and its irresistible aroma would waft through the air for miles, as if calling out to me. In northern Nigeria where this delicacy originates from, the Hausa-Fulnai tribes traditionally called it *tsire*. Now (and especially down south in Lagos), it is commonly known as suya. I remember as a young child and teenager, my hunger for suya would be raging by early afternoon but the *mai suya* (the grill master) wouldn't start grilling until 5 or 6pm. Luckily for me, the local *mai suya* in my father's neighborhood knew our household and had watched me grow from a toddler, despite the many gaps when I was away from the country. And so, I could often sneak my order through and beat the inevitable queue! Every *mai suya* has their own secret blend and after many years of testing I created my own from memory and with guidance from some of the best grill masters in Nigeria. When you have loved something all your life, you just know when you've got it right.

It is not essential to use the most expensive cut of meat for suya. I love a tender cut with good marbling of fat, such as rib eye, but leaner sirloin is also good. By all means, use a fillet if you wish, but I don't think the expense is necessary. Less costly cuts, such as flank or flat iron steak, are also excellent. The best suya is tender, juicy and grilled to perfection—not charred and chewy. Although using both my first and second marinade really accentuates the flavors, cooking with just the second marinade is perfectly fine if you are in a rush. Once it is out of the grill and still sizzling, I love to brush over a final helping of oil, as they do in the famous Glover Court Suya spot in Ikoyi, Lagos, before a final generous shower of my bewitching **Suya Spice Blend**.

SERVES 6

500g rib eye steak (thick cut)
500g chicken thighs, skinless and
  boneless, cut into 1-inch chunks
Vegetable oil, for frying

MARINADE

2 garlic cloves, peeled and roughly
  chopped
2-inch piece of ginger, peeled and
  roughly chopped
2 tbsp vegetable oil
75g unsalted roasted peanuts
100g **Suya Spice Blend** (see page
  272)

TO SERVE

4 large tomatoes, quartered or sliced
1 large red onion, peeled and cut
  into wedges
1 small red cabbage, shredded
Juice of 1 lemon
1 tbsp olive oil

YOU WILL NEED

Metal or wooden skewers, soaked
  to prevent burning

Variation

For a plant-based version, slice
500g king oyster mushrooms
lengthways into three strips.
Prepare the paste as above using
only half the ingredients and
omitting the salt. Place the
mushrooms in a bowl with the
paste and 2 tablespoons **Suya
Spice Blend**. Mix well and set
aside for 15–20 minutes. Thread
onto skewers and cook on a
smoking hot griddle for 2 minutes
on each side, pressing down.
Continue to cook, turning, until
browned all over and with a good
char. Remove from the heat and
brush lightly with oil, season with
fine sea salt and sprinkle with
1 tablespoon **Suya Spice Blend**.

1. Place the steaks in the freezer for 30 minutes to firm up, then thinly slice lengthways against the grain. If necessary, press the slices lightly with a rolling pin or heavy object to flatten them further, then place in a bowl with the chicken. Season with fine sea salt and set aside.

2. Place the garlic and ginger in a food processor with the oil, 60ml water and the roasted peanuts and blend to a smooth and runny paste. Tip into the bowl with the meat and sprinkle 3 tablespoons **Suya Spice Blend** over the top. Mix well to coat, cover and leave to marinate in the fridge for at least 2 hours, or overnight.

3. Remove from the fridge, sprinkle with 3 tablespoons more **Suya Spice Blend** and leave to come up to room temperature. Meanwhile, place a griddle pan over a medium-high heat.

4. Thread the chicken onto half the skewers, and the beef onto the remaining skewers. Once the griddle is sizzling hot, brush all sides of the chicken with oil and cook in batches for 13–15 minutes, until deeply golden and cooked through with a good char. Resist the urge to turn the skewers too soon. I typically leave the meat undisturbed for at least 6 minutes. Remove from the pan and place on a serving plate. Brush with a little more oil and shower the chicken with 1 tablespoon more **Suya Spice Blend**. Pat the skewers together to make sure the extra spices adhere to the meat, and leave to rest while you cook the beef.

5. Clean any burnt residue from the pan, return to a medium-high heat and brush all sides of the steak with oil. Cook the beef in batches for 2–3 minutes (5 minutes for well done). Remove from the pan and place on a serving plate. Brush with a little more oil and shower with 1 tablespoon **Suya Spice Blend**. Pat the skewers together to make sure the spices adhere to the meat, and leave to rest while you prepare the salad.

6. Return the griddle pan to a medium-high heat and brush the tomatoes and onions lightly with oil. Char them briefly without cooking through.

7. Dress the cabbage with the lemon juice, olive oil and season with a pinch of sea salt flakes.

8. Serve your sizzling suya on a bed of cabbage, charred tomatoes and onions. I adore this with **Baked Plantain** (see page 278) or tucked into a flatbread. (See photo on page 115.)

Bird of Paradise

Bird of paradise is a dream of a roast that delivers as promised. A dish I fantasized about for quite some time before bringing it to life. I wanted a "simple" yet sumptuous roast to transport you to paradise, journeying through Africa with wondrous spices from West Africa to the Horn of Africa and around the archipelagos and spice farms of Madagascar, Comoros and East Africa. It is a succulent and deeply aromatic roast with the peppery citrus grains of paradise and sweet warmth of turmeric, ginger and ground makrut lime leaves, brought together to make **Paradise Spice**, a spice blend I created for this recipe. Spatchcocking the bird ensures much quicker cooking and that the prized marinade permeates every nook. This is one of the easiest recipes in this book, and with two accompanying sauces, it truly is the gift that keeps on giving.

SERVES 4-6

1 1.8kg chicken, spatchcocked (see
Cook's Tips on page 275 or ask
your butcher)
12 small shallots, peeled, trimmed
and halved
1 red Romano or bell pepper,
stemmed, deseeded and halved
8 mild red and green chilies,
stemmed, pierced and left whole
1 tsp **Paradise Spice** (see page 270)

FOR THE MARINADE
1 tbsp freshly ground grains of
paradise or black pepper
2-inch piece of ginger, peeled and
finely grated
4 garlic cloves, peeled and finely
grated
4 tsp **Paradise Spice** (see page
270)
2 tbsp tomato puree
1 tsp dried thyme
3 tbsp vegetable or olive oil

Lerato's Tip

To make sure the bird is cooked
through, cut into the joint
between the thigh and the leg; if
the juice runs clear, the chicken is
ready. The flesh can sometimes
have a pink tinge even when
cooked through, especially in
organic or free-range chickens, so
you could use an internal
thermometer for a safe-to-eat
reading of 165°F.

---

1. Season the flesh of the chicken with 1½ teaspoons fine sea salt, massaging it into both sides, then place skin-side up in an oven dish. Set aside for no more than an hour while you prepare the marinade; otherwise, cover and keep in the fridge.

2. To make the marinade, place all the ingredients in a bowl and mix well. Reserve 2 tablespoons then spoon the rest onto the bird. Brush to coat all sides. Cover and refrigerate for 2 hours or overnight, if possible.

3. Preheat the oven to 400°F and remove the chicken from the fridge to come up to room temperature.

4. Place the shallots in the middle of a high-sided roasting tray and rest the chicken on top, skin-side up. Place the red pepper in the tray and tuck the chilies around the bird. Roast for 45 minutes in the middle of the oven, brushing with 1 tablespoon of the reserved marinade after 25 minutes, until cooked through (see Lerato's Tip below). Turn on the grill for the last 5 minutes and move the roasting tray higher up in the oven for a lovely, charred skin.

5. Carefully lift the chicken onto a serving board to rest and use a small fine sieve to sprinkle the fragrant **Paradise Spice** evenly over the bird. Return the veggies to the oven for a 5-minute blast under the grill.

6. Scoop out the pepper, chilies and just a few pieces of the shallots. Remove the seeds and scoop out the membrane from the chilies if you prefer less heat, then finely mince everything together to make a paste and set aside in a small bowl. Pour the roasting liquid and remaining shallots into a saucepan, scraping any thick sauce stuck to the tray. Add the remaining reserved marinade and pour in 60–125ml water, depending on how much roasting liquid you have left. Simmer for 10 minutes over a medium heat to reduce. Taste and season to perfection.

7. Serve the chicken with small bowls of the shallot sauce and chili paste alongside golden roasted potatoes or your favorite grains and a zesty salad. I love serving this roast with **Bejeweled & Aromatic Fried Rice** (see page 210) and **Mango & Cabbage Slaw** (see page 166) for an explosion of flavors.

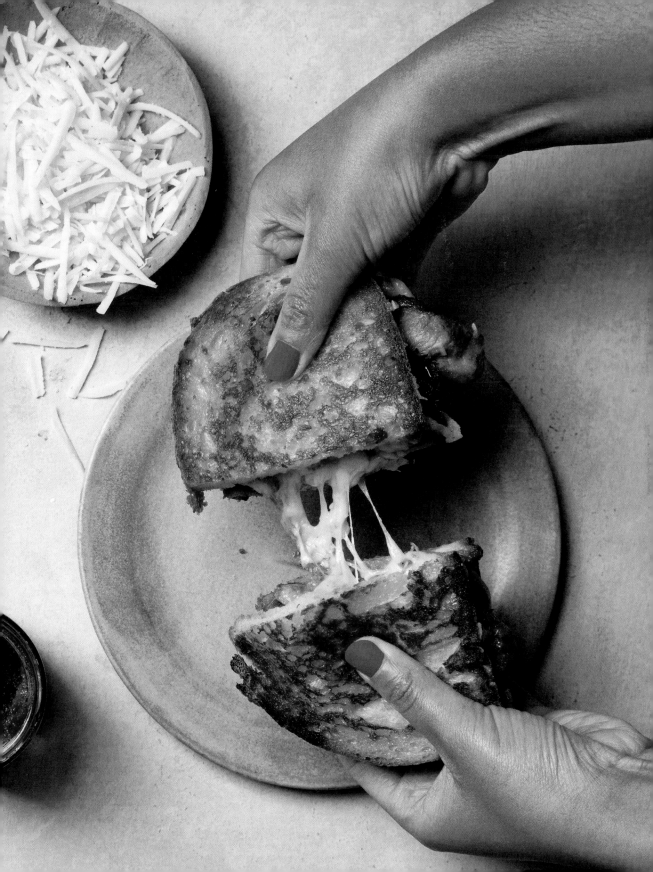

Braaibroodjies
South African Grilled Steak & Cheese Sandwich

A South African *braai* (barbecue or grill) is not complete without *braaibroodjies* (pronounced at braaibookies)—cheese sandwiches finished off on the grill. My ultimate steak sandwich, with generously buttered sourdough and either beef or a large portobello mushroom "steak," is a tad more substantial and indulgent, topped with the delectable **South African Mother Sauce—***Chakalaka* (see page 189) and **Smoky Tomato & Date Jam** (see page 257). Impress guests at your next barbecue with your new favorite sandwich.

SERVES 2

225g sirloin steak, trimmed of fat
    and sinew (reserving the fat)
Pinch of freshly ground grains of
    paradise or black pepper
1 tbsp vegetable or olive oil
4 tbsp unsalted butter, softened
2 fat garlic cloves, peeled and
    slightly smashed
2 sprigs of thyme
4 slices sourdough or your favorite
    bread (each about ½ inch thick)
4 tbsp **Smoky Tomato & Date Jam**
    (see page 257)
150g Gruyère cheese, grated, or a
    semi-soft cheese or grated
    mature cheddar
2 tbsp **South African Mother
    Sauce—***Chakalaka* (see
    page 189)

Variation
For a decadent vegan "steak"
sandwich, cook portobello
mushrooms as above over a high
heat, until charred and cooked
through using oil instead of
butter. Use your favorite vegan
spread and cheese. Finish
with the already plant-based
Smoky Tomato & Date Jam and
Chakalaka.

1. Place a heavy-based frying pan over a high heat.

2. Pat the steak dry and season with sea salt flakes and a
   generous amount of freshly ground grains of paradise
   or black pepper on both sides. Rub the steak with the
   oil and place in the sizzling hot pan. Throw in the
   cut-out fat to render alongside. Sear each side of the
   steak undisturbed for 1 minute, then reduce the heat
   to medium–high and add 1 tablespoon of the butter,
   the garlic and thyme. Baste the steak with the
   rendered fat and infused butter and continue to cook
   to your liking (3 minutes in total for rare, 4–5 minutes
   for medium and 7–8 minutes for well done). The
   cooking time will depend greatly on the type of steak
   and thickness. Transfer the steak to a chopping board
   and leave to rest.

3. Spread some butter on one side of each slice of bread
   and spread 1 tablespoon of **Smoky Tomato & Date
   Jam** over the buttered side of each slice. Top two
   slices with a quarter of the cheese and season with
   freshly ground grains of paradise or black pepper.

4. Slice the steaks into strips and divide between the
   two slices of bread with cheese. Top the steak with
   a tablespoon of *Chakalaka* and finish with the
   remaining cheese. Place the remaining slices of
   bread on top and press down.

5. Place a griddle pan over a high heat, or wipe the
   previously used pan clean and return to the heat.

6. Melt 1 tablespoon of butter in the pan, then add the
   sandwiches to brown for 2–3 minutes on each side,
   until golden and wonderful with the cheese melting.
   Brush the top of each sandwich with butter and turn
   carefully, butter-side down, onto the sizzling hot
   griddle pan. Press down for 15 seconds, then cook
   for up to 2 minutes. Brush the top with butter, then
   carefully turn over once again and press down for
   15 seconds before continuing to cook for 2–3 minutes,
   or until nicely charred with cheese oozing out. Leave
   to cool slightly, then cut in half and dig right in! (See
   photo on pages 120–1.)

Lamb Cutlets

WITH YASSA BUTTER, GRILLED VEGETABLES & POMEGRANATE

SERVES 2

Yassa brings sunshine to your plate in this luxuriously creamy butter sauce. I have always loved this tangy sauce with leg of lamb, marinated in a mix of spices, citrus and Dijon, before roasting. Another firm favorite at my feasts, but for this book I wanted a knockout dish with a little less work, and lamb cutlets or chops are a great alternative to a leg of lamb. Although slightly mellowed by the cream, the citrusy sauce with its sweet, caramelized onions is reawakened by the juicy pomegranate jewels. This is a great dish for an African-inspired dinner party, whether you are feeding 2 or 20.

FOR THE YASSA BUTTER

2 tbsp vegetable or olive oil
1 medium brown onion, peeled and sliced
1 carrot, scrubbed and chopped into small pieces
4 sprigs of thyme, leaves picked
2 garlic cloves, peeled and roughly chopped
2 tbsp unsalted butter (about 30g), softened
Zest of 1 lemon and 2 tbsp lemon juice
1 tbsp Dijon mustard
250ml chicken or vegetable stock
45ml heavy cream
¼ tsp cayenne pepper

1. To prepare the **Yassa Butter**, heat the oil in a pan over a medium heat. Add the onion, carrot and fresh thyme with a pinch of fine sea salt and cook for up to 10 minutes, stirring often, until softened and starting to take on color. Continue to cook for a further 10–15 minutes, adding 2 tablespoons of water now and again to moisten and prevent burning, while stirring occasionally, until the onions are soft, sticky and golden brown.

2. Add the garlic and butter, stirring for a few minutes until fragrant. Stir in the lemon zest and juice and mustard and pour in 200ml of the stock. Simmer over a low heat for 10 minutes, until slightly reduced, then add the heavy cream and simmer for another minute until thickened.

3. For a little tingling heat, stir in the cayenne pepper and season with a pinch of fine sea salt and freshly ground black pepper. Stir and take the pan off the heat. Leave the sauce to cool for 10–15 minutes, then blend until smooth. If it is too thick, adjust with a tablespoon at a time of the remaining stock until spreadable. Set aside.

2 tbsp vegetable or olive oil
1 tbsp unsalted butter, softened
2 tbsp Dijon mustard
1 large garlic clove, peeled and crushed
½ tsp cayenne pepper
1 tsp paprika
1 tsp dried thyme
1 red or yellow bell pepper, stemmed, deseeded and cut into quarters lengthways
2 shallots, peeled and halved
8 lamb cutlets
Small handful of fresh flat-leaf parsley, finely chopped
2 tbsp pomegranate seeds

4. In a large bowl, whisk 1 tablespoon of the oil and 1 tablespoon of water with the softened butter and mustard for the grilled lamb. Add the garlic, cayenne pepper, paprika, thyme and about ¼ teaspoon freshly ground black pepper. Add the pepper, shallots and lamb cutlets to the bowl and brush all sides with the marinade. It is perfectly alright to grill these immediately, but I find that marinating enhances the flavors. Cover and refrigerate for at least 1 hour, or overnight.

5. Preheat the grill or a griddle pan to sizzling hot, or prepare an outdoor barbecue and remove the lamb from the fridge to bring to room temperature.

6. Brush the lamb, pepper and onion with the remaining oil and season with fine sea salt. (See tips on grilling page 275.)

7. Grill the lamb in batches for 1½ minutes on each side for rare, 3 minutes on each side for medium well done with a slight blush (which I prefer), and 5 minutes on each side for well done, depending on the thickness of the cutlets. Shake off any excess marinade and add the pepper and shallots to grill alongside the lamb until softened and with a good char. Once the lamb is cooked to your liking with a lovely, charred crust, place on a warm dish to rest as you grill the remaining cutlets.

8. To serve, gently reheat the **Yassa Butter** in a saucepan for a few minutes and season to perfection. Spoon onto a serving plate or individual plates and rest the lamb on top. Dress with the grilled shallots and roasted peppers, and scatter over the parsley and pomegranate seeds for a delightful zing. I love this with a side of simple smashed or sautéed potatoes to soak up the tangy butter sauce. You can also enjoy it like a traditional yassa with rice or couscous. (See photo on page 126.)

Lerato's Tip

Once the **Yassa Butter** is completely cooled, store in an airtight container, refrigerate and use within 5 days. The sauce can be served hot or cold. Spread on to your favorite sandwiches or wraps.

Kefta

WITH SPICED BUTTER

Kefta of some kind is on weekly rotation in my home, grilled and stuffed into flatbread with harissa and yogurt, browned and cooked as meatballs in a rich lava of tomatoes and peppers, or encased in filo parcels, brushed with spiced butter and baked for the most addictive Moroccan *briouate*. I can never get enough of kefta and I find it rather therapeutic mixing and rolling meatballs. It comforts me to know that we will enjoy dinner and the next day's lunch from this single preparation, as there are always leftovers in my home. Combine lamb and beef for nuanced flavor. A good amount of fat is vital, not only for great flavor but to keep the meat beautifully moist. I love to add natural yogurt to my mix, especially if using leaner cuts of meat, which gives the kefta a slight tang and extra moisture, but this is entirely optional. You can easily get away with using leaner cuts when rolling the mixture into balls and adding to a sauce (such as **Juicy Berbere Meatballs in Tomato Sauce** on page 96). To perfect your kefta, roll one or two small balls and fry to taste test, before committing to a whole batch.

SERVES 4–6

FOR THE KEFTA
4 tbsp roughly chopped flat-leaf
   parsley leaves
4 tbsp roughly chopped cilantro
4 mint leaves
1 medium brown onion, peeled
3 garlic cloves, peeled and crushed
500g lamb mince
45ml natural yogurt
2 tsp paprika
1 tsp **Imperial Ras el Hanout Spice
   Blend** (see page 269 or a fragrant
   store-bought blend)
1 tsp ground cumin
½ tsp ground cinnamon
¼ cayenne pepper
1 tsp fine sea salt
Vegetable oil, for grilling

**FOR THE RAS EL HANOUT
   SPICED BUTTER**
1 tbsp butter
1 tsp **Imperial Ras el Hanout Spice
   Blend** (see page 269 or a fragrant
   store-bought blend)

YOU WILL NEED
6–8 bamboo or metal skewers

Lerato's Tip

This lamb mixture also makes great
meatballs or patties, and chicken or
mushrooms are excellent alternatives
to the lamb mince. Simply mince in
the food processor with the other
ingredients. To prevent the mince
mixture sticking to your hands, use
wet or oiled hands.

1. Soak the bamboo skewers in water for at least 30 minutes before using.

2. Place the fresh herbs, onion and garlic in a food processor and chop finely. (You could do this by hand.) Tip into a large bowl and add all remaining ingredients except the oil. Mix thoroughly with your hands or a spoon to distribute all the flavors and textures evenly.

3. Preheat the grill or place a griddle pan over a medium-high heat.

4. Shape the lamb mixture into logs and thread onto the skewers. You can shape the mixture into 18 small logs, 12 medium-sized logs or 6–8 large logs. The smaller logs are easier to pierce, while the larger logs can be flattened and molded around the skewers. You can also grill the logs and thread onto the skewers afterwards.

5. Brush the kefta with oil and place under the grill or on the sizzling hot griddle pan. Cook for 4–5 minutes, depending on the size of your kefta. Leave the kefta unturned for at least 2 minutes, then turn halfway through cooking for a good char on both sides.

6. Meanwhile, melt the butter in a small saucepan over a medium heat. Add the **Imperial Ras el Hanout Spice Blend** and mix well.

7. Arrange the hot kefta on a serving platter and brush with the spiced butter. Serve with **Medina Bread** (see page 194) or pitta, **Roasted Pepper Salad** (see page 179) and **Golden Chermoula & Yogurt Dip** (see page 35). (See photo on page 127.)

Harissa Leg of Lamb

WITH HIBISCUS & CUMIN SALT

SERVES 6–8

The first time I had *méchoui* lamb in Marrakech, after meandering through narrow passageways and streets within the Medina walls to the most enchanting restaurant with towering fragrant orange trees, it was a case of my eyes being bigger than my stomach. And so I created this recipe to marry the tangy, fruity hibiscus with the traditional cumin dipping salt served to cut through the richness of the lamb. And the hibiscus excels beautifully. I hope this makes your lips tingle and your heart sing as it does mine.

2kg leg of lamb on the bone
2 brown onions, peeled and cut into
   large chunks
2 carrots, scrubbed and cut into
   large chunks
500ml hot lamb or beef stock
1 bay leaf
6 sprigs of thyme

FOR THE MARINADE
75g natural yogurt
4 tbsp **Red Harissa** (see page
   260 or shop-bought)
6 garlic cloves, peeled and finely
   grated
2 tsp dried thyme
2 tbsp ground coriander
2 tsp ground cumin
1 tbsp cumin seeds, lightly crushed
2 tsp ground ginger
2 tsp paprika
¾ tbsp sea salt flakes, crushed
¼ tsp freshly ground black pepper
3 tbsp vegetable oil

1. To make the marinade, mix all the ingredients except the oil in a bowl to form a paste.

2. Trim any excess fat from the lamb and use a small sharp knife to make deep incisions all over the fleshiest part of the meat. Place the rough chunks of onion and carrot in the middle of a roasting tray and rest the lamb on top. Rub the marinade all over the lamb, heavily coating all sides and pushing some into the incisions you have made. Finally, drizzle and rub the oil onto the lamb. Cover and leave to marinate in the fridge for a few hours or overnight.

3. Preheat the oven to 450°F and bring the lamb up to room temperature.

4. Pour the stock around the sides of the roasting tray and drop in the bay leaf and thyme. Roast in the middle part of the oven for 30 minutes.

5. Reduce the temperature to 350°F and roast for a further 50 minutes for medium rare, 1 hour 20 minutes for medium, or 2 hours for well done, spooning the juices from the roasting tray over the lamb on a few occasions to keep it moist. Carefully remove the tray from the oven, cover the lamb with baking parchment and a clean kitchen towel and leave to rest for up to 20 minutes before carving.

FOR THE HIBISCUS & CUMIN SALT

1 tbsp cumin seeds
1 tbsp ground dried hibiscus
2 tbsp sea salt flakes

6. Meanwhile, to make the **Hibiscus & Cumin Salt**, place a dry frying pan over a medium-high heat and toast the cumin, swirling frequently, until fragrant. Grind with a mortar and pestle or spice grinder and tip into a small bowl with the hibiscus and crushed sea salt flakes. Mix well to combine.

7. Carefully lift out the lamb and place on a board. Carve and arrange on a platter. Sprinkle lightly with the **Hibiscus & Cumin Salt**. Serve the roasted carrots and onions alongside. This is a dream to eat with **Saffron Potatoes & Peas** (see page 186) and **Herb Salad with Hibiscus & Pomegranate** (see page 162). (See photo on pages 130–1.)

Lerato's Tip

To check the lamb for doneness, pierce the fattest part of the joint with a skewer and if the juices are pinky-red, the meat is medium rare, if slightly blushing pink, then it's medium, and if clear, then it is well done. I typically aim for well done with the slightest blush, and so I start checking after 2 hours. It is best to have a meat thermometer to ensure your lamb is at the safest temperature to eat. If the lamb is rarer than you will like after carving, place it back in the oven for a few minutes. The lamb will be succulent and crispy on the outside and juicy inside, with the onions and carrots meltingly soft and delicious.

Fabulous Fish & Seafood

Plantain & Crab Salad

WITH MANGO & LIME PIRI PIRI DRESSING

**SERVES 2 AS A LIGHT MAIN OR
4–6 AS SHARING PLATES**

Sweet plantains, creamy crab meat and tangy yogurt, with fragrant aromatics and warming chilies, all come together in another one of my delicious fantasies brought to life. Mango and lime piri piri is tamed with yogurt and fragrant limes to create a refreshingly piquant dressing. You can also serve the piri piri and yogurt separately if you wish. The scented leaves, herbs and edible flowers used to adorn this dish are beautiful, yes, but not merely decorative. The peppery, fruity flowers complement the sweet and spicy herbs and flavors that abound in this dish. This is certainly one to impress at a dinner party, or to treat oneself, as I do.

2 ripe yellow plantains, peeled
   (see page 277)
2 tbsp avocado or olive oil
2 garlic cloves, peeled and finely
   chopped
1-inch piece of ginger, peeled and
   grated
1–2 green or red chilies, stemmed
   and diced
4 spring onions, trimmed and
   chopped
300g fresh crab meat, any shell or
   cartilage discarded
100g natural yogurt, plus 1 tbsp
Sea salt flakes
Freshly ground grains of paradise
   or black pepper
Juice of 1 lime (about 2 tbsp)
25g fresh cilantro, chopped
4 tbsp **Mango & Lime Piri Piri** (see
   page 110)

TO SERVE
Small handful of edible nasturtium
   and pansy flowers
Small handful of fresh cilantro
   leaves
Small handful of scented leaves
   (e.g., African clove basil, Thai basil
   or basil)
1 lime, cut into wedges

1. Cook the plantains to your preference by frying or baking (see page 278).

2. Place a frying pan over a medium heat and add the oil. Once shimmering, add the garlic, ginger, chilies and spring onions, turn down the heat to medium-low and fry for 2 minutes, until fragrant and softened.

3. Stir in the crab meat, 1 tablespoon of the yogurt and 1 tablespoon of water, increase the heat to medium-high and sauté for about 1 minute, stirring frequently.

4. Season to perfection with crushed sea salt flakes and freshly ground grains of paradise or black pepper. Remove from the heat and stir in 1 tablespoon of lime juice and the chopped cilantro.

5. Meanwhile, mix the **Mango & Lime Piri Piri** with the 100g yogurt and add a dash of the remaining lime juice. Season with crushed sea salt flakes and spoon into small dipping bowls.

6. Serve the crab with a beautiful bouquet of torn fragrant peppery flowers, cilantro and scented leaves, the fried or baked plantains, lime wedges and the mango and lime piri piri dressing alongside.

Langouste à la Vanille
Lobster in Vanilla & Rum Butter

SERVES 2–4

125ml unsalted butter

1 garlic clove, peeled and crushed

1 red chili, stemmed and finely sliced

1 tbsp fresh lime juice

4 tbsp dark rum

1 vanilla pod, seeds scraped and pod reserved

4 lobster tails or 6–8 langoustines (prepared as page 275) or 6–8 large raw tiger prawns (prepared as page 275)

3–4 makrut lime leaves, ribs removed and leaves finely sliced, or 2 tsp lime zest

1 lime, cut into wedges

Lerato's Tip

Butter can be replaced by vegetable, olive or coconut oil. Brandy or white wine are wonderful as an alternative to rum, although the vanilla and rum are a match made in heaven.

Langouste à la vanille is one of the great culinary adventures of the East African island nation of Comoros and is known as the island's national dish. It also celebrates the distinctively smoky, fruity and sweet vanilla, similar to that found in neighboring Madagascar. Like a cross between a lobster and a langoustine, Comoros *langouste* is spiny and caught in local waters around East Africa. The meat soaks up the wonderfully buttery vanilla sauce that has heat from the rum and chilies and aromatics from the makrut lime leaves for a fragrant dish. Feel free to use lobster tails, langoustines or tiger prawns. This is a decadent dish that will bring the African tropical islands to your home.

1. Melt the butter in a frying pan set over a medium-low heat, then add the garlic, chili, lime juice, rum and the vanilla bean seeds with its pod. Mix well and bring to a simmer for 1 minute, then swiftly remove from the heat. Leave to infuse while you prepare the lobster, langoustines or prawns.

2. Preheat the grill to high and place an oven rack just below the grill.

3. Place the lobster tails, langoustine or prawns in the grill pan and season the meat with sea salt flakes and freshly ground black pepper. Brush some of the vanilla and rum butter sauce on the shellfish, then grill for 10 minutes (lobster) or 4 minutes (langoustine and prawns), until cooked through.

4. Remove from the grill, transfer to a platter and drizzle any sauce left in the grill pan over the top. Place the remaining butter sauce over a medium-low heat and simmer for 1 minute. Add the makrut lime leaves or lime zest and season to perfection. Remove from the heat.

5. Drizzle the vanilla and rum butter sauce over the shellfish and serve with lime wedges. I thoroughly enjoy this with simply sautéed baby potatoes and lemon or lime squeezed onto a small bouquet of cilantro and parsley.

Slow-Roasted Salmon

WITH HIBISCUS, HARISSA & CITRUS

SERVES 6

4 oranges, 1 thinly sliced, 2 zested
and juiced, and 1 cut into wedges
3 limes, 1 thinly sliced, 1 zested and
juiced, and 1 cut into wedges
6 tbsp olive oil
4 heaped tbsp **Red Harissa** (see
page 260 or store-bought)
1 tbsp ground dried hibiscus
1 tbsp ground coriander
2 tsp fennel seeds, toasted and
lightly crushed
2 fat garlic cloves, peeled and
grated
2-inch piece of ginger, peeled and
grated
2 tsp sea salt flakes
Grains of paradise or black pepper
1–1.2kg side of salmon, or 2 600g
sides (skin removed)
½ tsp chili flakes

I love the luxurious ease of roasting a whole side of fish, as it always looks like more work than it is. I created this recipe to be a showstopper that can be easily achieved and it has become a staple on my summer menus, dinner parties and at our family Christmas celebrations. Slow roasting the salmon in this beautiful mix of tangy hibiscus, warming harissa and two kinds of citrus creates the most wonderful flavorful and tender fish.

1. Place the orange zest and 2 tablespoons of the juice in a bowl with the lime zest and 1 tablespoon of the lime juice. Add 3 tablespoons of the oil, the **Red Harissa**, ground hibiscus, ground coriander, fennel seeds, garlic and ginger. Mix together and season with the sea salt flakes and a good grinding of grains of paradise or black pepper.

2. Line a large roasting tray with baking parchment (it will need to fit the salmon comfortably) and arrange the orange and lime slices around the center. Rest the salmon on top, skinned-side down. Spread the citrus marinade onto the salmon to coat the top and sides heavily. Cover and place in the fridge for 30–60 minutes, but no longer, otherwise the acids in the citrus will begin to cook the fish.

3. Preheat the oven to 400°F. Remove the salmon from the fridge to come up to room temperature before cooking.

4. Drizzle the fish with 1 tablespoon of the oil and season with freshly ground grains of paradise or black pepper. Reduce the oven temperature to 340°F and roast the salmon for 20 minutes.

5. Remove from the oven and drizzle 2 tablespoons of orange juice over the salmon. Return to the oven for another 10–15 minutes, until the internal flesh is flaky and opaque. The top may still look translucent and raw, as a result of slow roasting.

6. Whisk the remaining orange juice (about 2–2½ tablespoons) with 1 tablespoon of the remaining lime juice. Add the chili flakes and the remaining olive oil, season with a good pinch of sea salt flakes and whisk to make a dressing. Serve the salmon with the dressing and wedges of sweet orange and tart lime. I love sweet green peas with fish, so serve with **Saffron Potatoes & Peas** (see page 186) or **Kachumbari with Hibiscus Pickled Onion** (see page 160).

Grilled Fish

WITH MAKRUT LIME LEAVES & WATERMELON KACHUMBARI

SERVES 2

1 whole sustainable sea bass
    (800g), descaled, gutted and
    gills and tails trimmed
1 lemon, sliced
1 lime, sliced
1 tbsp olive oil
1 bunch of parsley, leaves picked
5 mint leaves

FOR THE MARINADE
2 tsp fennel seeds
1 tsp aniseed
1 brown onion, peeled and chopped
3 fat garlic cloves, peeled and
    roughly chopped
1-inch piece of ginger, peeled and
    grated
1 scotch bonnet pepper, stemmed
    and deseeded with membrane
    scooped out
1 mild red chili, stemmed and
    roughly chopped
2 spring onions, trimmed and
    chopped
6 makrut lime leaves, ribs removed
    (or African clove basil or Thai basil)
5 tbsp vegetable or olive oil
Zest and juice of 2 limes

FOR THE KACHUMBARI
150g seedless watermelon, peeled
    and cut into ½-inch chunks
1 small cucumber, cut into ½-inch
    chunks
4 medium vine-ripened tomatoes,
    cut into ½-inch chunks
Juice of 1 lemon
1 green jalapeño, deseeded and
    finely sliced
3 spring onions, trimmed and finely
    sliced

I love this recipe, as it combines the warmth, freshness and sweetness of chilies, aromatic spices and herbs, and fruits that complement the fish perfectly. With the watermelon kachumbari bursting in your mouth after a mouthful of the spicy fish—just glorious!

1. Season the fish inside and out with sea salt flakes.

2. To make the marinade, grind the fennel and aniseed using a mortar and pestle or a spice grinder. Tip them into a food processor with the onion, garlic, ginger, scotch bonnet, chili, spring onions and 3 of the makrut lime leaves. Pour in the oil and blend to a puree. Pour into a bowl and season with 2 teaspoons sea salt flakes and 1 teaspoon of freshly ground grains of paradise or black pepper. Add the lime zest and juice and mix well.

3. Cut three or four deep diagonal slashes into the thickest part of each side of the fish. Brush a generous amount of marinade onto the fish and inside the cavity, pushing some of the marinade into the slashes. Stuff the remaining makrut lime leaves and the lemon and lime slices inside the cavity.

4. Leave the fish to stand at room temperature for 15 minutes, or cover and leave in the fridge to marinate for up to 2 hours.

5. Preheat the grill to high.

6. Place a grilling rack over a heavy-duty roasting tray. Brush the rack and both sides of the fish with oil. Place under the grill to cook for 6–7 minutes on each side, until the flesh turns opaque. Check the thickest part of the fish and, if flaky, your fish is cooked through. Otherwise, place back under the grill to cook for another minute and check again.

7. Meanwhile, place the watermelon, cucumber and tomatoes in a bowl and drizzle over the lemon juice. Season with a pinch of sea salt flakes and scatter over the jalapeño and spring onions. Toss, cover and place in the fridge to chill and soak up the lemon juice until ready to serve.

8. Transfer the fish to a warm platter. Tuck the parsley and mint leaves inside the cavity while the fish is hot and serve with the watermelon kachumbari and **Twice-Cooked Yam & Cassava Chips** (see page 38).

Spice Island Coconut Fish Curry

This curry is reminiscent of the beautiful coast of Zanzibar, also known as Spice Island. Its warming and aromatic flavors will have you looking out the window in search of the *dhows*, some docking in and others setting sail, as they did when wondrous spices traveled from Asia through Africa to the rest of the world. The warmth of chilies and sweetness of tropical coconuts are embodied in the curries enjoyed across East Africa and the archipelagos on the Indian Ocean. Tomatoes give the sauce a good body and there's a double dose of tartness from limes and tamarind to accompany the firm fish. I enjoy serving this with white rice or **My East African Chapati** (see page 196) to soak up the creamy golden sauce while being transported to this wondrous Spice Island.

SERVES 4

500g monkfish or firm white fish, deboned and skin removed, cut into 1-inch chunks

FOR THE MARINADE
1 tsp ground turmeric
1 tsp garam masala
1 tsp chili powder
Juice of 1 lime

FOR THE CURRY SAUCE
3 tbsp coconut oil (cold-pressed and flavorful)
1 large brown onion, peeled and diced
2–3 green and red chilies, stemmed and diced
1-inch piece of ginger, peeled and grated
4 garlic cloves, peeled and crushed
1 tsp ground turmeric
1 tbsp garam masala or curry powder
2 vine-ripened or plum tomatoes, diced
150ml fish, vegetable or chicken stock
1 400ml can coconut milk
2–3 tsp tamarind paste
12 large raw king prawns, peeled and deveined (defrosted if frozen)
150g green beans, trimmed

TO SERVE
Small handful of fresh cilantro, leaves torn
4 tbsp coconut flakes, toasted
1 red chili, stemmed and thinly sliced

1. Combine all the marinade ingredients in a large bowl. Add the fish and some freshly ground black pepper and turn to coat on all sides. Cover and set aside while you prepare the curry sauce, or keep in the fridge for 1–2 hours.

2. Heat the coconut oil in a wide shallow saucepan over a medium heat. Add the onion and 1 teaspoon fine sea salt and cook for up to 10 minutes, or until softened and translucent, stirring every few minutes. Add the chilies, ginger and garlic and cook for 2 minutes, stirring frequently. Add a splash of water if it begins to stick. Stir in the turmeric and garam masala or curry powder and cook for a further minute, until fragrant and wonderful.

3. Tip in the tomatoes and their juices, stir and leave to cook for 5 minutes, until the tomatoes begin to break down slightly. Pour in the stock and the coconut milk and bring to a boil. Reduce the heat and simmer for 15 minutes, stirring occasionally, until the sauce begins to thicken a little.

4. Stir in the tamarind paste, then add the fish and cook for 3 minutes.

5. Finally, add the prawns and green beans and cook for 3–4 minutes, until the fish is flaky, the prawns are pink and plump and the beans have softened but with a little crunch.

6. Season to perfection and serve sprinkled with cilantro, toasted coconut flakes and slices of red chili, alongside steaming bowls of rice or **My East African Chapati** (see page 196). (See photo on page 144.)

Lerato's Tip

If you want to make the curry in advance, prepare the sauce up until the end of step 3, then leave the sauce to cool. Store covered in the fridge for up to 3 days until ready to cook and serve.

Fisherwoman's Okra

This is a celebration of the sea, inspired by my paternal origins of Akwa Ibom, a coastal state in southern Nigeria, known for some of the best seafood and seafood delicacies in the country. This recipe is also a personal triumph, especially for someone who is not a fan of mucilaginous food. Locally pronounced as "okro" and called *gumbo* in francophone countries such as Benin, the sweet and mildly grassy green pods are from the mallow family to which cotton and hibiscus also belong. My parents adore okra, the slimier the better. I quickly realized this was not for me and decided to create a recipe that I love. In my recipe, the okra is cut a little chunkier, cooked gently and swiftly to retain a little bite. The fresh and smoked seafood add wonderful flavor to the broth alongside smoky palm oil, which brings this dish together beautifully.

SERVES 4–6

1 tbsp vegetable oil
750g raw tiger prawns, peeled
    (keep the shells) and deveined
    (300g shelled weight)
500ml fish stock
4 sprigs of thyme
1 bay leaf
1 red Romano pepper, stemmed
    and deseeded
1–2 scotch bonnet peppers,
    stemmed and roughly chopped,
    or pierced and left whole
1 brown onion, peeled and roughly
    chopped
4 tbsp **Red Oil** (see page 262) or
    sustainable palm oil
1–2 tbsp ground dried shrimp or
    crayfish (depending on stock
    strength)
600g monkfish, cut into 1-inch
    chunks
400g okra, trimmed and cut into
    ¼-inch rounds
250g amaranth (callaloo) or
    spinach, tough stalks removed
    and leaves roughly chopped
150g smoked mackerel, deboned
    and flaked into chunks (or
    smoked cod, haddock)
150g shrimp

1. Place a large saucepan over a medium heat. Add the vegetable oil and, once the oil sizzles, stir in the prawn shells. Cook for 10–15 minutes, stirring occasionally to prevent sticking, until the shells are brown on all sides. Pour in the fish stock to deglaze the pan, scraping the bottom to release any prawn shells stuck there, and add the thyme and bay leaf. Increase the heat to medium-high and bring to a strong simmer. Reduce the heat and simmer gently for 10 minutes.

2. Use a fine mesh colander to strain the stock into a heatproof bowl. Squeeze out every drop of stock from the shells and herbs, then discard them. Set the stock aside.

3. Place the red pepper, scotch bonnet, if not leaving whole, and onion in a food processor and blend to a coarse puree. Place the unwashed saucepan used to prepare the stock over a medium heat and drizzle in the **Red Oil** or palm oil. Pour in the puree and cook for 15 minutes, stirring occasionally, until slightly reduced. Pour in half the stock, add the ground dried shrimp or crayfish and bring to a gentle simmer.

4. Add the monkfish and top up with more stock or water, if needed. Add the scotch bonnet, if using whole. Poach the fish for 2 minutes, then remove with a slotted spoon and set aside. Add the tiger prawns and poach for 1 minute, then remove with a slotted spoon and set aside with the fish.

5. Place the okra, amaranth or spinach, and smoked mackerel in the pan and add the poached monkfish. Add more stock or water, if needed, and stir gently. (Avoid stirring too much if you prefer little or no okra slime.) Cook for 5 minutes.

6. Season to perfection with sea salt, then add the poached prawns and the shrimp and simmer for 2 minutes, or until the prawns are plump and pink and the fish is cooked through and flaky.

7. Serve hot with **Pounded Yam** (see page 74) for a classic Nigerian feast, or with steaming hot rice. (See photo on page 145.)

Rougaille
Paradise Prawns in Creole Sauce

**SERVES 4 AS A MAIN OR
6 AS SHARING PLATES**

Rougaille is a humble creole dish popular in Mauritius, Madagascar, Comoros, Seychelles and neighboring island countries on the Indian Ocean, all geographically part of the African continent. With a base of tomatoes, onion and chilies, additions of either peas or beans, salt fish or shrimp became more popular depending on a family's economic standing. Cooking styles have since developed with an increasing amount of aromatics and herbs, smoked sausages, other meats and even rock lobster or langoustines added. As a deep lover of tomato stews, this is a quick meal I enjoy rather often. My version includes ground makrut lime leaves for an intensely aromatic sauce. I love to cook the peeled prawn shells in the sauce to extract as much of the briny and wonderful natural flavors of the sea as possible. Fish or shrimp stock is a perfectly suitable alternative. This dish is pure paradise on a plate.

4 tbsp vegetable or olive oil
1 large brown onion, peeled and
    sliced
4 garlic cloves, peeled and crushed
2-inch piece of ginger, peeled and
    grated
4 green chilies, stemmed and
    diced, or pierced and left whole
8 sprigs of thyme
800g fresh plum tomatoes or
    2 400g cans plum tomatoes
24–30 raw king prawns, peeled and
    deveined (see page 275) or 500g
    peeled prawns
3 spring onions, trimmed and
    chopped
2 tsp **Paradise Spice** (see page 270)
Small handful of fresh cilantro and
    flat-leaf parsley, chopped

1. Drizzle the oil into a wide sauté or frying pan, for which you have a lid, and place over a medium heat. Add the onion with a pinch of sea salt. Fry for 8–10 minutes, stirring occasionally, until softened and golden. Add the garlic, ginger, chilies and thyme and fry for 1 minute to release the wonderful oils and fragrance.

2. Pour in the tomatoes and stir to release any bits stuck to the bottom of the pan. If you have the prawn shells, add them to the tomatoes and bring to a strong simmer. Reduce the heat to medium, cover with a lid and simmer for 20–25 minutes, until the tomatoes begin to break down in the sauce.

3. Fish out the shells and the thyme stalks and place them in a bowl. Pour 100ml water over the shells, to rinse them, then strain the liquid and add to the tomatoes. Bring back to a simmer, add the prawns and spring onions and stir to combine. Season with sea salt flakes and the bewitchingly fragrant **Paradise Spice**. Cover and cook for 3–5 minutes, until the prawns are pink, plump and cooked through.

4. Scatter the cilantro and parsley over the top and serve with **My East African Chapati** (see page 196) or with rice and the refreshing **Kachumbari with Hibiscus Pickled Onion** (see page 160).

Lerato's Tip

For a plant-based variation, prepare a batch of sauce without prawns and finish off with roasted, grilled or sautéed vegetables. You can also freeze batches of the sauce for up to 1 month.

Fragrant Fish in Banana Leaves

I first created this dish for a live cooking appearance in Nigeria in 2017. It was the biggest food fair in Africa at the time and the first time I had cooked live in front of a physical crowd and not on television. In Nigeria we cook steamed beans called *moin moin*, carefully wrapped in sweet banana-like leaves known as *elewe*, both names from the Yoruba dialect. I was inspired to use this steaming technique to cook fish. I thought it was unique at the time, until I discovered *liboké de poisson,* a fish delicacy also cooked in banana leaves enjoyed in the region of the Congo Basin. It is worth the effort to stock up on banana leaves for the sweet flavor and fragrance they impart to whatever is encased within. Buy a packet online or from your local Asian store. You can freeze and defrost them when needed. Otherwise, baking parchment is just as effective at trapping moisture and allowing the fish to cook gently.

SERVES 4

4 thick halibut fillets (each about
170g), or any sustainable firm
white fish, skin removed
Sea salt flakes
Freshly ground grains of paradise
or black pepper
3 tbsp olive, coconut or vegetable
oil
Zest and juice of 1 lime
4 12-inch fresh or frozen banana
leaves
8 thin orange slices
4 thin lime slices
8–12 scented leaves (e.g., African
clove basil or Thai basil)
Handful of fresh cilantro, chopped

FOR THE MARINADE

4 shallots or 1 medium brown onion,
peeled and roughly chopped
3 garlic cloves, peeled and roughly
chopped
2-inch piece of ginger, peeled and
sliced into thin matchsticks
1 scotch bonnet pepper, stemmed
and deseeded
2 tsp **Paradise Spice** (see page 270)

1. Place the fillets in a wide bowl, pat dry and season both sides generously with sea salt flakes and freshly ground grains of paradise or black pepper. Drizzle the oil over the fish and add the lime zest and juice.

2. To make the marinade, crush the shallots or onion, garlic, ginger and scotch bonnet pepper using a mortar and pestle, or place in a food processor and chop using the pulse setting. Mix in the **Paradise Spice**, then tip the marinade over the fish and gently coat all sides. If you have time to do so, leave the fish in the fridge to marinate for 2 hours, otherwise it is perfectly all right to cook immediately. If you do marinate, make sure to bring the fish to room temperature before cooking.

3. Preheat the oven to 400°F and line a deep roasting tray with baking parchment.

4. Cut the banana leaves crossways to create leaves about 12 inches long. If using fresh banana leaves, soak them in hot water to soften, then pat dry. If using frozen leaves, gently defrost with warm water, then rinse and pat dry. Take one banana leaf at a time and place lighter side up. Place 2 orange slices in the center of each leaf, then place a slice of lime in the middle. Top with 2 or 3 scented leaves, then rest a fillet on top with a good coating of the marinade. Carefully fold in the sides of the banana leaves, until tightly wrapped with the folded sides facing up. You can tie the parcels with twine to secure them, if you wish.

5. Turn the parcels over and place them on the prepared roasting tray (so the citrus is on top and the folded sides are facing down). Place in the oven to roast for 30 minutes, until the fish is cooked through and flaky.

6. Carefully turn the parcels over and place in a deep plate to unwrap and catch any juice. Serve in the leaves or transfer to a plate. Scatter over the fresh cilantro and enjoy with a little bowl of **Sauce Piment** (see page 259) on the side. (See photo on pages 150–1.)

Variation
To steam, stack the parcels in a steam basket lined with baking parchment, and place over a pan of simmering water. Cover and steam for 40 minutes until the fish is cooked through and flaky.

Sticky Apricot Glazed Grilled Fish

**SERVES 4 AS A MAIN OR
6–8 AS SHARING PLATES**

Fire up the grill for this recipe inspired by a South African summer classic of *braaied* (grilled/barbecued) snoek. Snoek is a long, thin fish of the mackerel family, with a strong and distinctive flavor and aroma. Even though mackerel would be a more obvious choice here, I am not a big fan of bony fish, so I prefer to use sweet and succulent hake instead. If you can get your hands on snoek or mackerel, expertly cleaned and deboned, then do use that for a feast closer to a traditional *braai*, otherwise my version is just divine.

3 lemons, 2 thinly sliced and 1 halved
800g hake fillets, divided into 4 or 8
    pieces
½ small bunch of fresh cilantro,
    ½ chopped and ½ torn
½ small bunch of fresh flat-leaf
    parsley, ½ chopped and ½ torn
Hibiscus Pickled Onion (see page
    160), to taste (optional)

FOR THE APRICOT GLAZE
3 tbsp unsalted butter
2 large garlic cloves, peeled and
    finely chopped
1 red chili, stemmed, deseeded and
    finely chopped
3 tbsp apricot jam
2 tbsp fresh lemon juice
¾ tbsp balsamic vinegar

1. To prepare the glaze, melt the butter in a saucepan over a medium heat. Add the garlic and chili, and stir for about 1 minute, until fragrant. Add the apricot jam, lemon juice and balsamic vinegar and stir until well combined. Reduce the heat and simmer for 3 minutes. Taste and season to perfection with sea salt flakes and freshly ground black pepper. Set aside while preparing the fish for the grill.

2. Preheat the grill to high and brush the grill tray with oil. Arrange the lemon slices on top. Pat the fish dry and season lightly with sea salt flakes and freshly ground black pepper.

3. Brush the fillets with a generous amount of the apricot butter glaze and rest on top of the lemon slices. Grill the fish for 3–4 minutes on each side, depending on the thickness of your fillets, basting the fish with glaze halfway through cooking. Place the halved lemon to grill alongside.

4. Remove from the grill when the fish is cooked through, deep golden and flaky. Transfer the fish to a warm platter, placing the grilled lemon slices on top and spooning over any remaining glaze.

5. Squeeze the juice from one of the roasted lemon halves into the unwashed saucepan used for the glaze. Place over a low heat and stir to loosen the wonderful glaze stuck to the pan. Remove from the heat, add the cilantro and parsley and mix well to coat the leaves. Spoon onto the platter with the fish and scatter the remaining torn herbs over the top. Serve with the **Hibiscus Pickled Onion**, if using.

Variation

To grill on coals or the barbecue, place the fish on foil, banana leaves or a greased heavy-duty grilling tray. Brush both sides of the fish with oil and a generous amount of the glaze. Grill for up to 10 minutes. Watch the fish closely and baste again with the glaze. Turn the fish and grill the other side for 3–5 minutes. Brush the cut side of the halved lemon with oil, and grill over an indirect flame until charred.

Beniseed Stew

Fish in Sesame Sauce

WITH CHILI RED OIL

In Nigeria, sesame seeds are used in a variety of ways, such as in honey-sweetened snacks and *beniseed* soup or stew, a luxurious delicacy in parts of the middle belt and the northwest of the country. These versatile seeds are hulled after harvest, roasted and ground to a paste, then used in the rich stew with meat or seafood. There is also a plant-based version with ground dried papaya (called paw paw), which is popular among the Tiv tribes in and around Benue and the middle belt of Nigeria. I was first introduced to this regional food by Sister Margaret, a nun and dearest family friend who raised me and who is from the Idoma tribe in Benue state, Nigeria. For my version, I was inspired to use the jar of tahini I always have on hand, along with my trusted smoky **Red Oil** (see page 262) in place of palm oil. This dish is quite the doppelgänger for *egusi*, as *Beniseed* Stew is considered to be a richer version of that popular West African dish.

4 tbsp vegetable or olive oil
600g firm white fish loin or fillets
   (e.g., hake, halibut or cod), skin on
1 medium brown onion, peeled and
   finely chopped
4 garlic cloves, peeled and crushed
4 tbsp sesame seed paste (tahini)
300ml warm fish, chicken or
   vegetable stock
½ tsp cayenne pepper
1 tsp smoked paprika
200g spinach or kale, tough stalks
   removed
Sea salt flakes
Freshly ground grains of paradise
   or black pepper
2 tbsp **Chili Red Oil** (see page 262)
1 tsp nigella seeds

1. Drizzle 2 tablespoons of the oil into a large frying pan set over a medium-high heat. Pat the fish dry and, once the pan is hot, carefully place the fish skin-side down in the pan. Leave undisturbed for 3–4 minutes as the fish hisses and begins to curl up. The skin will stick at first but will release once it is crisp and the flesh has started to turn opaque. Once crispy, remove the fish from the pan and rest flesh-side down on a large plate. The fish will be finished in the sauce.

2. Place the frying pan back over a medium heat. Pour in the remaining oil and, once hot, add the onion. Sauté for 5 minutes, until softened and translucent. Add the garlic and stir until fragrant.

3. Meanwhile, whisk the sesame paste in a jug with 200ml of the warm stock until smooth.

4. Add the cayenne pepper and smoked paprika to the pan, stir for just under a minute, then pour over the tahini-stock mix. Add the remaining warm stock and bring to a gentle simmer over a medium-low heat.

5. Meanwhile, place the greens in a large bowl and pour boiling water from a kettle over them to blanch for 5 minutes. Drain in a colander or sieve and use a wooden spoon to squeeze out as much liquid as possible.

6. Chop the greens into smaller pieces and add them to the sauce. Arrange the fish with the crispy skin-side up, season with sea salt flakes and freshly ground grains of paradise or black pepper and simmer uncovered for 5 minutes, or until the fish is completely cooked, with the flesh opaque and flaky.

7. Serve in the sauté pan or individual shallow bowls. Drizzle the **Chili Red Oil** around the sauce and sprinkle the nigella seeds on top.

Spectacular Salads & Sides

Kachumbari

WITH HIBISCUS PICKLED ONION

SERVES 4-6

Kachumbari is a fresh and vibrant salad with plump tomatoes, onions and, more often than not, tingling and piquant green chilies. Most of the countries in the African Great Lakes region enjoy this delicacy in different variations. It is typically served as a salad to accompany rice dishes, roasted or grilled meat (known as *nyama choma*) and a cornmeal mash (known as *ugali* in Kenya and Tanzania, *posho* in Uganda and *mealie pap* in South Africa). I love adapting kachumbari to incorporate seasonal fruits and a variety of textures, such as creamy avocado or thirst-quenching watermelon. The possibilities are endless. See page 140 for a sweeter **Watermelon Kachumbari**.

FOR THE PICKLED ONION
1 large red onion, peeled and finely sliced
125ml red wine vinegar or apple cider vinegar
Pared zest of ½ lemon
1½ tbsp **Hibiscus Syrup** (see page 267)
1 tsp sea salt flakes
1 bay leaf
3 sprigs of thyme

FOR THE SALAD
450g mix of large and cherry vine-ripened tomatoes
1 cucumber, trimmed and cut into small pieces
1 green chili, stemmed and finely chopped
40g fresh cilantro, finely chopped

FOR THE DRESSING
Zest of ½ lemon and juice of 1 lemon
2 tbsp olive oil

YOU WILL NEED
1 500ml sterilized jar

1. Place the sliced onion into a sterilized glass jar or bowl and set aside.

2. Pour 125ml hot water and all the pickling ingredients into a small saucepan over medium heat and bring up to a slow simmer. After 5 minutes, remove from the heat, pick out the herbs and set aside. Pour the pickling liquid into the jar of onions, top with the saved herbs, cover and leave to sit in the fridge for at least 1 hour before using (for maximum flavor, however, make a few days before needed).

3. Halve the cherry tomatoes and chop the larger tomatoes into small chunks. Tip them into a serving dish and add the cucumber. Throw in the chili for some heat.

4. To make the dressing, place the lemon zest and juice and the oil in a separate small bowl, season to perfection with sea salt and freshly ground black pepper and whisk to combine.

5. Pour the dressing over the salad and toss to coat well. Place in the fridge to chill until ready to serve.

6. Once sufficiently pickled, add the onion to the salad and toss to combine. Scatter over the cilantro and serve alongside lots of different recipes in this book, such as **Slow-Roasted Salmon** (see page 139), **Smoky Jollof** (see page 206) and **Paradise Prawns in Creole Sauce** (see page 148), or enjoy with your favorite roast.

Lerato's Tip

The onion can be stored in a sterilized jar and kept in the fridge for up to 2 weeks.

Herb Salad

WITH HIBISCUS & POMEGRANATE

SERVES 4-6

60g lamb's lettuce
50g fresh cilantro leaves
50g fresh flat-leaf parsley, leaves
  picked and torn
1 small bunch of dill, torn
Small handful of mint leaves, torn
20g fresh chives, finely chopped
Seeds of 1 pomegranate

FOR THE DRESSING
Zest and juice of 1 orange (about
  70-80ml)
1 tbsp grated fresh ginger
40g dried apricots, chopped into
  small pieces
1 tbsp **Hibiscus Syrup** (see page
  267)
2 tbsp olive oil

I love this combination of peppery, sweet and fragrant herbs served as a salad. With the help of sweet apricots, the wonderful dressing with ginger, citrus and **Hibiscus Syrup** and a scattering of pomegranate jewels, you can whip up this standout salad in no time. Serve alongside spiced dishes, such as **Kefta** (see page 128), **Harissa Leg of Lamb** (see page 132) and *Mrouzia* (see page 94).

1. To make the dressing, place a small saucepan over a low heat and add the orange zest and juice, the ginger and 1-2 tablespoons of water (depending on the quantity of juice in your orange) to make about 100ml liquid. Heat until just warm, then remove from the heat.

2. Add the apricots to the pan and set aside for 10 minutes for them to soften and absorb the gingery citrus juice.

3. Stir in the **Hibiscus Syrup** and olive oil and season with ¼ teaspoon sea salt flakes and freshly ground black pepper. Mix well to combine, then leave to cool completely or store covered in the fridge for up to 3 days, if not using immediately.

4. Arrange the lamb's lettuce in a large bowl and add the assortment of herbs.

5. Spoon the plump apricots out of the dressing and scatter over the salad. Drizzle just enough of the dressing to coat the salad, toss to mix well, then scatter over the pomegranate seeds to serve.

Attiéké
African Grain Salad

SERVES 6

This recipe is heavily inspired by *attiéké* (pronounced ah-cheh-keh), a gluten-free dish of dried, fermented and grated cassava from Ivory Coast and popular across neighboring francophone countries. Precooked grains are sold in packets and sometimes referred to as *couscous de manioc* or *semoule de manioc*. *Attiéké* does bear a striking resemblance to couscous, but it possesses a significant tang as a result of fermentation. It is regularly eaten with fried fish or chicken and accompanied by a fiery tomato salsa called *moyo*. I wanted this vibrant salad to be as versatile as possible for you to prepare with a variety of grains. Here, I have used garri—dried and ground cassava without fermentation. The lemon juice and pomegranate brighten the salad with a sweet and refreshing tang.

200 garri, or fonio, couscous or precooked *attiéké*
4 tbsp olive oil
125ml stock, plus more for drizzling
Zest of 1 lemon and 4 tbsp fresh lemon juice
1 fat garlic clove, peeled and crushed
½ tsp freshly ground black pepper
1 cucumber, trimmed and cut into tiny cubes (peeled and deseeded, if you prefer)
1 jalapeño pepper, trimmed, deseeded (optional) and finely chopped
400g vine-ripened cherry tomatoes (mixed colors are wonderful), halved or quartered
4 spring onions, trimmed and chopped
Small handful of fresh flat-leaf parsley, leaves roughly chopped
4 mint leaves, roughly chopped
Handful of pomegranate seeds

1. Pour the grains into a large bowl and add 2 tablespoons of the oil. Using your hands, thoroughly rub the oil into the grains to keep them plump while steaming.

2. Add 2 tablespoons of stock at a time to the bowl and rub in. You want to add just a little moisture to the grains without soaking them. The grains may form clumps as you add the stock; this is perfectly all right. Keep massaging and running them through your fingers until all the grains are moistened.

3. Meanwhile, half fill a saucepan with water (one that will fit a steamer basket) and set over a medium heat. Place a cheesecloth or scrunched and flattened baking parchment into the basket and pour in the grains. Cover and steam for 10 minutes. Check the grains by gently fluffing with a fork. Drizzle with a few more tablespoons of stock, if needed, then fluff once again and steam for another 5 minutes, until the grains are plump. Larger grains may take slightly longer to cook. Carefully tip the steamed grains into a large bowl while you prepare the salad and dressing.

4. In a large bowl, combine the lemon zest and juice, the remaining oil and the garlic, and season with the freshly ground black pepper and a pinch of fine sea salt. Whisk thoroughly and check the seasoning.

5. Add the cucumber, jalapeño and tomatoes to the dressing and toss to soak up those wonderful flavors.

6. Finally, drizzle enough dressing to coat the grains and toss to combine. Scatter over the chopped spring onions, fresh herbs and pomegranate seeds and toss once more.

Black-Eyed Pea Salad

WITH ROASTED PEPPERS, TAHINI & LIME

SERVES 4

2 Romano peppers, or half a 450g jar roasted peppers
1 tbsp olive oil
250ml vegetable stock
1 bay leaf
1 fat garlic clove, peeled and lightly smashed
2 400g cans black-eyed peas, drained and rinsed
3 spring onions, trimmed and chopped
40g fresh flat-leaf parsley, leaves picked
½–1 scotch bonnet pepper, preferably yellow, stemmed, deseeded and diced
300g vine-ripened cherry tomatoes, halved
1 cucumber, trimmed and diced

FOR THE DRESSING
3 tbsp sesame seed paste (tahini)
Zest of 1 lime and juice of 2 limes
4 tbsp olive oil

Black-eyed peas are one of the great hallmarks of African culture and they have traveled with its people to faraway lands. From the Caribbean to the Americas, this "poor man's meat" is a much-loved staple and its influence is visible in many dishes across and beyond the continent. This recipe was inspired by Senegalese chef Pierre Thiam's *Salatu Niebe*, a refreshing salad where the precious peas sit in a zingy dressing. In my version, roasted red peppers, garlic and fresh herbs enliven the beans, with creamy tahini and fragrant limes, for an explosion of flavors. Leaving the salad to sit in the dressing for a while before tucking in allows the flavors to meld wonderfully. Serve with a crusty roll or your favorite roast.

1. If using fresh peppers, preheat the oven to 400°F.

2. Place the whole peppers in a roasting tray and brush with oil. Roast for 25–30 minutes, turning halfway, until shriveled and tender.

3. Meanwhile, bring the vegetable stock to a boil over a medium heat. Add the bay leaf, whole garlic clove and the black-eyed peas. Season with a generous pinch of fine sea salt and simmer uncovered for 5 minutes.

4. Drain the beans, reserving the stock and garlic, and tip into a wide bowl to cool slightly. Toss the spring onions, parsley and scotch bonnet into the bowl of beans.

5. To make the dressing, squeeze the poached garlic out of its skin and place in a small bowl. Crush to a puree, then add the tahini. Pour in a little of the reserved stock to loosen the puree, then add the lime zest and juice and season with fine sea salt. Pour in the oil and whisk thoroughly to combine. Pour the dressing over the beans and stir. The longer the beans soak in the dressing, the better they will be for devouring.

6. Remove the stalks from the peppers, scoop out the seeds and membrane and chop the flesh into small pieces, then add to the bowl with the beans.

7. Add the tomatoes, toss well and, once the beans are completely cooled, add the cucumber, too. Toss again and season with a pinch of fine sea salt and ground black pepper. Cover and set aside for 20–30 minutes, for the flavors to meld together before serving, or keep covered in the fridge for up to 3 days.

Mango & Cabbage Slaw

WITH HIBISCUS & ORANGE DRESSING

SERVES 4-6

½ red cabbage, tough center removed and leaves finely sliced into ribbons
½ red onion, peeled and finely sliced
1 jalapeño pepper, stemmed and diced
1 large or 2 small mangoes, ripe but firm, peeled, destoned and flesh sliced or julienned into thin strips
5 scented leaves (e.g., African clove basil or Thai basil)
5 mint leaves

FOR THE HIBISCUS & ORANGE DRESSING

Zest and juice of 1 medium orange
Juice of 1 lime
2 tbsp extra-virgin olive oil
2 tbsp **Hibiscus Syrup** (see page 267)

In many African cultures, it has been most common to eat your fruits as they are and not mix them into salads or cook with them. This recipe is a reflection of how modern cooks increasingly find ways to cook with the best of the season. I have combined mangoes with two of my favorite flavors—hibiscus and orange—for a beautiful slaw that pairs wonderfully with fish and grills. In the absence of the necessary ripe but firm mangoes, papaya or apples are wonderful alternatives.

1. Place the sliced cabbage in a large colander over a bowl and season with a generous pinch or two of fine sea salt. Toss and set aside for 30–60 minutes.

2. To make the dressing, combine the orange zest and juice, lime juice, olive oil and **Hibiscus Syrup** in a bowl and mix well.

3. Tip the red onion into the hibiscus and orange dressing to macerate for 15 minutes. This will soften the harshness of the onion for a wonderful balance to this sweet slaw.

4. Place the jalapeño and mango in a serving bowl.

5. Pile the herb leaves in a single stack from larger to smaller leaf, roll into a cigar shape and finely slice. Add to the bowl with the mango.

6. Squeeze the cabbage in the colander to remove moisture, then add it to the bowl. Pour the onion and dressing into the bowl, toss, taste and season to perfection. Serve immediately. This is wonderful with the fragrant **Slow-Roasted Salmon with Hibiscus, Harissa & Citrus** (see page 139) or **Mango & Lime Piri Piri Chicken** (see page 110).

Variation

This recipe is perfectly adaptable to different seasons—you could swap mangoes for apples or carrots, for example. You can omit the tingling heat of chili in exchange for the warmth of fresh or roasted Romano or bell peppers. Sometimes I prefer it with spicier cilantro leaves and at other times with lighter parsley. Pair your flavors to suit your accompanying dish and enjoy a unique salad every time.

Serengeti Salad

WITH HIBISCUS & CITRUS DRESSING

SERVES 6–8

So, I asked myself, "What would I serve guests if I were lucky enough to be hosting the ultimate African dinner after exploring the Serengeti on safari together? Imagine a breathtaking day of wide-eyed discovery, trailing through 'endless plains' (the English translation of Serengeti). Awestruck after encountering the Big 5, Africa's most elusive animals, and coming face to face with the jaw-dropping baobabs—the most enduring, most giving tree, one of the longest lived in the world, and one of our most prized, also known as the 'tree of life'?" In response I created the ultimate fruit salad— a thirst quencher that celebrates some of the best of African diversity of flora and fruits that you can enjoy from anywhere in the world.

4 small sweet oranges, peeled and sliced into ¼-inch-thick rounds

1 large mango, peeled, destoned and cut into chunks

1 papaya, peeled, deseeded, quartered lengthways and sliced

½ small watermelon, peeled and cut into small cubes

250g strawberries, hulled and sliced

½ pineapple, peeled and sliced

Seeds of 1 pomegranate

Small handful of mint leaves, torn

FOR THE HIBISCUS & CITRUS DRESSING

2 tbsp **Hibiscus Syrup** (see page 267)

1-inch piece of ginger, peeled and finely grated

200ml fresh orange juice

Juice of 1 lime

1 tsp baobab powder (optional)

1. To make the dressing, place the **Hibiscus Syrup** in a small bowl and whisk in the ginger, orange and lime juices and baobab, if using. Place in the fridge to chill until ready to use.

2. Arrange the oranges, mango, papaya, watermelon, strawberries and pineapple in a wide platter. Sprinkle the pomegranate seeds onto the fruit.

3. Drizzle the chilled dressing all over the fruit platter and scatter with the torn mint to serve.

Lerato's Tip

The salad can be stored in an airtight container in the fridge for up to 3 days.

Tomato & Strawberry Salad

WITH HIBISCUS & SCOTCH BONNET BALSAMIC DRESSING

SERVES 4

I created this recipe for my very first supper club in Lagos back in 2015 and, as with many other recipes, my aim was to spark conversation. I wanted to highlight the wonderful, blushing and plump local strawberries I had found in Nigeria. Formerly elusive, strawberries are now grown across Africa in temperate regions, such as Jos Plateau in Nigeria, in parts of Senegal, Kenya, South Africa and Egypt. Do not be frightened by the scotch bonnet in the dressing, as it adds just a tingling tease of heat. I love to serve this with torn chicory leaves, for their bitter sweetness and crunch. The sweet, tart and spicy flavors also work wonderfully with roasts and a variety of vegetables, such as roasted peppers, creamy avocado and cooling cucumbers. This is a vibrant salad that you can certainly make your own!

FOR THE SALAD
300g cherry tomatoes, cut into quarters
200g strawberries, hulled and cut into quarters
Handful of fresh basil leaves, torn
Handful of fresh mint leaves, torn

FOR THE HIBISCUS & SCOTCH BONNET BALSAMIC DRESSING
1 tbsp **Hibiscus Syrup** (see page 267)
3 tbsp extra-virgin olive oil
1–3 tbsp **Scotch Bonnet & Turmeric Oil** (see page 262), according to taste
15ml balsamic vinegar
1 tbsp fresh lemon juice
1 fat garlic clove, peeled and crushed
½–1 tsp sea salt flakes

1. To making the dressing, place all the ingredients in an airtight jar, secure the lid tightly and shake vigorously.

2. Place the tomatoes and strawberries in a wide serving bowl.

3. Pour half of the dressing over the fruits and toss to coat well. Season with freshly ground black pepper and a little salt, if needed. Drizzle more scotch bonnet oil, if you like more heat.

4. Toss the fresh herbs into the fruits and serve immediately with the remaining dressing alongside.

Lerato's Tip
If making ahead, you can cover the salad and place in the fridge to chill, adding the dressing 30 minutes or just before serving.

Braised Greens

WITH SWEET RED PEPPERS

SERVES 4

This is a humble, verdant dish with so much love, goodness and sweet memories of family. I learned to cook braised greens from my mum when my grandma Theresa (whom I am named after in my middle name) had diabetes and lived with us until she gently passed away. Although she was kept on a strict diet and told to avoid starchy foods, my sweet grandma adored plantains, just like my mother and I, and she simply could not give them up. So, we were advised to feed her boiled unripe (low-sugar) green plantains (see page 278) with her favorite stewed greens. Although I was mostly out of the country and in boarding school at the time, when I returned, I insisted on being responsible for cooking her plantains and greens every day. I love them with sweet peppers, pureed and sliced for a little sauce and texture, and with a smoky flavor from the paprika. I call this *Skinny Efo!* Braised greens in various guises are emblematic across Africa: the spicy *efo tete* in Nigeria—amaranth cooked in a stew of red peppers and chilies, with an assortment of meat and fish; Ethiopian *gomen*—collard greens cooked in aromatics and spices; East African *sukuma wiki*, meaning "stretch the week"; Ghanaian *palaver sauce* with taro leaves; and viscous stews made with West African sorrel, otherwise known as bush okra. One can also find Jew's mallow used in delicacies like *ewedu* in Nigeria and *mulukhiyah* or *molokhia* in North Africa and the Middle East. I hope that this recipe, inspired by my grandma Theresa, will encourage you to cook and love greens.

1 large brown onion, peeled and halved

3 red Romano peppers, stemmed and deseeded

½–1 scotch bonnet, or 2–4 red chilies, stemmed, deseeded (optional) and finely diced or pierced and left whole

200ml chicken or vegetable stock

90ml vegetable oil

500g greens (e.g., Swiss chard, amaranth, wild spinach, kale or collard greens), tough stalks removed and thin stalks and leaves thinly sliced

2 tsp smoked paprika

1. Place half the onion, 1 of the Romano peppers and the scotch bonnet or chilies, if not keeping whole, in a food processor with 60ml of the stock and blend to a puree.

2. Heat the oil in a heavy-based saucepan over a medium heat. Thinly slice the remaining half onion and, once the oil is shimmering, add to the pan with a generous pinch of fine sea salt. Sauté for 10 minutes, stirring often, until softened and golden.

3. Slice the remaining Romano peppers in half lengthways and then crossways into strips. Add to the pan with the sliced green stalks and chilies, if keeping whole. Sauté for 3 minutes, stirring occasionally, then pour in the onion and pepper puree. Cover with the lid slightly ajar and simmer gently for 10 minutes, until

the peppers and stalks soften and the puree thickens. Stir occasionally, adding a few tablespoons of stock, if needed, to stop the sauce from drying out.

4. Add the smoked paprika and a generous pinch of fine sea salt and cook for 1 minute before adding the leaves of the greens. Cover and cook for 5 minutes, stirring occasionally, until tender. The greens may release a lot of moisture, creating their own stock. If not, add some stock, a little splash at a time, to keep it moist but not drenched. After 5 minutes, taste your greens to check for doneness and seasoning. If you are happy with the texture, remove from the heat and serve—if you want them more tender, cook for another 5–10 minutes, as needed. Don't forget to fish out the scotch bonnet if kept whole! (See photo on page 174.)

Variations

When cooked with more vegetables, fish or proteins this dish can truly be stretched for more meals or to feed up to 8 people. In the absence of red peppers or fresh chilies, or for a quick pot of braised greens, simply sauté the onion and add 1 teaspoon smoked paprika and ½ teaspoon chili powder alongside the remaining ingredients. You can enjoy this African-inspired delight in several guises.

Braised Greens with Mushrooms & Sweet Red Peppers

Sauté 400g sliced mushrooms with the peppers.

Braised Greens with Smoked Fish & Prawns

Omit the smoked paprika and add 2 tbsp ground crayfish with the puree. Scatter 400g smoked fish into the sauce just before adding the green leaves and stir in 200g fresh or frozen prawns 3–5 minutes before the end of the cooking time. Make sure the prawns are thoroughly defrosted before using. Cooked prawns will need a little less time to cook.

Braised Greens with Beef or Chicken

Add 500g cooked beef or chicken with the puree, before continuing to cook the greens as above. If using raw chicken breasts or boneless thighs, cook in the puree for 20 minutes before adding the greens.

Eggplant Yassa
Roasted Eggplants & Tomatoes
WITH ONION & LEMON SAUCE

Spongy and meaty eggplants love this tangy and sweet sauce.
I created this dish for vegan guests when I first started immersive
events and supper clubs. Our feast was served in platters spread
across a long table, with our guests passing around the dishes and
sharing with each other. While it was my intention to make sure
vegans never felt their options were an afterthought, I didn't expect
non-vegans to dip greedily into the vegan dishes, such as this
Eggplant Yassa. It has become a long-running joke for us in the
kitchen and for our returning guests. Regardless of the number of
vegans at the table, the irresistible vegan options soon became the
main options for all.

SERVES 4–6

FOR THE ROASTED EGGPLANTS
1 garlic clove, peeled and grated
½ tsp cayenne pepper
1 tbsp Dijon mustard
Juice of 1 lemon
2 tbsp olive, peanut or vegetable oil
4 eggplants
400g cherry tomatoes

FOR THE SAUCE
3 tbsp olive, peanut or vegetable oil
3 medium brown onions, peeled,
    halved and sliced (just under
    ½ inch thick)
2 garlic cloves, peeled and grated
Zest and juice of 1 lemon
1 tbsp Dijon mustard
250ml vegetable stock
4 sprigs of thyme or 1 tsp dried
1 scotch bonnet, pierced and left
    whole (optional)
½–1 tsp agave syrup (optional)

TO SERVE
Small handful of fresh flat-leaf
    parsley, roughly chopped, or
    Parsley & Baobab Herb Oil (see
    page 263), for drizzling

1. Preheat the oven to 400°F.

2. Combine the garlic, cayenne pepper, mustard, lemon juice and 1 tablespoon of the oil in a bowl and set aside.

3. Slice the eggplants in half and use the tip of a small knife to cut deeply but not all the way into the flesh in a crisscross pattern. Hold onto both sides of each eggplant and lightly push upwards to widen the cuts. Place the eggplants and tomatoes on a large roasting tray and brush with the remaining oil. Sprinkle fine sea salt into and around the cut side of the eggplants and on the tomatoes. Brush the lemon and mustard mixture onto the cut side of the eggplants, making sure they are well covered, and roast cut-side up for 40–45 minutes, or until tender and cooked through.

4. Meanwhile, to make the sauce, heat the oil in a wide saucepan and, once shimmering, add the onions and a generous pinch of fine sea salt. Cover and cook over a medium heat for 10 minutes, stirring often, until the onions are translucent. Add a splash of water if needed to prevent burning. Remove the lid and continue cooking for another 15 minutes, stirring often, until softened and golden. Add the garlic and stir until fragrant.

5. Add the lemon zest and juice and use a wooden spoon to loosen any sticky bits in the pan. Add the mustard, stock, thyme and scotch bonnet, if using, and season with a pinch of fine sea salt and freshly ground black pepper. Simmer for 10–15 minutes until the sauce is reduced.

6. Taste to adjust seasoning—not all lemons are equal so if you find your sauce too tart, scoop out 2 tablespoons of sauce into a small bowl and add ½ teaspoon of agave syrup, mix well and pour back into your sauce. Gently stir and taste again. Repeat with another ½ teaspoon, if needed.

7. Spoon some sauce onto a warm platter, individual deep plates or bowls and rest the roasted tomatoes and eggplants on top, cut-side up. Spoon some more sauce and caramelized onions onto each piece, then scatter over the chopped parsley or drizzle with delightful **Parsley & Baobab Herb Oil.** Enjoy warm or cold. (See photo on page 175.)

Fosolia
Braised Green Beans
WITH TOMATOES & CARROTS

SERVES 4–6

Fosolia or *fasolia* is an Ethiopian and Eritrean dish which translates as "beans" in Arabic. Also known as fine beans, string beans or haricots verts, these can be so much more than sad, boiled side dishes. *Fosolia* is a wonderful vegan addition to a Lenten feast, enjoyed in the Horn of Africa during and after the Easter fast. The beans are cooked in several different ways and are a classic accompaniment with injera to much-loved favorites such as **Berbere Chicken Stew** (see page 86), sumptuous **Spiced Butter Lentils** (see page 213) and more. My version is rich with contrasting tomatoes, using plum or chopped tomatoes for lots of juice and cherry tomatoes for their sweet fruitiness, all simmered into a heartwarming dish.

4 tbsp olive or vegetable oil
1 large brown onion, peeled and sliced
4 garlic cloves, peeled and crushed
1–2 jalapeño peppers, stemmed and diced
½ tsp ground turmeric
½ tsp ground fenugreek
½ tsp chili powder
1 tsp dried thyme
1 tsp dried oregano
400g fine green beans, trimmed
1 tsp black cardamom seeds, crushed (about 10 pods)
1 400g can plum or chopped tomatoes
150g cherry tomatoes, halved
3 large carrots, scrubbed and coarsely grated
Handful of torn basil leaves

1. Heat the oil in a large sauté pan over a medium heat. Add the onion with a pinch of fine sea salt, cover and cook for 10 minutes, stirring often, until softened. Add the garlic and fry until fragrant, then stir in the jalapeño, dried spices and herbs. Cook for 2 minutes, stirring often as they release a wonderful fragrance, and add a tablespoon or more of water if dry.

2. Add the beans to the pan and toss in the onion and spices and sauté for 2 minutes.

3. Stir in both kinds of tomato with their accompanying juices. Season with a good pinch of fine sea salt and freshly ground black pepper and bring to a simmer over a medium-high heat. Reduce the heat to medium, cover and simmer gently for 20–25 minutes, stirring occasionally, until the tomatoes break down into a lovely sauce and the beans are tender, adding a splash of water if the pan looks dry.

4. Stir in the grated carrot, season to perfection, cover and cook for 5 minutes. Remove the lid and cook for another minute to reduce slightly.

5. Scatter over the basil and serve warm or cold.

Salade Méchoui
Roasted Pepper Salad

SERVES 4

Méchoui means "to burn or to roast" in Arabic and this simple salad is similar to *taktouka*, a Moroccan cooked salad with tomatoes and peppers, popular across the region. Once the peppers are roasted and peeled, tear them into rough chunks or chop them for a coarse puree. Depending on what I intend to use roasted peppers for, I sometimes leave on some of the skin for the flavorful char, and only peel the extremely blackened parts. Although a smooth puree or soup would fare better without any char. I keep these roasted peppers in a jar in the fridge, ready to eat or use in a variety of dishes, from pasta, salads and soups, to roasts and grills. If serving as a salad or with bread, drizzle the peppers with your most precious extra-virgin olive or argan oil.

4 red Romano or bell peppers, halved and deseeded

2 green bell peppers, halved and deseeded

4 tbsp olive oil, plus more for drizzling

3 garlic cloves, peeled

2 red chilies, stemmed and deseeded (optional)

1½ tsp ground cumin

2 tsp paprika

Small handful of fresh flat-leaf parsley leaves, chopped

Small handful of fresh mint leaves, torn

1. Preheat the oven to 400°F.

2. Arrange the peppers on a large baking tray. Drizzle with the oil and season with fine sea salt and freshly ground black pepper. Tuck the garlic and chilies underneath the peppers to prevent burning and roast in the middle of the oven for 35–45 minutes, until the peppers are tender and slightly charred.

3. Transfer the peppers, garlic and chilies onto a chopping board. Remove the skin, if you wish, or any extremely charred bits. Tear or chop the peppers, finely chop the chilies and smash the garlic to a puree. Transfer all to a bowl, sprinkle over the cumin and paprika and mix well to combine. Top with a little more oil, then season to perfection and scatter over the herbs to serve.

Grilled Corn

WITH AVOCADO & TAMARIND BUTTER

Growing up, my youngest brother was in love with roasted corn and steamed African pear, also known as *ube* in my mother's Ibo/Igbo language. During the corn season, the streets are awash with corn sellers roasting them over fires, while the pear is often sold raw. My brother would buy some almost daily and prepare the pear himself at home. This was possibly his first "cooking" experience. The small oblong-shaped pear can be roasted, boiled or steamed in boiling hot water until tender, after which a squeeze of the flesh releases a creamy and tangy green "butter" that tastes like a cross between avocado and olives. He would sprinkle a generous amount of salt and bite in, squeezing his face and smacking his tongue. In my recipe, the corn is grilled in the oven and I use creamy avocado and tangy tamarind to replicate the taste and lip-smacking sensation of the African pear.

SERVES 4

4 corn on the cobs
50g unsalted butter, melted, or
    vegetable oil
1 lime, cut into small wedges

FOR THE AVOCADO &
** TAMARIND BUTTER**
½ medium avocado, peeled and
    destoned
1 tbsp fresh lime juice
1 tbsp avocado or olive oil
1 tsp tamarind paste

Lerato's Tip

Grill on the barbecue or on coals
for the most amazing char and
smoky flavor.
If you are able to buy corn from a
farmers' market, do try to pick out
the freshest corn you can and
don't shy away from engaging in
conversation with the farmer or
shop owner to suss out the age of
the corn. He or she may just bring
forth a fresher stash from the
back. They almost always do.
Trust me!

1. Half fill a large pot with water and bring to a boil. Using tongs if you have them, carefully lower the corn into the boiling water. Season with fine sea salt and bring the water back up to a boil. Cook for 3–5 minutes, depending on the freshness of the corn. Once cooked, the yellow kernels will be plump and tender and a much brighter yellow. Drain the corn and pat dry.

2. Preheat the grill to high. Move one rack a little above the middle rack, closer to the grill but not dangerously close. Line a baking tray with baking parchment and place on the middle rack to catch any butter or oil.

3. Brush the corn with a little melted butter and place directly on the top rack and grill for 5–7 minutes, until charred. Turn the cobs over, baste with the melted butter or oil, and grill for another 5–7 minutes. Repeat until all sides have taken on some color and with a good char.

4. Meanwhile, prepare the **Avocado & Tamarind Butter**. Place the avocado in a food processor with the lime juice, oil and half the tamarind paste. Add 1–2 tablespoons water and process until smooth. Taste to determine if it is lip-smackingly tangy enough for you. Add the remaining tamarind or another tablespoon of lime juice if you desire more tang. Season with crushed sea salt flakes to balance the sour flavors.

5. Sprinkle chili flakes over the grilled corn and serve with a small bowl of the **Avocado & Tamarind Butter** alongside and a tablespoon of crushed sea salt flakes to cut through the tang. (See photo on pages 180–81.)

Berbere Potatoes

WITH CARROT & SPINACH

SERVES 4

2 tbsp olive or vegetable oil

2 medium brown onions, peeled and sliced

3 garlic cloves, peeled and crushed

1-inch piece of ginger, peeled and grated

3 medium carrots, scrubbed and cut into small round chunks

2 tbsp **Ethiopian Spiced Clarified Butter** (see page 264), butter or vegetable oil

1½ tbsp **Berbere Spice Blend** (see page 273)

½ tsp ground turmeric

500kg baby potatoes, scrubbed or peeled and quartered

500g spinach, tough stalks removed and leaves chopped

1. Heat the oil in a wide saucepan, for which you have a lid. Add the onions with ½ teaspoon fine sea salt, cover and cook over a medium heat for 10 minutes, until softened. Add the garlic and ginger and stir for 30 seconds, until fragrant.

2. Add the carrots, **Spiced Clarified Butter** or oil, the **Berbere Spice Blend** and the turmeric and cook for 3 minutes, stirring frequently to prevent burning.

3. Add the potatoes and stir to coat all sides, then try to arrange the vegetables in a single layer in the pan. Pour over 90ml water, bring to a simmer, cover and cook gently over a medium heat for 20 minutes, until the potatoes and carrots are tender with little or no liquid left in the pan.

4. Stir in the spinach and cook for a few minutes. If the pan is dry, pour in 60ml water, cover and cook for 5 minutes, until softened.

5. Remove the pan from the heat, taste and season to perfection, then leave covered to steam for a few minutes before serving.

Variations

This is a versatile one-pot dish that can be cooked with any of your favorite greens. For an Ethiopian and Eritrean-inspired *tikel gomen*, swap the greens for shredded green cabbage and cook as above until tender. You can throw together leftover spuds to soak up the wonderful aromatics and Berbere spices. Use less of the **Berbere Spice Blend** for a milder dish.

Patate Douce
Spice Roasted Sweet Potatoes

SERVES 4

When I started writing this book, a flood of memories from my childhood came rushing in. Like the fondest memories of sweet potatoes, lovely and fluffy inside and crispy outside. My emotional association with food is more about the feeling the memory of the taste and my attachment to a particular time. While in francophone Benin Republic with our family friends, the d'Almeidas, we weren't really allowed to eat "outside food" or street food, just like at my mother's house. And so, since the forbidden is always sweeter, we would sneak out for *Patate Douce avec Sauce Piment*—sweet potatoes with a fiery red pepper sauce. The women would wrap the freshly fried potatoes in newspaper and sell them with a tub of freshly ground chilies. It was pure heaven. Thinking back now, I can't believe how madly in love I was with these sweet potatoes. And although I have created a slightly more spiced version, I still relish the memory!

4 medium sweet potatoes, peeled and cut into 1-inch chunks
1½ tbsp paprika
1 tsp garlic granules
1 tsp dried thyme
1 tsp onion granules
4 tbsp vegetable or olive oil
2 tsp sea salt flakes, crushed, or 1 tsp fine sea salt
1 tsp smoked paprika

1. Preheat the oven to 425°F. Line a very large roasting tray or 2 medium trays with baking parchment.

2. Place the sweet potatoes in a wide bowl. Add the paprika, garlic granules, thyme, onion granules and oil, and toss to coat the potatoes. Season with the salt and massage the potatoes thoroughly, coating them on all sides.

3. Tip the potatoes onto the roasting tray(s) and spread out, leaving space in between each piece to allow them to crisp properly. Roast for 40–45 minutes, until golden and crispy with a little char on the edges.

4. Sprinkle with a light dusting of smoked paprika and some more salt, if you wish, and serve with **Sauce Piment** (see page 259).

Lerato's Tip

You can also place all the dry ingredients and oil with the potato chunks in a Ziploc bag and toss to coat everything well. The spice blend is also wonderful with a variety of roasted vegetables, ideal for using up leftovers.

Saffron Potatoes & Peas

WITH RAS EL HANOUT

SERVES 4-6

For this dish I wanted saffron, the most expensive spice in the world, to sing and take center stage. The sweet and floral **Imperial Ras el Hanout Spice Blend** (see page 269) offers a beautiful complementary background of flavor and fragrance that still allows the saffron to remain the star, but feel free to use whatever Ras el hanout you have. While this makes for an excellent dinner party dish to impress your guests, I don't see why you couldn't enjoy it as part of a midweek meal to indulge yourself. On meat-free Fridays we often enjoy this with baked fish. Plant-based margarine or oil can be used instead of butter.

0.4g saffron strands
2 tbsp olive oil or neutral vegetable oil
4 banana shallots or 2 medium white onions, peeled and sliced not too thinly
4 garlic cloves, peeled and crushed
2 tbsp unsalted butter, softened
1 tsp **Imperial Ras el Hanout Spice Blend** (see page 269 or store-bought)
1kg baby potatoes, scrubbed and quartered
300g frozen green peas
Small handful of fresh flat-leaf parsley, leaves roughly chopped

1. Crumble the saffron strands into a bowl and pour over 90ml of water. Set aside to infuse.

2. Heat the oil in a large sauté pan over a medium heat. Add the shallots or onions with 1 teaspoon fine sea salt, cover and cook for 10 minutes, until softened.

3. Add the garlic, butter and **Imperial Ras el Hanout Spice Blend** and stir until fragrant. Add the potatoes, pour over the saffron-infused water and stir to coat well. Arrange in a single layer, cover and cook gently over a medium heat for 20 minutes.

4. Add the peas, stir and cook covered for another 5 minutes, until the potatoes are creamy and just wonderful.

5. Scatter over the parsley and serve hot or cold.

Slow-Roasted Carrots

WITH ORANGE & GINGER GLAZE

SERVES 4

I created these glazed carrots for our Moroccan cookery classes, inspired by the fragrant and sweet orange segments we would enjoy after a meal in Morocco. The land is flush with wonderful citrus, some of the best I have ever tasted, and like in many African countries, fresh fruit is as good a dessert as any. In this recipe, the carrots serve as a vessel for the sweet, fresh citrus juice, and the zest with all its comforting oils. I typically serve this dish alongside sharing plates as a refreshing side and palate cleanser between dishes, especially helpful in quelling the fires of spicier dishes. For a warming variation, stir in a generous pinch of ground cinnamon after roasting the carrots, or add a splash of orange blossom water to the glaze for a transfixing scent and flavor.

400g carrots, scrubbed and halved
2 garlic cloves, peeled
1 tsp fennel seeds
4 sprigs of thyme, leaves picked
1 tbsp olive oil
Zest of 1 orange and juice of 2 oranges
1-inch piece of ginger, peeled and grated
2 heaped tsp honey or agave syrup
1 small bunch of chives, finely sliced

1. Preheat the oven to 400°F and line a roasting tray with baking parchment.

2. Cook the carrots in boiling salted water for 5 minutes, then drain and transfer to the roasting tray.

3. Crush the garlic, fennel seeds and thyme leaves with a mortar and pestle. Add the oil and a pinch of fine sea salt and grind to a paste. Scoop onto the carrots and toss well, then place in the oven to roast for 30 minutes.

4. Meanwhile, place the orange zest and juice and the ginger in a small saucepan set over a low heat and simmer gently for 5 minutes, then stir in the honey. Simmer for 1–2 minutes, then remove from the heat.

5. Remove the carrots from the oven and pour the orange and ginger glaze over the top. Toss carefully to mix. Return to the oven and continue roasting for another 10 minutes, until the carrots are softened and caramelized.

6. Serve scattered with the chives and with any remaining cooking juices poured over the top.

Chakalaka
South African Mother Sauce

SERVES 6-8

When invited to a *braai*—the much-loved barbecue emblematic of South African feasting—expect the delicious trinity of a piquant relish known as *chakalaka*, served alongside barbecued meat of some kind, such as a coiled spiced sausage called *boerewors*, and a stiff porridge made of cornmeal called *mealie pap*. South Africans simply adore *chakalaka* and it is a warm reflection of the country's mélange of people and cultures. It originated from the townships, which were segregated and typically underdeveloped neighborhoods around the mining towns, reserved for the non-whites who worked in the mines, the biggest being Soweto in Johannesburg. This mother of all relishes is also a wonderful addition to "7 colors," the nation's equivalent of a heartwarming Sunday roast, with a variety of colors from the vegetables, rice dishes, salads and more. Slap it on just about anything!

2 tbsp olive or vegetable oil

1 large red onion, peeled and thinly sliced

3 garlic cloves, peeled and crushed

1-inch piece of ginger, peeled and grated

2 green chilies, stemmed and finely chopped

1 tsp ground turmeric

1 tsp smoked paprika

1 tsp ground cumin

2 tsp roasted garam masala or curry powder

¾ tsp fine sea salt

1 red bell pepper, stemmed and thinly sliced

1 yellow bell pepper, stemmed and thinly sliced

1 green bell pepper, stemmed and thinly sliced

5 large carrots, scrubbed and coarsely grated

2 400g cans plum or cherry tomatoes

1 tbsp fresh thyme leaves or ¾ tsp dried thyme

2 tbsp apple cider vinegar

1 400g can baked beans

½ tsp freshly ground black pepper

1. Heat the oil in a large, heavy-based saucepan over a medium heat. Add the onion with a pinch of fine sea salt. Fry for 10 minutes, until golden. Add the garlic, ginger and chilies, stirring until fragrant. Add the ground spices and salt and cook for 1 minute.

2. Add the chopped peppers and carrots, and cook for 3 minutes, stirring to coat the vegetables in the wonderful aromatics and spices.

3. Pour in the tomatoes, add the thyme and stir to combine. Simmer gently for 15 minutes, until the sauce has thickened.

4. Stir in the apple cider vinegar and baked beans. Season to perfection with sea salt and freshly ground black pepper and simmer for a final 5 minutes before taking the pan off the heat.

5. *Chakalaka* can be served warm or cold. Enjoy it in a **South African Grilled Steak & Cheese Sandwich** (see page 122) or alongside **Cheesy Maize Meal Cakes** (see page 202) and grilled sausages. Store any leftovers in an airtight container and keep in the fridge for up to 1 week.

Sweet Potato

WITH SUYA SPICED PEANUTS

SERVES 4

In Malawi, *nsinjiro* is a widely sold ground peanut powder used in soups and stews, most deliciously in a heartwarming dish known as *futali*, or creamy sweet potatoes. At the final stage of cooking, the tender spuds are mixed with the ground peanut and its natural oils thicken the potatoes into a luxurious mash. In my recipe, peanut butter and the bewitching suya-spiced roasted peanuts are the perfect combination for creamy decadence and crunch. This dish is good enough to enjoy on its own, or serve it with your favorite roasts.

1kg sweet potatoes, peeled and cut into small chunks
2 tbsp vegetable or coconut oil
2 fat garlic cloves, peeled and crushed
2 tsp grated fresh ginger
4–5 tbsp natural and unsweetened peanut butter

FOR THE SUYA SPICED PEANUTS
50g roasted peanuts, chopped
1 tsp ground ginger
½ tsp garlic granules
½ tsp onion granules
½ tsp paprika
¼–½ tsp cayenne powder

1. Bring a large pot of water to a boil over a high heat. Add the potatoes and cook for 20 minutes, or until tender.

2. Drain and reserve the water in a heatproof bowl. Place the potatoes in a separate bowl or in the bowl of your food processor or mixer.

3. Place the same pot used for the potatoes over a medium heat and drizzle in 1 tablespoon of the oil. Add the garlic and ginger and stir until fragrant. Add the peanut butter, stirring as it softens, and 60ml of the reserved potato water. Return the cooked potatoes to the pot, stir to combine, cover and reduce the heat to low. Cook for 5 minutes, adding more water, a tablespoon at a time, if necessary, to keep the potatoes moist and to prevent burning.

4. Remove from the heat and mash using a hand masher or wooden spoon. For a luxuriously creamy mash, place in a food processor or mixer, with the paddle attachment, and beat on low speed just until well combined, smooth and fluffy. Overbeating the mash may ruin its texture. Taste and season to perfection with fine sea salt and freshly ground black pepper.

5. Meanwhile, mix the chopped peanuts and spices in a small bowl, adding cayenne to taste. If using unsalted peanuts, grab a three-finger pinch of sea salt flakes, crush and mix into the spiced nuts.

6. Turn your beautiful mash into a warm serving bowl or individual bowls and use the back of your spoon to create "wells." Scatter over some of the **Suya Spiced Peanuts** and drizzle over the remaining oil. Serve the remaining nuts in a small bowl for extra helpings.

Vanilla Mashed Potatoes

SERVES 4–6

If you love mashed potatoes, you'll adore mashed potatoes with vanilla. Creamy and floury potatoes with a combination of cream and butter create a wonderful foundation for the caramel-perfumed tones of the vanilla—the second most expensive spice in the world! To make the most of your precious vanilla pod, after removing the seeds, add the pod to the milk for maximum infusion. The herby chives, reminiscent of onion and garlic, add a savory balance to the potatoes. For a dairy-free mash, you can easily use a plant-based milk, cream and butter.

150ml milk
1 vanilla pod or 1 tbsp vanilla bean paste
50ml heavy cream
1kg floury potatoes, peeled and cut into chunks
100g unsalted butter
2 fat garlic cloves, peeled
20g fresh chives, finely chopped

1. Pour the milk into a saucepan and bring to a boil. Place the vanilla pod on the chopping board and, using a paring knife, lightly slice into the pod. Open up and flatten and use the back of your knife to gently scrape the seeds out. Add the seeds and the pod to the milk and simmer gently for 5 minutes. Remove from the heat, add the cream and mix well to combine.

2. Meanwhile, place the potatoes in a large saucepan filled with cold salted water. Cover with a lid and bring to a boil over a medium heat. Remove the lid and cook for 15–20 minutes, until cooked through. Remove from the heat, drain the potatoes and return them to the hot pot. Cover to keep the potatoes steamed and dry.

3. Melt the butter in a small saucepan and add the garlic. Cook for 1 minute over a medium-low heat, then remove from the heat and leave to infuse for a few minutes.

4. Mash the potatoes until smooth—use the paddle attachment of your freestanding mixer, if you have one. Reserve 1–2 tablespoons of the garlic butter, then stir the remaining butter into the potatoes until well combined. Remove the vanilla pod from the cream and milk mixture, then pour the liquid over the potatoes. Season with fine sea salt and use a wooden spoon to fold the mix, then beat to wonderful fluffy clouds.

5. Spoon the mashed potatoes into a large serving bowl and use the back of your spoon to create "wells" in the mash. Drizzle the reserved garlic butter over the potatoes, so the butter collects in the wells, and season with freshly ground grains of paradise or black pepper. Scatter over the chives and dig in.

Breads,
Grains &
Pulses

Khubz
Medina Bread

MAKES 2 MEDIUM OR 4 SMALL LOAVES

If you spend a day getting lost in a typical medina in Morocco, be it in Essaouira or Marrakech, it won't be long before your curious nose leads you to something pleasantly unexpected. Through a maze of cobbled streets and narrow alleys, past vibrant textile and spice souks, smoky stalls with *kefta* and *méchoui*, and steaming *hammams* (local bath spas), you will eventually arrive at the neighboring *ferrans* where freshly baked bread awaits. These round and crusty puffed flatbreads are known as *khubz*. Meaning "bread" in Arabic and also known as *kesra* among the Berbers, it is an essential and delicious tool for mopping up tagines, stuffing with kefta, roasted sardines and much more. They are also called medina bread, as they are part of the enigma of those enduring fortresses. I love them baked with a mix of white bread flour and a nutty-tasting or malted flour, like barley or malted grains, with creamy and gritty semolina dusted on the baking sheet. The whiff of the malted loaves as they bake transports me to the "red city" every time.

300g white bread flour, plus more for dusting
100g barley or malted wheat flour
2¼ tsp instant yeast
1 tsp sugar
1 tsp fine sea salt
300ml lukewarm water
2 tbsp olive oil, plus more for oiling

TO FINISH
Semolina, for dusting
1 tsp nigella seeds
½ tsp sesame seeds
½ tsp fennel seeds, slightly crushed
60ml milk or water, for glazing

1. Place the flours, yeast, sugar and salt into a large mixing bowl or the bowl of your freestanding mixer and mix to combine. Create a well in the center and gradually pour in the water and oil, mixing until well combined. Use your hands or the dough hook of the mixer on low speed as you gradually pour in the liquid. If the dough is dry, add more water, a tablespoon at a time, up to an extra 60ml. If it feels too sticky, add a very light dusting of flour to correct the moisture level.

2. Either knead in your freestanding mixer on medium speed until the dough transforms to a soft, smooth and elastic ball, or very lightly flour a clean and smooth work surface and turn the dough out onto it. Sprinkle another very light dusting of flour onto the dough and start to knead by hand. Push the dough away from you then fold the top end up and back toward you. Turn the dough 90° and repeat. Continue kneading for up to 10 minutes, until the dough is soft, smooth and elastic.

3. Transfer to a lightly oiled bowl, cover with a wax or clean cloth and leave in a warm place to rise for 1 hour, until the dough is pillowy soft. (At this stage you can chill the dough in the refrigerator overnight. Bring back to room temperature before baking.)

4. Transfer the dough to a very lightly floured surface, punch to knock out any air, then roll the dough into a thick log. Divide into 2 or 4 equal pieces and lightly roll back into smooth balls. Beginning in the center, use the heel of your palm to flatten each ball into a disc, about ¾ inch thick, as even as possible on all sides. (If using plain or white bread flour, flatten the discs to about ¼ inch as they will rise more than a dough made with heavier flours like barley or malted grains.)

5. Line a baking tray with baking parchment and dust it with semolina. Place the flattened discs on the prepared sheet, cover with a wax cloth or clean napkin and leave in a warm place for 30 minutes for a final rise before baking.

6. Preheat the oven to 450°F.

7. Mix the seeds together in a small bowl. Very lightly brush the top of each disc with milk or water, then scatter some seeds on top, pressing lightly so they stick to the dough. Using a mesh strainer, very lightly dust the top of the discs with semolina or flour. Use a paring knife to cut a few light incisions across the discs, then slide the baking tray into the middle of the oven and bake for about 20 minutes, until golden on top.

8. Transfer to a wire rack to cool slightly, then tear open and enjoy with your favorite dips, with **Plantain Shakshuka** (see page 62) or dipped into the most wonderful extra-virgin olive or argan oil.

My East African Chapati

MAKES 8

East African chapati, also known as Kenyan chapati, is an important tool for mopping up the curries, stews and roasts enjoyed across East Africa. Essential for **My Golden Ugandan Rolex** (see page 66), these are a cross between an Indian chapati and the flaky, layered paratha. Stretching the dough plays a big part in creating its distinctively buttery layers. I prefer to mix it with milk instead of water, to create a slightly enriched dough, while I use oil or butter, instead of ghee, to cook them to perfection in a smoldering hot pan. As this delicious bread is a labor of love, see my tips for storing and freezing the dough so you can enjoy them at a moment's notice.

225g fine wholewheat or
   chapati flour
225g plain flour
1 tsp fine sea salt
¾ tsp granulated sugar
50ml lukewarm milk
200ml lukewarm water
2 tbsp vegetable oil (olive, peanut
   or sunflower oil)

TO SHAPE AND COOK
Plain flour, for dusting
Vegetable oil, for rolling and oiling
   hands
50g butter, melted, or 60ml
   vegetable oil

1. Put the flours, salt and sugar into a large bowl or the bowl of your freestanding mixer and mix to combine. Combine the milk, water and oil in a small jug. Create a well in the center of the dry ingredients and pour in the liquid, a little at a time, while mixing. Once combined, use your hands to keep mixing or use the dough hook of the mixer on low speed as you pour in the liquid, then increase to medium speed. Mix for a few minutes until the dough transforms from crumbly to a sticky ball. If the dough is dry, add water a tablespoon at a time (up to 60ml). If it feels too sticky, add a very light dusting of flour.

2. Very lightly flour a smooth work surface and turn the dough out. Sprinkle a little flour onto the dough and start to knead. Push the dough away from you, then fold the top back toward you. Turn the dough 90° and repeat. Continue for 5–8 minutes, until the dough is super soft, smooth and ever-so-slightly sticky.

3. Roll into a medium-sized log and divide into 8, using a sharp knife or a dough cutter. Roll each piece into a ball, then lightly oil your hands to roll and coat each ball. Brush the surface of a tray with oil and transfer the balls into it, in a single layer. Cover with a clean cloth and leave in a warm place to rest for 1 hour.

4. Transfer one dough ball to a very lightly floured surface, leaving the rest covered. Very lightly dust the top of the ball with flour, then flatten it with the bottom of your wrist. Roll the dough out as thinly as possible into a rectangle without tearing. Brush the entire surface with oil and sprinkle with a very light dusting of flour. Holding the bottom of the dough,

To prevent your chapati from drying or shrinking, you can roll out half your batch and start cooking, stopping halfway through to roll and cook the remaining half. If you roll all the chapatis at once, make sure you stack and cover them.

Chapatis are best eaten immediately while warm and supple, but if you don't eat them all in one sitting, you can store them in the fridge or freezer with my handy tips:

To store in the fridge, shape your dough into coils up to step 4, lightly oil a tray or airtight container and arrange the coils in one single layer. Cover tightly with a wax cloth or secure the lid of the container and keep in the fridge for a maximum of 48 hours before cooking.

To freeze your chapatis, prepare up until step 8 where you cook the chapatis. Cook each dough in a dry frying pan for 20–30 seconds on each side, until the chalky-white raw surface disappears. Remove and place on a tray and repeat until you have precooked all your chapatis. Leave to cool completely and wrap each one individually tightly with a wax cloth or baking parchment. Store in an airtight container or wrap once again in a wax cloth. To defrost, remove from the freezer and leave out at room temperature for up to 15 minutes or until softened. Continue from step 8, first cooking each side for 10 seconds before proceeding to the oiling stage.

start rolling it up, like a cinnamon roll. Continue to roll and stretch the dough into a slim rope, then starting from one end, roll into a coil or spiral-shaped disc. Tuck the second end across the top of the coil and into the center. Transfer to the oiled tray and press to flatten slightly. Repeat until you have rolled and shaped all the balls. By the time you have prepared all the dough balls, the first one should be rested and ready to cook. (They should rest for at least 15 minutes.)

5. Line a tray or large plate with kitchen paper and have a clean cloth on hand to keep the chapatis warm after cooking. Cut out two 10-inch pieces of baking parchment and set aside.

6. Lightly dust a clean work surface with flour, transfer one of your coils onto the surface and lightly dust the top with flour. Roll and turn clockwise to form a circle 8 to 9 inches in diameter and about ⅛-inch thick. Carefully peel the chapati from the surface and place on one of the pieces of parchment. Repeat with the other coils, stacking the chapatis as you roll. Place the second piece of parchment on top of the last rolled dough, then flip the pile over to start cooking the first.

7. Heat a large nonstick frying pan or flat pancake pan over a high heat.

8. Carefully place a chapati in the pan. Watch as it puffs up after about 30 seconds. Flip and wait for it to puff up again after about 30 seconds. Once the flecks of raw flour have all but disappeared, brush the surface with melted butter or oil and flip again. Cook for about 40 seconds, pressing down with a spatula and rotating the chapati in the pan to regulate the heat. Brush this side with butter or oil and flip, cooking for another 30–45 seconds, until both sides are golden with dark caramel spots. Flip a few more times, if necessary.

9. Transfer the chapati to the tray lined with kitchen paper to prevent sweating at the bottom and cover with the clean cloth to keep it warm and soft. Heat your pan again until smoldering hot before repeating with the other chapatis, stacking them as you cook.

10. Serve your soft and flaky "chapos," as they are called on the street food circuit in Kenya, immediately. Use them to scoop up your favorite curries or as an essential conduit to roll up **My Golden Ugandan Rolex** (see page 66). (See photo on page 198.)

Medfouna
Berber Buns

MAKES 4

When exploring the land of the Berbers, or *Imazighen* meaning "free people," one of the most delicious and enchanting discoveries you'll experience is *medfouna/madfouna*, meaning "buried" in Arabic. My version of this "buried" bread are delightful buns inspired by the fondly named Berber pizza, a stuffed flatbread typically baked in a sand fire pit or mud oven. Yeasted dough is kneaded and stuffed with anything from wild mushrooms, goat's or ewe's cheese and meat, to nuts, spices, aromatics and more, depending on what flora and fauna the people are blessed with. I especially love salty and creamy goat's cheese, but you could use feta or a vegan cheese. These buns are just wonderful with a crispy exterior and rich flavors that remind me of Moroccan *briouate*, with which I am completely obsessed.

FOR THE DOUGH
200g plain flour
100g fine semolina flour
½ level tsp fine sea salt
2¼ tsp instant yeast (17g sachet)
200ml lukewarm water
1 tbsp olive oil

FOR THE LAMB
2 tbsp olive oil
1 brown onion, peeled and sliced
350g lamb mince
3 garlic cloves, peeled and crushed
2 tsp Ras el hanout
1 tsp ground cumin
1 tsp paprika
½ tsp freshly ground black pepper
¼ tsp cayenne pepper
1 tsp dried thyme
3 tbsp chopped fresh parsley leaves
3 tbsp chopped fresh cilantro
   leaves

TO SHAPE AND COOK
Fine semolina, for dusting
Oil, for rolling and oiling hands
1 tbsp **Ras el Hanout Oil** (see
   page 263)

1. Start by preparing the dough. Place the flours, salt and yeast into a large bowl or the bowl of your freestanding mixer and mix to combine. Create a well in the center and gradually pour in the water and oil while mixing with your hands, a wooden spoon or the mixer on low speed. If the dough is dry, add water a tablespoon at a time, up to 60ml. If it feels too sticky, add a very light dusting of flour to correct the moisture level.

2. Either knead in the freestanding mixer on medium speed until the dough transforms into a soft, smooth and elastic ball, or very lightly flour a clean and smooth surface and turn the dough out onto it. Sprinkle another very light dusting of flour onto the dough and start to knead. Push the dough away from you, then fold the top end toward you. Turn the dough 90° and repeat. Continue kneading by hand for 10 minutes, until soft, smooth and elastic.

3. Transfer the dough to a lightly oiled bowl, cover with a wax or clean cloth and leave in a warm place to rise for 1 hour or until increased in size. (At this stage you can leave the dough to chill in the refrigerator overnight. Bring it up to room temperature before baking.)

4. To prepare the lamb filling, heat the oil in a large pan over a medium heat and add the onion with a small pinch of fine sea salt. Cook for 10–15 minutes, stirring occasionally, until softened and golden. Add the lamb and fry for 10 minutes, stirring often, until well cooked. Stir in the spices and thyme and cook for 3 minutes,

Variation

For a caramelized onion and mushroom version, replace the onion and lamb mince with 2 red onions, peeled and sliced, and 750g sliced mixed mushrooms. Heat 2 tablespoons oil in a large pan set over a medium heat. Add the onions with a small pinch of fine sea salt and cook for 10 minutes, until softened. Reduce the heat to medium-low and cook for 15–20 minutes, stirring occasionally, until dark golden and caramelized. Add another tablespoon of oil and increase the heat to medium. Once hot, add the garlic and stir until fragrant. Add the sliced mushrooms and cook for 10 minutes, stirring occasionally, until well cooked. Stir in the spices and thyme, cook for 3 minutes, then take the pan off the heat. Add the fresh herbs and stir to combine. Set aside to cool completely before breaking 150g goat's cheese or vegan cheese into the mixture, using a fork to break it up. Continue as above to fill and cook the buns.

adding a small splash of water, if necessary, to keep the mixture moist. Remove the pan from the heat, add the fresh herbs and mix well to combine. Leave to cool completely.

5. Transfer the dough to a very lightly floured surface and punch to knock out any air. Roll the dough into a thick log and divide into 4. Very lightly dust the top of each piece and roll back into a ball. Return the balls to the oiled bowl—if not wide enough to fit the individual dough balls in one single layer, use an oiled tray. Cover and leave to rest for another 15 minutes.

6. Preheat the oven to 400°F and line a baking tray with baking parchment. Brush them with olive oil, dust with fine semolina and place in the oven to heat.

7. Place each dough ball on a very lightly oiled surface, flatten with the heel of your palm and roll out to about 6-inch rounds. Spoon a quarter of the cooled filling into the center of each piece of flattened dough, then gently pull the edges of the dough into the center and pinch to seal together. Gently roll the filled dough into a ball, brush with **Ras el Hanout Oil** and place on the preheated tray.

8. Increase the oven temperature to 425°F and bake the buns in the middle of the oven for 15–20 minutes, until golden and crusty. Serve immediately. These buns are just wonderful with **Smoky Tomato & Date Jam** (see page 257). (See photo on page 199.)

Cheesy Maize Meal Cakes "Mealies"

MAKES 20

South Africans love *mealie pap*, best described as a stiff porridge made out of coarsely ground cornmeal, which is also known as maize meal. *Pap* comes in different varieties from a soft porridge for breakfast to crumbly and stiff for soups and stews. My cheesy maize meal cakes are the perfect addition to the classic trio of *pap*, *chakalaka* and *boerewors*, South Africa's favorite sausage.

1 liter vegetable or chicken stock
200g maize meal or cornmeal (white or yellow)
4 tbsp vegetable oil
2 garlic cloves, peeled and crushed
50g unsalted butter, softened
20g fresh chives, finely chopped
20g fresh flat-leaf parsley, leaves finely chopped
100g semi-soft cheese (Gruyère, Fontina, Gouda), cut into ¾-inch cubes

1. Start by cooking the "pap." Pour 900ml of the stock into a large saucepan and bring to a boil. Mix the remaining 100ml stock in a bowl with the maize meal until smooth. Gently pour the thick maize mixture into the boiling stock, whisking continuously to prevent lumps. Once the mixture turns into a very thick mash consistency, abandon the whisk and use a wooden spoon to keep mixing. Mix thoroughly to dissolve any lumps, then cover and cook over a medium heat for 10 minutes, stirring occasionally, and making sure it does not burn. Continue to cook for another 10–15 minutes, or until the maize is less sticky and coming away at the sides.

2. Meanwhile, heat a tablespoon of the oil in a frying pan and sauté the garlic until fragrant. Add to the cooked maize meal, along with the butter, chives and parsley. Mix thoroughly until well combined. Season to perfection with fine sea salt and freshly ground black pepper.

3. Divide the dough into 20 heaped tablespoonfuls and place on a large oiled tray. Roll each one into a ball and then flatten. Place a cube of cheese in the center of each, pinch to seal and roll into a ball once again. Press down to form a patty and arrange on the tray. Repeat until all the maize dough and cheese are used up.

4. Heat a large frying pan with the remaining oil over a medium heat. Once hot, add the maize cakes and fry for 3 minutes on each side, until golden and crisp. Cook them in batches and drain on kitchen paper.

5. Serve with your favorite relish, such as **South African Mother Sauce—*Chakalala*** (see page 189), alongside grilled sausages and vegetables.

Quick Injera

MAKES 8–10

Teff is a heritage grain native to the Horn of Africa. A grass species and one of the earliest domesticated plants in the area, the mildly nutty, tiny seeds are ground and cooked as a porridge or patiently fermented and cooked like a pancake to become injera. The distinctively spongy and sour bread is a fond conduit for almost all meals in the area. Traditional injera is a labor of love with a sour starter that needs several days to ferment. This task is typically left to the most skilled home cooks, who tend to be aunties and grandmas, but I know exceptional Ethiopian and Eritrean cooks who happily buy injera ready-made from their local suppliers. This is a quick version for you to whip up at home!

200g brown teff flour
100g white teff flour or plain flour
2¼ tsp instant yeast
2 tsp baking powder
½ tsp fine sea salt
600ml lukewarm water, plus 1 tbsp

1. Sift the dry ingredients into a large bowl. Add the water and use an electric whisk to combine. Blend for up to 1 minute, or until smooth. The batter should be runny, yet just slightly thicker than a crepe batter. Cover the bowl with a wax or clean cloth and leave to rise for 30 minutes–1 hour, until the surface has lots of bubbles and a foamy top. (The longer the batter rests, the more fermented it becomes.)

2. Heat a 12-inch nonstick frying pan over a medium heat. (No oil will be required if using a nonstick pan, or use kitchen paper to rub a little oil over the surface.) Gently stir the batter back to a uniform consistency, then swiftly pour 125ml into the middle of the frying pan, using a ladle or measuring cup. (If using a 10-inch pan, reduce the quantity to 80ml.) Immediately swirl the pan to thin out the batter and cover the entire surface of the pan. Regulate the heat between medium and medium-low to prevent burning. After about 1 minute, bubbles will have erupted on the surface. Do not turn over—continue to cook on the same side. After 1–2 minutes, the batter should be well cooked and coming away at the sides, and the surface will become dry to the touch, losing its shiny wet look. Remove from the pan and set aside on a wide plate.

3. Bring the frying pan back to a high heat before cooking the next injera. Continue until all the batter is used.

4. The cooled injera can be stacked in batches without sticking or arranged overlapping on a large platter. Serve with your favorite stews, like the **Berbere Chicken Stew** (see page 86) and **Spiced Butter Lentils** (see page 213) for a classic Ethiopian/Eritrean feast.

Lerato's Tip

The distinctive sourness of traditional injera is a result of quite a few days of fermentation. You can add a touch of sourness to your quick injera by including 3 tbsp white vinegar in the mix, or leaving the batter to ferment a little longer than an hour and up to overnight. If leaving overnight, omit the baking powder and vinegar and mix with only half the amount of water. The next day, when ready to cook, add the baking powder; vinegar, if the extra sourness is needed; and remaining water and whisk thoroughly before cooking.

A Note on Jollof...

There are some dishes that must come with bells and whistles, marching bands and circus troops, with a reverence that cuts across borders and ethnicities. Jollof is one of them. A humble one-pot of rice, tomatoes and peppers, it has become an infamous part of many nations' sense of identity. So infamous, in fact, that it is at the center of culture "wars" across West Africa, especially between hyper-visual Nigeria and its neighbor Ghana, who contest for the title of best jollof.

My jollof truly is the best there is, though! And so will yours be, after cooking this recipe time and time again. After years of cooking and teaching, I assure you that practice does make perfect. The secret to perfect jollof is time, care and attention. Take your time to cook each ingredient and build the rich flavor, from creating a deeply rouge and aromatic puree, to cooking the onions patiently, frying the puree and spices, and cooking the rice gently. It is a labor of love that requires your commitment.

When teaching, I find it most helpful to divide this recipe into three stages. The first stage is picking the base ingredients, starting with the tomatoes and peppers. Select the very best richly ripened, sweet and juicy tomatoes—in Nigeria, the plum variety is most commonly used but at home in the UK, I cook with vine-ripened tomatoes of different varieties. In the absence of fresh tomatoes, a top-quality passata is a magical store-cupboard alternative, and jarred or canned tomatoes are also suitable substitutes that will considerably cut down your cooking time. In terms of peppers, I love Romanos, and they are a great substitute for the peppers used in Nigeria, commonly known by their Yoruba name *tatashe*. Red bell peppers are a great alternative if you cannot find the sweeter Romano peppers. Scotch bonnets add a tingling heat and fruity flavors that elevate the sauce. Although other ingredients, including the rice and stock, will dilute the heat of the scotch bonnet, for those who are new to cooking with them, simply piercing one and adding it to the sauce is a measured way to extract some of those warming oils without the full heat of the chili. You can also replace the scotch bonnets with one or two warmer chilies, such as Thai chilies, or cayenne or chili powder. If I haven't convinced you by now, then omitting chilies altogether will be just fine. The tomatoes, peppers and chilies are blended into a puree with onion, garlic and ginger. To this rich puree, a fragrant curry powder, most commonly a Caribbean blend with allspice (pimento), and other spices and herbs are added to make the base. This is the important foundation for creating color and building flavor in your jollof. I also add smoked paprika to mimic the almost inimitable smoky flavors of jollof cooked over coals or wood fire.

The second stage is the cooking, and you must avoid the temptation to pour in too much water, and make sure you don't stir your rice while cooking. This would create mushy rice that you can never remedy. After gently cooking and soaking up the wonderfully aromatic puree, each grain of rice should be plump and separated, with a deep, orange-red hue just screaming to be devoured. You must also choose the very best quality of rice that you can. While, traditionally, long-grain rice is used to cook jollof, I personally love the fragrance of basmati, even though many cooks find it trickier. When using basmati rice, simply start with just enough liquid to submerge the rice, cover tightly and cook low and slow, adding a little more liquid as needed throughout the course of the cooking time.

For the final finishing touch, adorn your jollof with thinly sliced red onions and slices of tomato, or chopped fresh or chargrilled spring onions. I love to throw in defrosted green beans to steam for the final 5 minutes of cooking for an extra burst of sweetness. Inspired by a Somali penchant for serving bananas with pasta or rice and sauces, at my cookery classes I often leave fresh bananas on the table, knowing that if anyone did try it, they might just fall in love with the combination. And they do! This is not dissimilar to pairing jollof with plantains and I remain forever loyal to my sweet plantains.

Smoky Jollof

SERVES 4-6

300g long-grain or basmati rice, thoroughly rinsed
250-400ml chicken or vegetable stock

FOR THE PUREE

6 medium vine-ripened tomatoes or 1 400g can plum tomatoes
2-3 red Romano or bell peppers, stemmed, deseeded and roughly chopped
1 large brown onion, peeled and roughly chopped
1-2 red or yellow scotch bonnet peppers, stemmed and roughly chopped, or pierced and left whole
2-inch piece of ginger, peeled and roughly chopped
5 garlic cloves, peeled and roughly chopped

FOR THE JOLLOF BASE

90ml coconut or vegetable oil
1 small red onion, peeled and finely sliced
2 tbsp tomato puree
2 tsp curry powder
2 tsp smoked paprika
1 bay leaf
1 tsp dried thyme
4-6 sprigs of thyme, some thyme leaves picked and kept for garnish

Lerato's Tip

The smoked paprika is a cheat to add the smoky flavor that is typically achieved through cooking on firewood or coals. I love adding vegetables to jollof. Raid your fridge for leftovers.

1. Place all the puree ingredients in a food processor, except the scotch bonnets, if using whole, and blend to a thick and aromatic puree.

2. Place the oil in a wide large saucepan, for which you have a tightly fitting lid, and set over a medium heat. Add the red onion and a pinch of fine sea salt. Cook for 15 minutes, stirring often, until softened and golden. If it starts to get dry, add a little splash of water to prevent the onion from burning.

3. Stir in the tomato puree and cook for 2-3 minutes, until the puree starts to separate.

4. Add the spices and herbs and cook for 2 minutes, stirring continuously.

5. Gently pour in the blended puree, stirring well, cover and cook for up 20-25 minutes, until the puree is reduced to a drier sauce. Keep a close eye on it and stir.

6. Add the rice and stock (about 250ml for basmati rice and up to 400ml for long-grain rice), ensuring there is enough water to just submerge the rice. Season with 2 teaspoons of fine sea salt and stir just once. Add the scotch bonnet, if using whole. Bring to a boil, then reduce the heat, cover and simmer over a medium-low heat for up to 30 minutes. The sauce must be visibly simmering to ensure the rice cooks properly. Jollof rice is at its best cooked low and slow for perfectly plumped grains. Check at 15-minute intervals as the rice may start to catch at the bottom. If the sauce dries out and the rice is still not cooked, add a little more water or stock around the edges, gently pushing the grains from the sides to the center without stirring. A burnt bottom is perfectly acceptable and encouraged, as it infuses a wonderful smoky flavor into the grains.

7. Once the rice is cooked, remove the pan from the heat and leave covered to steam for a few minutes. Fluff with a fork, scatter over the reserved thyme leaves and enjoy your wonderful creation with a fresh salad like **Kachumbari with Hibiscus Pickled Onion** (see page 160) and **Fried** or **Spiced Roasted Plantains** (see pages 278 and 280), because jollof and plantains are a match made in heaven.

Seafood Jollof

SERVES 4–6

300g long-grain or basmati rice,
   thoroughly rinsed
400–600ml chicken or vegetable
   stock

FOR THE PUREE
6 vine-ripened tomatoes or 400g
   passata or tinned plum tomatoes
1 red Romano or bell pepper,
   stemmed, deseeded and roughly
   chopped
1 large red onion, peeled and
   roughly chopped
1–2 yellow scotch bonnet peppers,
   or 3–4 chilies, stemmed and
   roughly chopped, or pierced and
   left whole
2-inch piece of ginger, peeled and
   roughly chopped
5 garlic cloves, peeled and roughly
   chopped

FOR THE SEAFOOD JOLLOF
60ml vegetable oil
1 small red onion, peeled and finely
   chopped
1 red Romano or bell pepper,
   stemmed, deseeded and sliced
2 tbsp tomato puree
½ tsp cayenne pepper or chili
   powder (optional)
1 tsp smoked paprika
250g smoked fish, deboned (e.g.,
   salmon, haddock or cod)
100g smoked prawns or shrimp,
   heads and tails removed

1. Place all the puree ingredients in a food processor, except the scotch bonnets, if using whole, and blend to a thick and aromatic puree.

2. To make the jollof, heat the oil in a large heavy-bottomed saucepan over a medium heat and add the finely chopped red onion with a pinch of fine sea salt. Cook for about 10 minutes, stirring occasionally, until softened. Add the sliced red pepper and cook for a further 5 minutes, until the onion is golden and the pepper softened.

3. Add the tomato puree and 2 tablespoons of water and stir as it cooks for 2 minutes. Carefully pour in most of the blended puree, keeping 125ml back for later. Cook for 20–25 minutes, stirring often, until thickened, reduced and a little sweeter. Keep a close eye to avoid burning.

4. Add the cayenne or chili powder, if using, and smoked paprika, then add the chunks of smoked fish and smoked prawns. Stir and cook for a few minutes to enrich the base sauce.

5. Add the rinsed rice and pour in the stock (400ml for basmati rice and up to 600ml for long-grain rice), season with 1½ teaspoons of fine sea salt and bring to a boil. Add the scotch bonnet, if using whole. Cover with a lid, reduce the heat to medium–low and simmer gently for 30 minutes, until all the sauce is absorbed and the rice is plump and cooked. If the sauce dries out and the rice is still not cooked, add a little water or stock at a time around the edges, gently pushing the grains from the sides to the center without stirring.

6. While the rice is cooking, prepare the prawns. Blanch the spinach in hot water for up to 10 minutes. Drain and squeeze out the water, then finely slice.

FOR THE PRAWNS

Small handful of spinach

2 tbsp vegetable oil

5 spring onions, trimmed and
chopped, separating the white
and green

2 garlic cloves, peeled and crushed

1 tsp grated fresh ginger

12–15 large raw prawns, defrosted if
frozen

½ tsp chili flakes

½ tsp smoked paprika

5 scented leaves (e.g., African basil
or Thai basil, finely sliced, or 2
tbsp chopped flat-leaf parsley)

7. Heat the oil in a large frying pan over medium heat
and, once hot, add the white part of the spring onions,
the garlic and the ginger, stirring continuously for a
few minutes until fragrant and softened. Add the
reserved blended puree and bring to a simmer. Stir in
the prawns, chili flakes, smoked paprika and blanched
spinach, season with fine sea salt, stir and cook over a
medium heat for up to 3 minutes, until the prawns are
pink and the sauce has thickened. Finally, stir the
scented leaves into the prawns and greens.

8. Once the rice is cooked with all the sauce absorbed,
tip in the prawns with their sauce and, using a fork,
gently mix to combine. Cover and leave to steam for
3 minutes before taking off the heat. Fluff gently for
a final time before serving.

Lerato's Tip

Stack and roll the scented leaves
into a cigar, in order to cut them
into fine shreds.

Crank up the heat for the final 5
minutes of the cooking time to
burn the bottom of your rice, not
only to add a smoky flavor but to
leave behind a crispy bottom for
those who love it!

Bejeweled & Aromatic Fried Rice

This recipe is inspired by Nigerian fried rice, one of my favorites as a child. An aromatic dish with a rainbow of vegetables, peas and peppers, and the rice stir-fried in curry spices. This is a classic in Nigerian cooking, prepared in several different ways, from vegetable-based fried rice to varieties with meat and prawns.

SERVES 4-6

3 tbsp coconut or vegetable oil

2-3 pods of selim pepper, smashed, or 3 black cardamom pods, lightly bashed leaving the seeds intact inside

½ tsp ground turmeric

1 tbsp curry powder

1 bay leaf

300g basmati rice, rinsed and drained

400ml coconut milk, shaken

200-300ml chicken or vegetable stock

1 medium brown onion, peeled and diced

3 garlic cloves, peeled and crushed

1-inch piece of ginger, peeled and grated

1 tsp dried thyme

3 red or green chilies, stemmed and finely chopped

100g green beans, trimmed and sliced into ½-inch pieces

4 small-medium carrots, scrubbed and diced

1 red bell pepper, stemmed, deseeded and diced

1 yellow bell pepper, stemmed, deseeded and diced

300g peeled prawns, defrosted, if frozen

100g frozen green peas, defrosted

2 spring onions, trimmed and sliced into ½-inch pieces

1. Heat 2 tablespoons of the oil in a heavy-based saucepan set over a medium heat. Add the selim or cardamom pods and toast for 2 minutes.

2. Add the turmeric and half the curry powder and stir for 1 minute. Now add the bay leaf and drained rice and toast for 3-4 minutes, stirring frequently.

3. Pour in the coconut milk and 100ml of the stock (you can use less coconut milk, if preferred, so long as you increase the amount of stock at this stage to make 500ml liquid). Season with ¾ teaspoon fine sea salt and bring to a boil. Reduce the heat, cover tightly and simmer for 10 minutes, until softened but not quite cooked, with just a little bite.

4. Meanwhile, heat the remaining oil in a wide sauté or frying pan set over a medium-high heat. Add the onion with a pinch of fine sea salt and fry for 8 minutes, until softened. Stir in the garlic, ginger and thyme for 1 minute, until fragrant. Add the remaining curry powder and cook for 2 minutes, stirring frequently.

5. Stir in the chilies, beans, carrots and peppers, season with ½ teaspoon fine sea salt and sauté for 2 minutes, before taking off the heat.

6. Remove the selim or cardamom pods from the rice and discard. Add the sautéed vegetables to the rice and mix gently until well combined. Add a little more stock, about 100-200ml, depending on the texture of the rice, then cover tightly and continue to cook until the rice and vegetables are tender.

7. Finally, add the prawns and peas and cook for 5 minutes, until the prawns are pink and plump.

8. Remove the pan from the heat and fold in the spring onions. Cover and continue to steam for 5 minutes. Taste and season to perfection, then fluff the rice with a fork to serve.

Geelrys
South African Yellow Rice

SERVES 4–6

300g basmati rice
1 tbsp vegetable oil
45g butter (about 3 tbsp), softened
1 tsp cumin seeds
3 cardamom pods, smashed
4 cloves
1 cinnamon stick, broken in half, or
   1 tsp ground cinnamon
3 fat garlic cloves, peeled and finely
   grated
1-inch piece of ginger, peeled and
   finely grated
1 tsp ground turmeric
1 tsp fine sea salt
650ml hot chicken or vegetable
   stock
50g raisins (preferably golden) or
   pitted dates, finely chopped

Lerato's Tip

Although butter makes this dish rich and indulgent, you can swap it for virgin coconut oil or vegetable oil, if you prefer. Brown, long-grain and other rice varieties will do just fine, but may not be as fragrant and fluffy as basmati. If using brown rice, increase the liquid and cooking time. You can bulk this dish up with lots of chopped vegetables, like carrots, mushrooms and peas, or stir fry leftovers with roast chicken or vegetables.

South African yellow rice, known locally as *geelrys* in Afrikaans, is a staple in Cape Malay cooking and a classic accompaniment to bobotie, with its distinctive golden hue from the added turmeric and sweetness from raisins. My version includes a bit more spice and aromatics and I often swap the raisins for dates, for their bolder caramel flavor.

1. Thoroughly wash the rice in a colander under cold running water until clear, then leave to drain.

2. Heat the oil and 2 tablespoons of the butter in a wide saucepan, over a medium heat. Once the butter melts, add the cumin seeds, cardamom pods, cloves and cinnamon. Toast the whole spices for 1 minute, stirring continuously, as they release their wonderful fragrance, then add the garlic, ginger, turmeric and salt. Cook for 2 minutes, stirring continuously to prevent burning.

3. Add the thoroughly drained rice, stirring well to coat every grain in the aromatic butter. Toast over the heat for about 5 minutes, stirring frequently to prevent sticking, then pour in the hot stock. Add the raisins or dates and bring to a strong simmer. After a few minutes, reduce the heat to medium–low, cover and simmer gently for about 20 minutes, until the liquid is fully absorbed and the rice is perfectly plumped with a glowing golden hue.

4. Add the remaining butter and gently fluff with a fork. Pick out the whole spices and serve the rice with typical South African flair, alongside **South African Vegan Bobotie** (see page 216), or my personal favorite, the mellow, spiced and apricot-sweetened **Cape Malay Chicken Curry** (see page 88).

Misir Wot
Spiced Butter Lentils
WITH BERBERE

SERVES 4

This rich lentil stew is wonderful and comforting. Cooked in spiced butter and seasoned with fragrant Berbere spices, it is a vegetarian delight from Ethiopia and Eritrea that is traditionally served on sheets of spongy injera, alongside **Berbere Chicken Stew** (see page 86), braised greens like *Fosolia* (see page 178) and more.

3 tbsp vegetable oil or **Ethiopian Spiced Clarified Butter** (see page 264)

1 large brown onion, peeled and roughly chopped

2 garlic cloves, peeled and crushed

1½ tbsp **Berbere Spice Blend** (see page 273)

6 vine-ripened tomatoes, chopped, or 1 400g can plum tomatoes

250g red lentils

500ml vegetable stock

1 tsp **Ethiopian Finishing Spice** (see page 270) or fragrant curry powder

1. Heat 2 tablespoons of the oil or **Spiced Clarified Butter** in a medium saucepan over a medium heat. When hot, add the onion and leave to cook for 5 minutes until softened.

2. Stir in the garlic and **Berbere Spice Blend** and cook for 3 minutes to build a wonderful base for your stew.

3. Tip in the tomatoes and cook for 10 minutes, stirring occasionally as they break down beautifully.

4. Stir in the lentils along with the stock and bring to a strong simmer. Cover with a lid and leave to simmer for 20–30 minutes, stirring occasionally, until the lentils are plump and all liquid is absorbed.

5. Stir in the **Ethiopian Finishing Spice** or fragrant curry powder and the remaining oil or spiced butter for a luxurious finish. Season with fine sea salt and leave to steam for a few minutes before serving as a vegan or vegetarian main meal with bread or injera (see page 203 for a quick version), alongside **Braised Greens with Sweet Red Peppers** (see page 172) or **Berbere Potatoes with Carrot & Spinach** (see page 184) for a heartwarming feast.

Waakye
Ghanaian Red Rice & Beans

SERVES 4-6

Ghanaians adore *waakye*. Pronounced *waa-chay*, it is an abbreviation of the Hausa *shinkafa da wake*, which simply means rice and beans. The Hausas, a Northern tribe predominantly in Nigeria, Niger and sub-Saharan Africa, are responsible for transfixing Ghanaians with what has become one of the most popular breakfast choices, sold at street stalls and chop bars. *Waakye* sellers begin cooking well before dawn, with several components prepared some days in advance. In my recipe, beets replace the commonly used sorghum leaves, which give the dish its ubiquitous oxblood hue. It is served with a variety of accompaniments: *waakye stew*, or Hausa stew, a deeply flavored and rich stew; sometimes with *wele*, the traditional name for tripe; garri (dried and ground cassava); *talia* (spaghetti); *kelewele*, like my **Spiced Roasted Plantains** (see page 279); and *shito*, a more pungent version of my Togolese-inspired **Blackened Red Pepper Sauce** (see page 52). By all means enjoy yours on its own, throw some or all the above on top and don't forget the boiled eggs!

250g dried red kidney beans, thoroughly washed
1 bay leaf
150g cooked beets, roughly chopped
1 small red onion, peeled and halved
3 garlic cloves, peeled and roughly chopped
2.5g piece of ginger, peeled and roughly chopped
1 liter chicken or vegetable stock
250g jasmine or short-grain rice, lightly rinsed
1 tbsp virgin coconut oil

TO SERVE
6 free-range eggs, soft-boiled, peeled and halved

1. Place the beans in a large saucepan. Add 600ml water, place over a medium heat and bring to a boil. Season with 1 teaspoon fine sea salt and tuck in the bay leaf. Cook for 30 minutes with the lid slightly ajar. Add a little more water if the liquid dries up before the cooking time is over. Carefully scoop out a few beans to check the texture—they should be just a little tender yet firm when pressed between your fingers.

2. Meanwhile, place the beets, onion, garlic and ginger in a food processor and blend to a puree. Add a little stock to loosen the puree, if needed.

3. Add the rice to the pan with the beans, along with the beet puree and stock. Season with ½ teaspoon fine sea salt and bring to a boil. Reduce the heat to medium-low and simmer gently for 30 minutes.

4. Taste and season to perfection, then add the coconut oil. As this is intended to be a sticky rice, stir as vigorously as you desire. Remove from the heat and leave to stand covered for another 10 minutes.

5. Fluff with a fork before serving with soft-boiled eggs, **African Grain Salad** (see page 164) and any of your favorite stews and sauces, especially those with a tomato base.

South African Vegan Bobotie

WITH LENTILS & MUSHROOMS

SERVES 6-8

Bobotie is rather meat-heavy, so I created this plant-based version of one of South Africa's most popular traybakes. With a variety of mushrooms cooked alongside lentils, spices and dried fruits, there is abundant flavor and richness to the dish. I use a food professor to make light work of dicing the mushrooms. This Cape Malay favorite is typically enjoyed with **South African Yellow Rice** (see page 212) and extra helpings of fruit chutney on the side.

250g green lentils

5 bay leaves

60g dried porcini mushrooms

350ml hot vegetable stock

Plant-based butter or oil, for greasing

3–4 tbsp vegetable oil

750g chestnut mushrooms, diced

2 brown onions, peeled and roughly chopped

4 garlic cloves, peeled and crushed

1½-inch piece of ginger, peeled and grated

½ tsp dried oregano

½ tsp dried thyme

1 carrot, scrubbed and grated

1 tsp ground turmeric

2–3 tbsp garam masala or mild curry powder

¼ tsp ground allspice

3 tbsp mango or fruit chutney

Zest of 1 lemon and 1 tbsp lemon juice

50g raisins

50g dried apricots, finely chopped

2 thick slices of bread, crusts removed

100ml warm plant-based milk

50g toasted almond flakes

1. Thoroughly rinse the lentils, place in a large saucepan with 1 liter of water and 1 of the bay leaves and bring to a boil. After a few minutes, reduce the heat and simmer for 20–30 minutes, or until tender but not mushy. Drain and set aside.

2. Meanwhile, place the dried porcini mushrooms in a bowl and pour over the hot stock. Leave to soak for 30 minutes, drain and reserve the stock (about 300ml should be left). Finely chop the mushrooms and set aside.

3. Preheat the oven to 400°F and grease an 11- to 12-inch baking dish with plant-based butter or oil.

4. Heat 3 tablespoons oil in a large sauté or frying pan over a medium–high heat and add the mushrooms. Sauté for about 5 minutes until browned all over. Remove the mushrooms from the pan and set aside.

5. Add the onions to the pan with an extra tablespoon of oil, if needed, and sauté for 5–8 minutes, until softened and golden.

6. Add the garlic, ginger, dried oregano, thyme and 1 bay leaf, and stir until fragrant. Now add the carrot, turmeric, 2 tablespoons of the roasted garam masala or mild curry powder, the allspice, mango chutney and lemon zest and juice, and cook for 3 minutes.

7. Return the browned mushrooms, the rehydrated dried mushrooms and the drained lentils to the pan. Mix well to combine and pour in the reserved stock from the dried mushrooms. Add the raisins and chopped apricots and bring to a boil. Reduce the heat and simmer for 15–20 minutes, until the mushrooms and lentils have absorbed all the liquid.

FOR THE TOPPING

100ml vegetable oil

100g chickpea flour or cornstarch

850ml unsweetened plant-based
milk

1 fat garlic clove, peeled and
crushed

½ tsp ground turmeric

8.   Meanwhile, soak the bread in the warm milk for 10 minutes. Squeeze the bread (reserving the milk) and add to the mushrooms and lentils, along with half of the almonds. Pour the mixture into the prepared oven dish and level it out, but avoid pressing it down too firmly—you do not want a dense base.

9.   To make the topping, warm the oil in a saucepan over a medium heat. Add the flour and whisk. Gradually pour in the milk and any milk left from soaking the bread, until smooth, whisking all the time. Bring to a boil, then reduce the heat and simmer to thicken slightly.

10.   Remove the pan from the heat, season to perfection with fine sea salt and freshly ground black pepper. Add the garlic and turmeric and whisk thoroughly. Pour into your baking dish over the lentils and mushrooms and place the remaining bay leaves on top. Cover with foil and bake in the oven for 40 minutes, then remove the foil and bake for a final 15 minutes, until golden and firm.

11.   Scatter over the remaining almonds and leave the bobotie to rest for 10 minutes before serving "Cape Malay" style with **South African Yellow Rice** (see page 212) and extra helpings of mango, a fruit chutney or the **Smoky Date & Tomato Jam** (see page 257).

Slow-Cooked Beans

WITH PLANTAIN & CRISPY ONIONS

SERVES 4

This recipe is "home." When I am sad and weary, I turn to these slow-cooked beans to nourish my heart, body and spirit. As a baby, my mother weaned me on this with smashed potatoes and mackerel. The secret is cooking the beans until buttery soft and finishing with blended peppers, crayfish and red oil. My father's late sister, Auntie Vic, taught me to throw in a chunk of onion to soften the beans as they cooked. While I have not been convinced of the efficacy of this tip, I have strived to obey my auntie and enjoy the wonderful flavor the onion does impart to the beans.

300g dried black-eyed peas, brown beans or Nigerian honey beans, picked and thoroughly rinsed

1 large red or brown onion, peeled and halved

1 bay leaf

1 red Romano or 1 bell pepper

1-2 scotch bonnet peppers or habanero chilies, or 2-4 red chilies, stemmed and roughly chopped

1-inch piece of ginger, peeled and roughly chopped

125ml sustainable palm oil or **Red Oil** (see page 262), plus a drizzle to serve, or 2-3 tsp smoked paprika

½ small red onion, finely sliced

2-3 tbsp ground dried shrimp or crayfish

200ml fish, chicken or vegetable stock

2 ripe yellow plantains, peeled (see page 277) and sliced into ¼-inch rounds or ½-inch diagonal strips

1 spring onion, trimmed and sliced into pieces

1. Place the dried beans in a large saucepan with 1.25 liters of water and bring to a boil over a medium-high heat. This can take up to 10 minutes. Skim off any foam that forms on the surface.

2. Tuck half the large onion into the pan along with the bay leaf and season with 1 teaspoon fine sea salt. Cover with a lid slightly ajar to avoid bubbling over and cook over a medium heat for 50 minutes–1 hour. Check the beans after 25 minutes and pour in another 500ml water. Continue cooking until softened and easily squashed when pressed between your thumb and index finger.

3. Meanwhile, prepare a pepper puree. Place the red pepper, scotch bonnet, ginger and the remaining half onion with a splash of water in a food processor and blend to a puree.

4. Heat the palm or **Red Oil** in a separate small saucepan over a medium-low heat. Add the sliced red onion and fry for up to 8 minutes, stirring often. Keep a close eye to ensure it does not burn. As soon as it begins to curl up and darken, swiftly remove the onion from the oil with a slotted spoon and place on kitchen paper to drain.

5. Pour the pepper puree into the pan with the red oil and fry for 10 minutes over a medium heat, stirring frequently. Add the ground dried shrimp or crayfish and fry for another 10 minutes, stirring frequently, until thickened.

6. Transfer the cooked puree to the pot of beans and add the stock. Season with a pinch of fine sea salt and stir gently to combine. Cover and cook over a medium

heat for 10 minutes, then reduce the heat to low and simmer for a final 10 minutes, until most of the moisture is absorbed, leaving a bit of sauce on the top layer.

7. Once the beans are meltingly soft, remove from the heat and set aside for 20 minutes. The sauce on top will set as it cools.

8. Meanwhile, to fry the plantains, heat about 1 inch of oil to 375°F (see page 275) in a shallow frying pan or deep fat fryer. Carefully place the plantain pieces into the hot oil without overcrowding. Leave to fry for a few minutes, then use a turner or slotted spoon to peek at the bottom of the plantains. Once golden brown on the bottom, swiftly turn to fry the other side. Remove when the plantains are deep golden brown on both sides and drain on kitchen paper. Season with fine sea salt while still hot.

9. Serve the beans with a drizzle of palm or **Red Oil**, fried plantains and the crispy onions and spring onions scattered on top. (See photo on page 220.)

Lerato's Tip

I often cook this heartwarming dish with the plantains added to the beans at its final stage of cooking. Cut the plantains into small 1-inch chunks and add to beans with the pepper puree and 300ml stock. Stir to combine and cover to cook over a medium heat until the plantains are tender and thoroughly cooked. A wide variety of beans can be cooked or mixed together for this dish, as well as lentils, chickpeas or, for a sweeter dish, add corn, which is a popular variation in many regions across West Africa and similar to the Kenyan *githeri*.

Benachin
Senegalese 7 Veggie One-Pot Rice

SERVES 6–8

Embrace the joys of feasting together with this Senegalese one-pot rice. *Benachin*, enjoyed in Senegal, Gambia and neighboring countries, simply translates into "one pot" in Wolof language. This is the big sister of the famous jollof rice, with several versions across West Africa, including rice with fish, which is called *tiep* in Senegal, short for *thieboujienne* (pronounced as che-bou-jen). In my version, the vegetables are poached in a tangy, aromatic and rich sauce with tomatoes, sweet peppers and tamarind before the rice is cooked within.

300g long-grain rice, thoroughly rinsed
2–3 tsp tamarind paste
1 lime, cut into wedges

FOR THE PUREE
6 medium vine-ripened tomatoes, or 1 400g can plum tomatoes
3 red Romano or bell peppers, stemmed, deseeded and roughly chopped
1 large onion, peeled and roughly chopped
1–2 red or yellow scotch bonnet peppers, stemmed and roughly chopped, or pierced and left whole
2-inch piece of ginger, peeled and roughly chopped
8 garlic cloves, peeled and roughly chopped

FOR THE SAUCE BASE
90ml coconut or vegetable oil
1 large red onion, peeled and finely sliced
6 tbsp tomato puree
2 tsp smoked paprika (optional)
2 bay leaves
2 tsp dried thyme
800ml–1 liter chicken or vegetable stock

1. Place all the puree ingredients in a food processor, except the scotch bonnet if leaving whole, and blend to a thick and aromatic puree.

2. To make the jollof, place the oil in a wide and large heavy-based saucepan, for which you have a tightly fitting lid, and set over a medium heat. Add the red onion with a pinch of fine sea salt and cook for 15 minutes, stirring often, until softened and golden. If it looks dry, add a little splash of water to prevent the onion from burning. Stir in the tomato puree and cook for 2–3 minutes, until the paste starts to separate.

3. Add the paprika and herbs and cook for 2 minutes, stirring continuously, then pour in the blended puree, stir well and cook for up to 20 minutes, until the puree is reduced to a drier texture. Keep a close eye on it and stir often.

4. Pour in half of the stock, bring to a boil, then reduce the heat and simmer for 20 minutes, until the sauce is slightly reduced.

5. Add 1 teaspoon fine sea salt to the broth, then add the carrots, squash and cabbage, and simmer with the lid slightly ajar for 5 minutes. Now add the eggplant, zucchini, shallots and jalapeños and cook for 15–20 minutes, until fork tender but not mushy. Use a slotted spoon to transfer the vegetables onto a plate and set aside for later. You can cover to keep warm or heat in a preheated oven 15 minutes before serving.

6. Add the rice to the pan and pour in the remaining stock, just enough to submerge it, and bring to a strong simmer. Stir in the tamarind paste and taste to check the levels of salt. Stir just once, add the scotch

3 medium carrots, scrubbed and
   cut into quarters

250g crown prince or butternut
   squash or pumpkin, deseeded
   and cut into 1-inch thick wedges

½ small red or green cabbage, cut
   into 3 wedges

6-10 baby eggplants, halved, or
   1 large eggplant, trimmed and cut
   into 1-inch round chunks

1 zucchini, trimmed and cut into
   1-inch round chunks

4 small banana shallots, peeled and
   halved

4 jalapeño peppers

bonnet, if left whole, and season, if needed. Bring to a boil, then reduce the heat, cover tightly and simmer gently for 20–30 minutes. The sauce must be visibly simmering to ensure the rice cooks properly. Check at 15-minute intervals, as the rice may start to catch at the bottom. If the sauce dries out and the rice is not cooked, add a little more reserved stock or water around the edges, gently pushing the grains from the sides to the center without stirring. A burnt bottom is perfectly acceptable and encouraged as it infuses a wonderful smoky flavor into the grains.

7. Remove the pan from the heat and leave covered to steam for a few minutes. Fluff with a fork and transfer to a warm platter. Pile some of the vegetables on top of the rice and serve with lime wedges for extra zest. (See photo on page 221.)

Chocolate, Cakes & Puddings

Candied Peanuts

MAKES ABOUT 200G

These sugar-coated caramel peanuts bring back sweet memories of my childhood in Lagos. My mum would take us to the local baker, who sold the most buttery-soft loaves and vanilla-rich sponge cakes. She also sold moreish deep-fried, cookie-like dough known as *chin chin* and then there were these candied peanuts, wrapped in small bags or cone-shaped greaseproof paper if they were freshly made and still warm. These are one of the easiest treats you can make for a dazzling snack to serve with drinks, to embellish ice cream, yogurt or a salad with their nutty sweetness and crunch, or simply to share with friends and family as a thoughtful gift. Most importantly, these candied peanuts are essential for crowning my decadent **Candied Peanut Butter Chocolate Cake** (see page 228).

75ml water
100g caster sugar
100g roasted unsalted peanuts, half broken in pieces

1. Pour the water into a wide heavy-based saucepan and set over a medium heat. Add the sugar and leave to dissolve. Once the liquid starts to bubble and crystallize, stir, then add the roasted peanuts. Leave for about 50 seconds, then begin stirring the peanuts. Reduce the heat to medium-low to avoid smoking and take the pan off the heat. Return it to the heat to continue cooking as the syrup darkens.

2. Keep stirring often and, after 5 minutes, the peanuts and sugar will begin to form clumps. At 7 minutes, the peanuts will harden and the syrup will be very grainy. At this point, watch out for smoke and be careful not to let it burn. Take the pan off the heat and keep stirring. After 30 seconds, return the pan to the heat for 1 final minute to caramelize and, after 8½ minutes, swiftly take it off the heat. Trust what you can see and smell; time this recipe mindfully and you will soon be in ecstasy with these beautifully bronzed treats.

3. Enjoy as a snack, crumble onto salads or ice cream, and don't forget to save some to crown your **Candied Peanut Butter Chocolate Cake** (see page 228).

Variation
For salted candied peanuts, add crushed sea salt flakes once removed from the heat and stir to combine. And for a warming treat, sprinkle with ground cinnamon or ginger.

Candied Peanut Butter Chocolate Cake

SERVES 6-8

I love this cake enriched with peanut butter and dates. There are four secrets to its perfection: the first is the base of sticky dates and peanuts, chilled in the fridge, with no baking needed. The second is the body of the cake: moist, delicate and dark, with a very good-quality cocoa and natural peanut butter. The third secret is to let the cake cool slightly in its tin, then cover and chill in the fridge. This will allow the delicate cake to set to a firmer texture, making it easier to decant, while the ganache adheres beautifully to a chilled cake. And finally, adorn the cake with the glistening, candied peanuts for flavors that mimic the peanut and date base, bringing it all together harmoniously.

Softened unsalted butter or oil, for greasing
Candied peanuts (see page 226), to decorate

FOR THE PEANUT & DATE CRUMB BASE
2 tbsp hot milk
100g medjool dates, pitted
250g roasted unsalted peanuts
50g golden caster sugar

FOR THE PEANUT BUTTER CHOCOLATE CAKE
150g medjool dates, pitted and chopped
450ml hot milk
200g peanut butter (smooth or chunky)
1 vanilla pod, seeds scraped, or 1 tbsp vanilla bean paste
125ml vegetable or coconut oil, melted
75g plain flour
75g good-quality fair-trade unsweetened cocoa powder
1 tbsp baking powder
Pinch of fine sea salt
50g golden caster sugar

1. Line two 9-inch springform tins with baking parchment and generously grease or oil the sides.

2. To prepare the peanut and date crumb base, pour the milk into a small saucepan and warm gently. Remove the pan from the heat and add the dates. Leave to soak and soften for up to 10 minutes. Once softened, squeeze out all the liquid, using your hands or by pressing the dates into a fine mesh strainer. Place the dates, peanuts and sugar in a food processor and blitz until it comes together to form a very sticky and crumbly mixture.

3. Prepare a small bowl of hot water and place a tablespoon inside. Have a kitchen towel alongside for drying it. Tip the peanut and date crumb into the prepared tin. Use your hands to press and spread the crumb mixture to fill the entire base of the tin, then dry the warmed spoon and use the curved back to press and smooth the surface. Dip the spoon back in the warm water, dry and repeat until the crumb base is evenly spread and smooth. Place in the fridge to chill.

4. Preheat the oven to 350°F. Set a rack in the middle of the oven.

5. Place the dates in a bowl with 3 tablespoons of the hot milk to soak and soften for 5 minutes. Pour into a food processor and blend to a puree. Add the peanut butter, vanilla seeds or paste, and oil and blend again until well combined. Pour the mixture into a large bowl and sift in the flour, cocoa powder, baking powder and salt. Gently pour in the remaining hot milk, add the sugar and mix thoroughly.

FOR THE CHOCOLATE & PEANUT BUTTER GANACHE

100ml heavy cream
60g smooth peanut butter
2 tbsp golden caster sugar
100g fair-trade dark chocolate (70–75% cocoa solids), broken into small pieces
1 tbsp unsalted butter or coconut oil, melted

6. Pour the batter into the second tin and bake in the middle of the oven for 23–25 minutes, until the cake comes away from the sides of the tin and a skewer inserted into the center comes out clean or with some crumbs attached. Place on a wire rack to cool for 1 hour. The cake will still be too delicate to decant. Cover the cake tin and place in the fridge to chill for 1 hour before assembling.

7. About 15 minutes before removing the cake from the fridge, prepare the ganache. Warm the cream in a small saucepan over a gentle heat, then pour into a blender. Add the peanut butter and blend until smooth. Pour this mixture back into the saucepan, add the sugar and heat gently until dissolved. Remove from the heat, add the chocolate and leave to sit for 2 minutes as the chocolate melts. Finally, add the butter or coconut oil and stir until well combined. Leave to cool and thicken slightly.

8. Release the cake from its tin. Place a large plate on top of the cake and carefully flip it over. Remove the base of the tin, then peel off the baking parchment.

9. To assemble, release the peanut and date crumb base from its tin and place on a cake stand. Spoon 4–5 tablespoons of the chocolate and peanut ganache onto the base (or just enough to spread the top without dripping down the sides). Place the chilled cake on top of the base and pour just enough ganache to cover the top. Use a spatula or the back of a spoon to spread the ganache right to the edge. Finally, dot the top of the cake with as many glistening candied peanuts as you wish. Leave for an hour to set and for the cake to return to room temperature before tucking into your "crowned" jewel. (See photo on page 227.)

Lerato's Tip

This is an eggless cake and a vegan-friendly recipe. Although I use homemade oat milk when baking this cake, you can use any nut or plant milk, butter and cream alternative.

Hibiscus Chocolate Orange Cake

SERVES 6–8

Dark chocolate, citrus and tart hibiscus are a match made in heaven in this zesty cake. As someone who does not typically like cake, I have found joy in creating decadent chocolate cakes and desserts that celebrate rich, fairly traded cocoa and chocolate, especially of African origin. I adore this cake with its arresting flavors that marry beautifully. You will want seconds, then thirds and a naughty midnight snack. You will love this!

FOR THE CAKE
Softened unsalted butter, for greasing
225g plain flour
75g good-quality fair-trade unsweetened cocoa powder
1 tsp baking powder
2 tsp baking soda
½ tsp fine sea salt
125ml mild-flavored oil, like sunflower or olive
350g golden caster sugar
2 large free-range eggs, room temperature
400ml hot milk
Zest and juice of 2 medium oranges
Edible rose petals, crumbled, to decorate

FOR THE CANDIED ORANGE PEEL
1 medium orange
50g caster sugar

1. Preheat the oven to 350°F. Line the base of two 8-inch sandwich tins with baking parchment and generously grease the sides with butter.

2. Sift the flour, cocoa powder, baking powder, baking soda and salt into a large bowl.

3. Whisk the oil, sugar and eggs in a separate bowl for about 5 minutes, until pale and thick.

4. Pour the milk into a bowl, add 1 tablespoon of the orange zest and 2 tablespoons of the orange juice and leave for 5–10 minutes to curdle a little. Pour the curdled milk into a saucepan and heat gently.

5. Make a well in the center of the dry ingredients and, once the milk is simmering, remove from the heat and gradually stir into the dry ingredients until well incorporated. Add the remaining orange zest and gently fold in the oil, sugar and egg mixture. Be careful not to overmix in order to keep the cake light.

6. Divide the batter evenly between the two prepared tins and bake in middle of the oven for 25 minutes, until the cake pulls away from the sides of the tin and a skewer comes out either completely clean or with some crumbs attached. Place on a wire rack to cool for 20 minutes before carefully running a flexible spatula or round-bladed knife around the inside of the tins to loosen the cakes. Turn out onto the rack to cool completely for at least 2 hours.

7. Meanwhile, to make the **Candied Orange Peel**, cut long wide strips from the orange using a vegetable peeler, avoiding the pith. Cut the peel into thin matchsticks and place in a small saucepan with the sugar and 50ml water. Bring to a simmer and cook for 5 minutes, until the syrup is slightly reduced. Transfer the peel from the syrup to a plate or tray lined with

FOR THE HIBISCUS & CITRUS CREAM

Zest and juice of 2 medium oranges
  (about 125ml juice)
1 tbsp ground dried hibiscus
150g golden caster sugar
150ml heavy cream

FOR THE GANACHE GLAZE

200ml heavy cream
1½ tbsp orange zest
50g golden caster sugar
150g fair-trade dark chocolate
  (70–75% cocoa solids), broken
  into small pieces
2 tbsp unsalted butter or
  coconut oil

Lerato's Tip

Thoroughly rinse the oranges with hot water or scrub under running water to remove any wax. I like to chill the cakes in the fridge for an hour before filling and decorating to allow the ganache to adhere quickly and beautifully.

baking parchment. Leave to set for up to an hour before decorating the cake.

8. To make the **Hibiscus & Citrus Cream**, combine the zest and juice of the oranges with the ground hibiscus and 100g of the sugar in a small saucepan and bring to a simmer over a medium heat. Watch closely as the syrup simmers and thickens for up to 5 minutes. Leave to cool and thicken.

9. Meanwhile, whip the cream and remaining 50g caster sugar in a mixing bowl until just past soft billowy peaks. Fold in the thickened syrup, whipping once more to combine, then refrigerate until ready to decorate the cake.

10. To make the **Ganache Glaze**, heat the cream, orange zest and sugar in a small saucepan over a gentle heat. Once hot but not simmering, remove from the heat and add the chocolate pieces. Leave to melt for 2 minutes, then add the butter or coconut oil and stir until well combined and with a lovely glossy finish. Leave to cool and thicken slightly, while remaining runny enough to pour.

11. To decorate, place one of the cakes, flattest side up, on a wire rack with a tray resting underneath. Spoon the hibiscus cream filling onto the cake and spread out evenly with a spatula, leaving about ¾ inch space between the edge for the filling to spread. Place the second cake on top to align with the bottom. Drizzle a third of the ganache glaze over the cakes and use an offset spatula to spread the ganache out on top and around the sides of the cake. Drizzle some more and spread out to the sides once again to fill any cracks. Finally, drizzle over the remaining ganache and allow to smooth or run over the sides.

12. Decorate the top of the cake with the candied orange peel and scatter over the crumbled edible rose petals. Leave to set, then transfer to a large plate or cake stand. Cut to reveal and devour your wonderful creation. (See photo on pages 232-33.)

Coconut & Cardamom Rice Cakes

WITH CINNAMON & CARDAMOM SUGAR

My neighbor Maimouna would prepare rice cakes at the crack of dawn on Sunday morning, after soaking short-grain rice and blending it into a batter leavened with yeast. Their distinctive shape is created by cooking the batter in cast-iron dumpling pans. In Northern Nigeria, these rice cakes called *masa* are more savory and typically accompanied by stews. In East Africa where the cakes are much sweeter, they are known as *vitumbua*. You will find them at street food stalls across Tanzania and especially in Mombasa, Kenya, during Ramadan. In Madagascar they are known as *mofo gasy* and are sold across the island at breakfast. In this recipe, rice flour is used to save time, instead of soaking and blending the rice. Serve these delightful doughnut-pancake hybrids with **Kenyan Masala Chai (see page 32)** to transport you to the wondrous coast of East Africa!

1 400ml can full-fat coconut milk
1 vanilla pod, seeds scraped and
   pod reserved, or 1 tbsp vanilla
   bean paste
225g rice flour
2 tbsp cornstarch
100g light brown sugar
7g instant yeast
1 tsp ground cardamom
Oil, for greasing

**FOR THE CINNAMON &
   CARDAMOM SUGAR**
2 tbsp icing sugar
1 tsp ground cinnamon
½ tsp ground cardamom

YOU WILL NEED
An aebleskiver or dumpling pan

1. Pour the coconut milk and 90ml water into a saucepan. Add the vanilla seeds and pod and warm gently. Remove from the heat and leave to infuse for 5 minutes. Remove the vanilla pod and save to flavor warm milk another time or add to your chai—see page 32.

2. Place the rice flour, cornstarch, light brown sugar, yeast and ground cardamom in a bowl and mix well until combined. Create a well in the center and pour in the warm coconut milk, whisking until smooth, creamy and thick, like a very thick pancake batter. Cover and leave to rise in a warm place for 40 minutes–1 hour. Once risen, your batter should be bubbly.

3. Pour about ½ teaspoon of oil into each mold and generously brush onto the sides and top of the pan. Place over a medium heat. When the pan is hot, mix the batter lightly to a consistent texture, then use a measuring cup or jug to fill the "wells" of the pan with batter, leaving a little gap at the top for it to rise as it cooks. Reduce the heat to medium-low and cook for 3–4 minutes. Watch closely as bubbles appear and pop. Once the top is dry to the touch, carefully flip each cake, using a skewer or a spoon. As you flip them, the batter in the center might still be runny. Once flipped, cook for another 3 minutes, then flip a few more times for another minute, until golden on all sides and fluffy. Remove from the pan and place on a plate lined with kitchen paper. After each batch, fill the molds with more oil and repeat as above until you use up all the batter.

4. Mix the icing sugar, cinnamon and cardamom in a small bowl. Stack the rice cakes on a serving platter and use a fine mesh strainer to dust them with the spiced sugar. Serve with a warm cup of **Kenyan Masala Chai** (see page 32).

Honeycomb Pancakes

WITH ORANGE BLOSSOM & HONEY SYRUP

MAKES ABOUT 10

FOR THE PANCAKES
200g fine semolina
100g plain flour
2 tbsp caster sugar
2¼ tsp instant yeast
2 tsp baking powder
½ tsp fine sea salt
1 medium free-range egg, beaten
    (optional)
600ml lukewarm milk or water (add
    an extra 60ml if omitting the egg)

**FOR THE ORANGE BLOSSOM &
    HONEY SYRUP**
100g unsalted butter
125ml honey or agave syrup
¼ tsp ground cinnamon
Zest of 1 medium orange
1 tsp orange blossom water

Lerato's Tip

For a nutty treat, serve with
Almond & Honey Paste (see page
265) and toasted slivers of almonds
or chopped roasted almonds. Store
any unused syrup in a sterilized jar
and use within a week.

These pancakes, known locally as *baghrir*, always transport me back to the wonderfully fragrant breakfasts I enjoyed in Morocco. What makes these so special are the honeycomb-like holes that appear once the batter hits the pan, good for soaking up the delicious syrup I created to capture the essence of Morocco. Serve them with mint tea and fresh fruits for breakfast or brunch.

1. Sift the dry pancake ingredients into a large bowl and slowly whisk in the egg, if using, and milk or water until combined. Pour into a food processor and blend for 1 minute, or until the batter is smooth and wonderfully creamy. Pour back into the bowl, cover tightly and leave to rise in a warm place for 30 minutes, until the surface is foamy and covered with bubbles.

2. Meanwhile, prepare the syrup. Melt the butter in a small saucepan over a medium-low heat. After about 1 minute when the butter is foaming, whisk in the honey and cinnamon with 1 tablespoon of water. Simmer for 1 minute, until it begins to bubble and thicken, then add the orange zest and blossom water, whisking until well combined. Simmer for 1 minute. As the syrup begins to bubble, remove it from the heat and leave to cool slightly.

3. Pour half the syrup into a jug or bowl for serving, leaving the rest in the saucepan to brush onto the pancakes. The syrup will thicken once cooled.

4. Place a nonstick frying pan over a medium heat—no oil required. Gently stir the batter back into a uniform consistency then pour about 125ml swiftly into the middle of the pan (use a ladle or measuring jug). Leave to spread out on its own. Reduce the heat to medium-low and cook for 2–3 minutes, until bubbles start to erupt all over the surface. Do not flip! Test with your finger and when the top is dry to the touch remove the pancake from the pan. Leave to rest on a wire rack. Brush some syrup over the top.

5. Heat the frying pan for the next pancake and repeat as above until you have used up the batter.

6. Once slightly cooled, the pancakes can be stacked in small batches without sticking or arranged overlapped on a large platter. Serve the pancakes with orange wedges, fresh berries and the fragrant syrup alongside.

Om Ali
Sinful Bread Pudding

SERVES 6-8

Om Ali, the much-loved pudding and national dish of Egypt, directly translates into "Ali's mother." As the story goes, in the 13th century, Sultan Ezz El Din Aybak's wife prepared this dish as a victory celebration after getting rid of another woman. She fed it to the people and, since then, the legacy of this pudding has lived on. Although traditionally prepared with *rokak*, a light and crispy bread, my recipe uses filo pastry that is prebaked with a coating of sugar for a delicious caramel base to hold the layers of creamy custard sauce, dried fruits and nuts for a sinful pudding to tuck into.

160g unsalted butter, melted
440g filo pastry
200g caster sugar
500ml milk
1 tsp vanilla bean paste
4 green cardamom pods, smashed with seeds finely crushed
2 tsp rose water
500ml heavy cream
100g mixed roasted nuts (e.g., hazelnuts, pistachios, almonds), chopped
50g raisins or sultanas
50g dried apricots, chopped into small pieces
½–1 tsp ground cinnamon
Handful of edible rose petals, torn

YOU WILL NEED
9 × 13-inch baking dish or 10- to 12-inch nonstick ovenproof casserole or pan

1. Preheat the oven to 400°F and brush some of the melted butter all over the bottom and sides of your baking dish or pan.

2. Brush one side of each pastry sheet with butter, then carefully fold and scrunch up into a round shape, almost like a rose. Place in a single layer in the baking dish and repeat to fill every possible space.

3. Brush the remaining butter all over and into the scrunched pastry. The filo should be drenched in butter, so brush every possible corner and all around the sides. Now sprinkle 50g of the sugar all around the pastry and transfer the dish to the middle of the oven to bake for 20 minutes, until golden and crisp.

4. Meanwhile, combine the milk, vanilla paste, the remaining sugar and the crushed cardamom seeds in a saucepan and bring to a steady simmer over a medium heat. Whisk the mixture and reduce the heat to medium-low as the sugar dissolves and the milk begins to boil. Simmer for 10 minutes, whisking occasionally, to prevent sticking.

5. Once the milk is slightly reduced, pour in the rose water, remove from the heat and stir in the heavy cream.

6. Remove the pastry from the oven and scatter half the nuts and dried fruit over the top. Pour over the creamy mixture and return to the oven to bake for 20 minutes, until the pastry has soaked up most of the sweet milky cream and the top is browned and crunchy.

7. Finish with a light dusting of cinnamon and scatter over the remaining nuts and dried fruit along with the torn edible rose petals. Leave to cool for 5 minutes, then spoon into bowls to serve.

Malva Pudding
Sticky Apricot Pudding
WITH SPICED CREAM

SERVES 4–6

Malva pudding is South Africa's answer to sticky toffee pudding. The spongy and caramelized pudding with apricot jam is doused in a creamy sauce for quite the luxurious treat, especially at Christmas. I particularly love to add spices to my sauce and sometimes use half Amarula—a South African nut liquor made from the marula fruits. The plum-shaped fruits famously leave the elephants and animals in the surrounding woodlands tipsy. Tipsy elephants! What more must I say to convince you to serve this at your next dinner party?

250ml warm milk
1 tbsp apple cider vinegar
150g plain flour, plus more for dusting
1½ tsp baking powder
½ tsp baking soda
150g golden caster sugar
2 large free-range eggs
½ tsp fine sea salt
80g apricot jam (about 2 tbsp)
2 tbsp butter, melted, plus more for greasing

FOR THE SPICED CREAM
250ml heavy cream (or half heavy cream and half a cream liquor such as Amarula or Irish cream)
4–6 tbsp caster sugar
100g butter
1 tsp ground cinnamon
½ tsp ground cloves
A good grating of whole nutmeg, or ½ tsp ground nutmeg

1. Preheat the oven to 400°F and generously grease the inside of a 1-liter pudding tin or 6–8 small pudding tins or ramekins and dust with plain flour, covering the entire surface.

2. Gently warm the milk and apple cider vinegar in a small saucepan and set aside.

3. Sift the flour, baking powder and baking soda into a large bowl and whisk to combine.

4. In a separate bowl, beat the sugar, eggs and salt until pale and fluffy. Add the apricot jam and beat until well combined. Now gradually pour in the warm milk and vinegar mixture.

5. Add the flour mixture to the liquid ingredients in small portions, mixing all the time, until smooth. Pour the mixture into the prepared tin(s) and bake in the middle of the oven for 35–40 minutes (1-liter tin) or 25–30 minutes (small tins), until caramelized and a skewer inserted into the center comes out clean.

6. Meanwhile, prepare the spiced cream by heating the cream, sugar and butter gently in a small saucepan. Whisk in the spices, until dissolved and the sauce is thickened. Remove from the heat.

7. Use a small knife to carefully and deeply cut incisions into the pudding. Pour the spiced cream all over the pudding and into the cuts until it has had its fill. You will know when, as the cream will float on the top. Leave the pudding to cool for 15 minutes.

8. Carefully turn the pudding out of the tin onto a wide serving plate or cake stand. Serve warm or cold with any leftover spiced cream poured over the top or on the side. This is also wonderful with ice cream.

Lerato's Tip

This keeps very well in an airtight container in the fridge for a few days, but I doubt you will need to. To enjoy warm, simply reheat in a microwave or in a preheated oven at 350°F.

Christmas Pudding Puff Puffs

MAKES 25–30

This is a doughnut and Christmas pudding hybrid, one I created especially for haters of Christmas pudding, like myself. Puff puff is a much-loved Nigerian doughnut that "puffs" once the batter is dropped into hot oil. I have always found these round balls to be simply irresistible and have been similarly smitten with *olie bollen*—another dropped doughnut, which I enjoy on New Year's Eve with my Dutch family as part of a tradition in the Netherlands. Once, while making puff puffs for New Year, we had some Christmas pudding left over from our family dinner, so I decided to crumble the abandoned pudding into my puff puff batter. And just like that Christmas pudding puff puffs were born.

FOR THE SOAKED FRUITS
250g dried mixed fruits (e.g., raisins, apricots, prunes, sultanas and more), finely chopped
Zest and juice of 1 medium orange
25ml dark rum
1 tsp ground cinnamon
¼ tsp ground nutmeg
¼ tsp ground allspice
50g dark brown sugar

FOR THE PUFF PUFFS
300g plain flour
2¼ tsp instant yeast
65g caster sugar
½ tsp fine sea salt
¼ tsp ground cinnamon
¼ tsp ground nutmeg
300ml lukewarm water, plus 2 tsp
Vegetable oil, for frying

TO COAT THE PUFF PUFFS
50g caster sugar
1 tsp ground cinnamon

YOU WILL NEED
A 500ml sterilized jar

1. Place the dried fruits, orange zest and juice, rum, spices and sugar in the sterilized jar to soak until ready to use. You can do this as early as the day before.

2. To make the puff puffs, combine the flour, yeast, sugar, salt and the dry spices in a large bowl. Gradually pour in the lukewarm water and mix thoroughly with a wooden spoon or whisk until smooth. Cover loosely with a kitchen towel and set aside in a warm place to rise for 45 minutes–1 hour, until doubled in size.

3. Squeeze out any liquid from the soaked fruits and scatter them over the batter. Stir to combine and distribute the fruits evenly. The batter should be thick and runny.

4. Fill a deep pan with oil to the depth of 2 inches and heat to 350°F (see page 275). Lightly oil two tablespoons and use one to scoop the batter, then lower it toward the oil and use the second tablespoon to guide the batter into the oil. You could also use a retractable ice cream scoop, for ease. Once the batter hits the oil it should sink and puff back up. Fry for 1–2 minutes, until the bottom browns, then turn over to fry for another 1–2 minutes, until browned all over. Use a slotted spoon to remove the puff puffs and drain them on a tray lined with kitchen paper. Repeat in small batches until all the batter has been used.

5. Mix the sugar and cinnamon together in a bowl. When the puff puffs are slightly cooled, dust them with the cinnamon sugar to coat all over. Pile onto a serving dish and devour right away!

Spiced Chocolate & Coffee Mousse

WITH HIBISCUS GLAZED POPCORN

SERVES 4

Ethiopia and Eritrea are not known for desserts, but the much-loved and enchanting coffee ceremonies and floral nuance of the exceptional coffee beans grown in the region inspired this decadent mousse. Dark chocolate provides a good body and balance to the coffee, while the popcorn is reminiscent of the freshly popped corn traditionally served as a snack during the coffee ceremonies. This light and fluffy mousse will completely enchant you, dazzling your taste buds!

FOR THE MOUSSE

100g fair-trade good-quality dark chocolate (70–75% cocoa solids), chopped into small pieces
300ml heavy cream, chilled
2 tsp instant ground fair-trade Ethiopian Coffee (or good-quality coffee)
1 tsp ground cinnamon
½ tsp ground ginger
¼ tsp ground cloves
2 green cardamom pods, seeds crushed
½ tsp freshly ground black pepper
3–4 tbsp honey
1 vanilla pod, seeds scraped, or 1 tbsp vanilla bean paste
Pinch of sea salt flakes

FOR THE HIBISCUS GLAZED POPCORN

1 tbsp vegetable oil
75g popcorn kernels
½ tsp ground cinnamon
½ tsp ground ginger
4 tbsp **Hibiscus & Honey Syrup** (see page 267)

1. To make the popcorn, drizzle the oil in a large heavy-based saucepan over a medium heat. Add the corn and sprinkle in the spices. Cover with a lid and carefully shake or swirl around to coat the corn in the oil and spices. After a few minutes, the corn will begin to pop. Shake a few more times as it continues to pop. Remove from the heat when the popping stops and tip into a large bowl.

2. Drizzle 2 tablespoons of the **Hibiscus & Honey Syrup** over the top and toss to coat. Spread the popcorn out on a baking tray and leave to cool. Keep in an airtight container until ready to serve.

3. To prepare the mousse, place the chocolate in a medium glass or heatproof bowl. Pour half of the cream into a small saucepan and slowly heat until it begins to simmer gently. Remove from the heat and pour it over the chocolate. Set aside for 2 minutes while the chocolate melts.

4. Meanwhile, combine the coffee, cinnamon, ginger, cloves, cardamom and black pepper in a small jug with 2½ tablespoons hot water. Mix thoroughly until the coffee and spices dissolve. Stir the spiced coffee, honey and the vanilla into the melted chocolate and mix well to combine. Leave to cool completely, then place in the fridge to chill for 30 minutes, or until ready to serve.

5. Once chilled, whisk the chocolate and coffee mixture.

6. In a separate bowl, whisk the remaining cream to soft peaks. Using a metal spoon or rubber spatula, carefully fold the cream into the chocolate and coffee mixture until well combined.

7. Spoon the mousse into glass or coffee cups and place in the fridge to chill, until ready to serve. Top with a drizzle of the remaining syrup, the hibiscus glazed popcorn and a light sprinkling of crushed sea salt flakes.

Banana Fritters

WITH SPICED CHOCOLATE SAUCE

SERVES 4–6 (MAKES ABOUT 15 FRITTERS)

200g self-rising flour
50g cornstarch
½ tsp ground nutmeg
1 medium free-range egg, beaten
   (optional)
40g caster sugar
5–6 bananas, peeled and each cut
   into 3 pieces
Vegetable oil, for frying
1 tbsp hibiscus icing sugar (1 tsp
   ground dried hibiscus mixed with
   1 tbsp icing sugar)

FOR THE SPICED CHOCOLATE SAUCE

400ml heavy cream
50g caster sugar
150g fair-trade dark chocolate
   (70–75% cocoa solids), broken
   into small pieces
1 tsp ground cinnamon
½ tsp ground ginger
¼ tsp ground cloves
½ tsp freshly ground black pepper

Banana fritters can be found on the street food circuit all across Africa—sometimes the bananas are mashed into the batter and sometimes left whole, dipped in the batter, then deep fried. I created this recipe by chance for a dinner party, when I didn't have enough time to cook a mashed version. I quickly mixed a batter, cut the bananas into chunks, dipped them into the batter and fried them. They were a triumphant success! The batter was golden and crispy, and the bananas were meltingly soft inside. Serve these with a spiced chocolate sauce and an extra helping of black pepper for a surprising kick.

1. To prepare the spiced chocolate sauce, place the cream and sugar in a pan and heat gently. Once hot, remove from the heat and add the chocolate. Set aside for a few minutes while the chocolate melts. Add the spices and whisk until well combined. Set aside while you make the fritters.

2. Sift the flour and cornstarch into a bowl, add the nutmeg and mix well. Stir in the beaten egg and sugar, and mix with a wooden spoon or mixer. Slowly pour in 250ml water, mixing all the time, until the dough is smooth. You may need a little more water, depending on the liquid content of your egg, so add a tablespoon at a time, if needed. Your batter should be thick enough to stick to the bananas.

3. Fill a large frying pan with vegetable oil to the depth of 1½ inches and heat to 350°F (see page 275).

4. Dip the bananas into the batter one at a time until fully coated and lower carefully into the hot oil. Fry in batches for 2–3 minutes, turning halfway, until golden on all sides. Remove with a slotted spoon and place on kitchen paper to drain any excess oil.

5. Transfer the fritters to a platter and dust with the hibiscus sugar. Pour the spiced chocolate sauce into small bowls for dipping and grind a little black pepper on top to serve.

Variation

To bake these fritters instead, preheat the oven to 400°F and line a baking tray with baking parchment. Arrange the dipped fritters on the sheet and bake for 20 minutes, turning halfway, until the bananas turn golden brown.

Mango & Moringa Fool

WITH GINGER & BERRIES

SERVES 2–4

100g mix of strawberries and
  raspberries (fresh or frozen)
1 tbsp grated fresh ginger
2 medium ripe mangoes, peeled
  and destoned
Zest and juice of 1 lime
240ml natural yogurt or coconut
  yogurt
1 tbsp moringa powder
1 tbsp honey (optional)

TO SERVE
Small handful of strawberries,
  hulled and sliced
Small handful of raspberries, halved
1 tbsp coconut flakes, toasted

I first created this dessert after being inspired by the abundance of mangoes on a road trip with my mum (see page 108). At the time she was looking for more ways to enjoy moringa and she adores fresh fruits. Although she prefers to bite into them or drink them in the form of juice, I wanted to create a dessert. It has since transformed into a tropical delight with coconut, lime and berries.

1. Hull the strawberries and place in a food processor with the raspberries and ginger and blend to a puree. Spoon into glasses and place in the fridge to chill, if not already frozen.

2. Place the mangoes in the food processor with the lime zest and juice, yogurt or coconut milk and moringa powder and blend. (Although a very good ripe mango is naturally sweet, you can sweeten your fool with honey, if preferred.)

3. Pour into the chilled tall glasses on top of the berry puree and return to the fridge to chill.

4. When ready to serve, top with a few slices of strawberry and the raspberry halves and sprinkle with coconut flakes.

Strawberry, Hibiscus & Honey Ice Cream

MAKE ABOUT 1.2 LITERS

FOR THE HIBISCUS & ROSE SYRUP
1 tbsp ground dried hibiscus
Zest of 1 lemon plus 1 tbsp juice
200ml mild-flavored honey
1 tbsp rose water

FOR THE STRAWBERRY PUREE
500g strawberries, hulled, plus
    more to serve
1 tbsp fresh lemon juice
2 tbsp caster sugar

FOR THE ICE CREAM
600ml heavy cream
1 vanilla pod, seeds scraped, or
    1 tbsp vanilla bean paste
50g caster sugar

TO SERVE
Dried edible rose petals
Waffle ice cream cones (optional)

Lerato's Tip

I particularly enjoy serving this in two different shades of hibiscus-pink. To do that, after folding in the puree, divide the mixture into two bowls and drizzle another tablespoon of hibiscus and honey syrup in one for a slightly darker hue. Freeze as above.

This is one of my many recipes that celebrate the versatility of hibiscus. I make this wonderful ice cream with the abundant strawberries of summer or, in winter months, I keep a frozen stash handy. With no ice cream maker in sight, the honey does wonders for the texture of the ice cream, while a touch of rose water marries delicately and beautifully.

1. To make the **Hibiscus & Rose Syrup**, place the ground hibiscus, 125ml water and the lemon zest and juice in a saucepan over a medium-low heat and simmer gently. Once the liquid and hibiscus are well mixed, add the honey and rose water. Whisk thoroughly to combine and simmer gently for about 5 minutes to thicken. It should lightly coat the back of a wooden spoon. Although your hot syrup might be runnier than honey, it will thicken as it cools. Pour into a jug and set aside to cool completely before use.

2. Place the strawberries in a food processor with the lemon juice and caster sugar and blend to a puree. Place in the fridge to chill until ready to use.

3. To make the ice cream, place the heavy cream, vanilla and sugar in a large bowl and whisk until just past soft peak stage.

4. Add 125ml of the cooled **Hibiscus & Rose Syrup** and fold into the cream as it transforms from white to a delightful purple pink.

5. Fold in the pureed strawberry, leaving streaks of puree rather than incorporating it fully. Spoon the mixture into an airtight container and leave to freeze for a minimum of 5 hours. Within those first 5 hours of freezing, remove from the freezer and rake with a fork every 1½ hours (about 3 times) for a creamy consistency.

6. Remove from the freezer 10–15 minutes before serving or keep in the fridge for 30 minutes. Serve with fresh strawberries, a drizzle of **Hibiscus & Rose Syrup**, if you wish, and some dried edible rose petals scattered on top. I love to stack the ice cream in a waffle cone for a portable treat, especially on a summer's day by the seaside.

Black Pepper & Vanilla Chai Shortbread

I adore shortbread and I adore chai, and so I created a recipe to marry the buttery sweet crunch of this traditional Scottish biscuit with the aromatic magic of chai spices. The black pepper is a very pleasant surprise as it hits the tongue with a tingle, while the vanilla is fragrant and wonderful. This treat is sure to be a hit when served at your table or gifted to family and friends!

MAKES ABOUT 30

225g unsalted butter, softened
115g icing sugar, sifted
1 vanilla pod, seeds scraped, or
  1 tbsp vanilla bean paste
225g plain flour
95g cornstarch
50g light brown sugar

BLACK PEPPER CHAI BLEND
1½ tsp ground cinnamon
1½ tsp ground ginger
2 tsp freshly ground grains of
  paradise or black pepper
6 green cardamom pods, seeds
  ground, or ½ tsp ground
  cardamom
¼ tsp ground cloves

1. To make the **Black Pepper Chai Blend**, combine all the ingredients in a small bowl and mix well. Set 1 teaspoon aside for dusting at the end.

2. Cream the butter, icing sugar, **Black Pepper Chai Blend** and vanilla in a large bowl or in a mixer on low speed until light and fluffy. Add the plain flour, cornstarch and a pinch of fine sea salt and mix until well combined. Knead lightly until it forms a solid dough.

3. Divide the dough in two and roll each piece into a 2-inch-thick log. Wrap tightly in baking parchment, twisting the ends to secure, and chill in the fridge for at least 1 hour, or freeze in an airtight container for up to 2 months.

4. When ready to bake, preheat the oven to 340°F and line a large baking tray with baking parchment.

5. Cut the logs into ½-inch-thick rounds and arrange on the baking tray, leaving about ¾ inch between each shortbread to allow them to spread. Sprinkle a little bit of the light brown sugar on the tops of the biscuits and bake for 15 minutes, or until the edges begin to turn a light golden. Don't be tempted to bake them for longer.

6. Mix the remaining light brown sugar and reserved **Black Pepper Chai Blend** and use to dust the hot biscuits.

7. Transfer to a wire rack to cool. Store in an airtight container and enjoy for up to 5 days, if shockingly you have not devoured or shared them all already.

Spiced Banana Bread

WITH OATS, ALMONDS & DATES

MAKES 900G LOAF TIN

220g oat flour, plus 2 tbsp for
   dusting
½ tsp fine sea salt
2 tsp baking powder
½ tsp baking soda
1 tsp ground cinnamon, plus a pinch
   for dusting
1 tsp ground ginger
¼ tsp ground nutmeg
85ml olive or melted coconut oil,
   plus extra for greasing
170g date syrup, plus more for
   drizzling (optional)
100ml milk
2 large free-range eggs
2 large ripe bananas, mashed
100g pitted dates, rehydrated in
   hot water if dry, chopped
100g whole roasted almonds,
   chopped

Lerato's Tip

Avoid using too many bananas,
which may affect the texture of
your bake, and make sure you
bake it for long enough—
50 minutes at the very least.
For chocolate lovers, chop 100g
of your favorite chocolate into
small chunks and add to the
batter with the dates and nuts.
You could use a variety of nuts or
leave them out altogether.
This can also be baked as muffins,
in which case, reduce the baking
time to 30–40 minutes.

Do you need another banana bread recipe? I think you
do! I wanted to create something "naughty" enough for
dessert but "nice" enough for breakfast. This is pure
indulgence, with finely ground oats, the rich caramel
notes of dates and a whole lot of crunch. The warming
cinnamon and subtle heat from the ground ginger will
leave you feeling comforted but with your lips tingling.

1. Preheat the oven to 350°F. Grease a nonstick 900g
   loaf tin and dust it generously with oat flour, or line it
   with baking parchment.

2. Place the 220g oat flour, salt, baking powder, baking
   soda and spices in a large bowl
   and mix well.

3. Pour the oil and date syrup into a separate bowl and
   whisk until blended. Pour in the milk and then the
   eggs, one at a time, whisking all the time. Add the
   mashed bananas and mix well.

4. Pour a third of this mixture into the dry ingredients
   bowl, stirring well, then add another third, and stir
   again. Finally, add the remaining banana mixture and
   stir well.

5. Fold in the dates and half of the almonds and tip
   the mixture into the prepared loaf tin. Sprinkle the
   top with the remaining nuts, dust with a pinch of
   cinnamon and bake in the middle of the oven for
   50 minutes–1 hour, or until a skewer inserted in the
   center comes out clean.

6. Place the tin on a wire rack and leave to cool for
   30 minutes, before turning out, slicing and drizzling
   with date syrup, if you like, before devouring.

7. To store, wrap slices in baking parchment and place
   in an airtight container. It will keep for up to 3 days at
   room temperature and up to a week in the fridge.

Sauces &
Spice Blends

Hibiscus Pickled Onions

MAKES ABOUT 300G

1 large red onion, peeled and finely
  sliced

FOR THE PICKLING LIQUID
125ml red wine vinegar or apple
  cider vinegar
Pared peel of ½ lemon
1½ tbsp **Hibiscus Syrup** (see page
  267)
1 tsp sea salt flakes
1 bay leaf
3 sprigs of thyme

YOU WILL NEED
1 500ml sterilized jar

1. Place the onion in a sterilized glass jar or heat-safe bowl and set aside.

2. Pour 125ml hot water and all pickling liquid ingredients into a small saucepan and place over a low-medium heat. Bring up to a slow simmer. After 5 minutes, remove from the heat, pick out the herbs and lemon peel and set aside.

3. Pour the pickling liquid into the jar of onions, top with the saved herbs and peel, cover and leave to sit in the fridge for at least 1 hour before using. (For maximum flavor, however, make the onions a few days before needed.)

Smoky Tomato & Date Jam

MAKES 2 200ML JARS

400g vine-ripened tomatoes
  (plum, cherry or any red quality
  tomatoes)
100g pitted dates
1–2 green chilies, stemmed
2 tbsp grated fresh ginger
2 garlic cloves, peeled and crushed
1 tsp ground selim pepper, from
  3–5 pods
1 tsp cumin seeds
1 tsp fennel seeds
2 tbsp vegetable oil
60ml apple cider vinegar
½ tsp paprika
¼ tsp ground ginger
⅛ tsp ground cloves
¼ tsp cayenne pepper
½ tsp fine sea salt
100g sugar

YOU WILL NEED
2 200ml sterilized jars

This jam is a treasure I am thrilled to share with you. Dark, rich, smoky and sweet, this could well be your new favorite ketchup. A wonderful addition to an African afternoon tea or dolloped onto roasted plantains for canapés, served alongside chips or spread on a chapati for **My Golden Ugandan Rolex** (see page 66).

1. Place the tomatoes, dates, chili, ginger and garlic in a food processor and puree until smooth.

2. Add the selim, cumin and fennel seeds to a dry frying pan over a medium heat and toast for about 2 minutes, until fragrant. Tip into a mortar and pestle or a spice grinder and blitz to a fine powder.

3. Pour 1 tablespoon of the oil into a nonreactive saucepan then add the puree and apple cider vinegar. Stir in the toasted and ground spices, the paprika, ground ginger, cloves and cayenne pepper, season with the sea salt and bring to a gentle simmer. Cover with a lid and cook over a low heat for 10 minutes.

4. Add the sugar, stir well and leave to simmer with lid slightly ajar for another 30 minutes, stirring now and again. The puree will caramelize and reduce to a thick consistency.

5. While still hot, carefully scoop into warm sterilized jars and secure tightly with clean lids.

6. Store in a cool dark place and the jam will keep for up to 3 months. Once opened, keep refrigerated and use within a month.

Coconut, Ginger & Tamarind Chutney

MAKES ABOUT 200G

A mildly sweet, creamy, herbaceous chutney inspired by the coconut and cilantro chutneys served in Kenya and Zanzibar. Although fresh coconut tends to be sweeter, add a little sugar if you want more sweetness, and reduce the chilies for less heat.

50g freshly grated or unsweetened desiccated coconut

40g fresh cilantro

Small handful of mint, leaves picked

½ tsp ground cumin

2 tbsp coconut or vegetable oil

2 long green chilies, 1 stemmed and 1 pierced and left whole

1-inch piece of ginger, peeled and roughly chopped

2 garlic cloves, peeled and lightly smashed

½ tsp cumin seeds, lightly crushed

1 tsp tamarind paste or lime juice, to taste

1. Place the coconut, fresh herbs and ground cumin in a food processor and blitz to a coarse mixture. Adding a splash of water at a time, continue to blitz until the paste is as coarse or as smooth as you like. Desiccated coconut will need more water added than freshly grated coconut.

2. Heat the oil in a saucepan over a medium-low heat and add the pierced chili, ginger, garlic and cumin seeds. Toast for about 3 minutes, until fragrant.

3. Remove from the heat and transfer the stemmed chili and all the ginger and garlic to the coconut and herbs in the food processor. Add the tamarind paste or lime juice and blitz to combine.

4. Pour into a dipping bowl and season to perfection with sea salt flakes. Pour over the warm oil and cumin seeds from the pan, stir a little, then add the remaining whole chili to serve.

Lerato's Tip

Although best served immediately or within a day, you can keep any left over in the fridge in an airtight container. Consume within 2 days.

Sauce Piment
Chili Sauce

MAKES UP TO 2 200ML JARS

It was while living in francophone Benin Republic that I began to eat spicier foods. *Sauce piment*, which translates as "spicy/hot sauce," is frequently served with fried sweet potatoes, yam chips, and many other dishes. Chili sauces are ubiquitous across Africa and come in many wonderful variations. Across East Africa, southern Africa and parts of central Africa, chili and chili sauce is known as *pili pili*, which means "pepper pepper," now famously called "piri piri" across the world. Your chili sauce can be smooth or coarse, and as mild or as hot as you wish. You could also mix a variety of chilies for a nuanced flavor. Keep a jar handy to add to marinades and sauces, or to use as a dip. See page 22 for more about chilies.

FRESH CHILI SAUCE

10 scotch bonnet peppers (mix of yellow and red), stemmed and deseeded
2 medium ripe tomatoes, roughly chopped (optional)
1 small red onion, peeled and roughly chopped
3 garlic cloves, peeled
1-inch piece of ginger, peeled
¼ tsp ground grains of paradise or freshly ground black pepper
1 tbsp apple cider vinegar or white wine vinegar (optional)
Vegetable or olive oil, to cover

ROASTED CHILI SAUCE

2 red Romano or bell peppers, stemmed, deseeded, and halved, or 220g roasted red peppers from a jar
1 small red onion, peeled and quartered
Vegetable or olive oil, for roasting, frying and topping up
10 scotch bonnet peppers (yellow and red), stemmed and deseeded
3 garlic cloves, peeled
1-inch piece of ginger, peeled
½ tsp fine sea salt
¼ tsp ground grains of paradise or freshly ground black pepper

Fresh Chili Sauce

1. Combine all the ingredients except the vinegar and oil in a food processor and roughly chop to a coarse puree. Add the vinegar and some sea salt if using as a dip.

2. Tip into an airtight container, top with enough oil to cover and store for up to 5 days. Use a clean spoon to scoop out the quantity needed, then top up with oil and secure the lid.

Roasted Chili Sauce

1. Preheat the oven to 400°F.

2. If using fresh peppers, brush the pepper halves and onion with oil. Place the peppers cut-side down on a baking tray next to the onion and roast for 30 minutes.

3. Place the roasted veggies with the scotch bonnets, garlic and ginger in a food processor and chop to a coarse puree.

4. Heat 2 tablespoons of oil in a heavy-based pan and pour in the puree. Season with the sea salt and grains of paradise or black pepper and fry over a medium-low heat for 5 minutes, stirring frequently.

5. Tip into an airtight container or jar, top with enough oil to cover and store for up to 5 days.

Variations

For a fragrant chili paste known as *pâte de piment* in Madagascar, add 2 teaspoons ground makrut lime leaves. For a fragrant herb version, chop flat-leaf parsley or cilantro and mix it into the chili sauce.

Red Harissa

MAKES ABOUT 350G

Harissa is a Tunisian chili paste that has traveled from North Africa to the Middle East and beyond, transfixing us with its deepened red hue. The chilies are typically mild and predominantly grown in the Tunisian coastal towns of Gabés and Nabeul. Traditionally crushed with a meat grinder for a coarse texture, harissa can be found in many variations across North Africa with mild, hot and smoky chilies. Sometimes it is found simply seasoned or enlivened with a spice blend of cilantro, caraway seeds and cumin, known as *tabil*, which directly translates as coriander. I love making my own harissa, incorporating tips I picked up from my travels. Add harissa to sauces and stews, use it as a marinade, stir into dips or combine it with florals like in the transfixing **Slow-Roasted Salmon with Hibiscus, Harissa & Citrus** (see page 139).

120g mix of dried chilies (a mix of Kashmiri, Guajillo, New Mexico) or roasted fresh red chilies (or a mix of both)

6 garlic cloves, peeled

1 tbsp ground cilantro

1 tbsp ground cumin

1 tsp caraway seeds

1 tsp paprika

1 tbsp diced preserved lemon rind and flesh, or the zest and juice of 1 lemon

125ml olive oil, plus more for topping up

½ tsp fine sea salt (less when using preserved lemon)

1. If using dried chilies, remove the stems, slit open to remove and discard the seeds and soak the chilies in hot water for 10–20 minutes, or until softened. Drain and save the water to flavor soups and stews.

2. Combine the chilies, spices and oil in a food processor and pulse to a coarse paste. Season with the salt (reducing the amount if you have used preserved lemon).

3. Store in an airtight container and keep in the fridge for 5 days.

Lerato's Tip

To preserve your harissa for longer, tip into a sterilized jar and top up with olive oil, cover tightly with a lid and keep in the fridge. Keep sealed for up to 3 months and once opened use within 5 days. For a more herbaceous **Green Harissa**, add 1 roasted green bell pepper and fresh herbs—40g fresh cilantro and 1 tablespoon chopped fresh mint leaves or 1 teaspoon dried mint—and reduce the red chilies by half. Blend and store as above.

Golden Chermoula

MAKES ABOUT 300G

Chermoula is wonderful as a dip, mixed into salads, or as a marinade for meat, fish and vegetable roasts. Although traditionally ground in a mortar and pestle, using a food processor is perfectly fine. I call my recipe golden chermoula because of the amount of turmeric I include, which turns the oil a delightful golden hue. Whatever method you choose, start by roughly chopping the herbs and garlic to make them easier to process into an even mixture. Adapt your chermoula to the dish you intend to pair it with by holding back some herbs, spices or citrus, if required. When using preserved lemons, hold back on seasoning with salt, as they are already salty, and add at the end only if needed.

4 garlic cloves, peeled and roughly chopped
100g fresh cilantro, leaves and stalks roughly chopped
40g flat-leaf parsley, leaves picked and roughly chopped
1 tbsp diced preserved lemon rind and flesh, or the zest and juice of 1 lemon (optional)
2 tsp ground cumin
1 tbsp paprika
1 tsp ground turmeric
60ml olive oil

1. If using a mortar and pestle, place the garlic and a pinch of salt in the mortar and grind to a puree. Add the herbs, preserved lemon or lemon zest, and the spices in small batches and grind until bruised to your liking. Drizzle in the oil and lemon juice, if using, and mix well.

2. If using a food processor, place the garlic, herbs, spices and preserved lemon or lemon zest and juice in a food processor. Pulse to finely chop the herbs and drizzle in the oil a little at a time to loosen the mixture.

3. Season to perfection with freshly ground black pepper and sea salt flakes to taste.

4. Store the chermoula in an airtight container or jar. Keep topped up with oil and use within 5 days.

Red Oil

MAKES 4 TBSP

60ml vegetable oil
1 tsp smoked paprika

YOU WILL NEED
1 sterilized jar or bottle

This is a wonderful alternative to palm oil, as the smoked paprika works wonders to mimic its smoky flavors. Use in dishes such as **Braised Greens with Sweet Red Peppers** (see page 172) or **Aromatic & Soothing Chicken Pepper Soup** (see page 70).

1. Gently heat the vegetable oil in a pan over a low heat.

2. When it is warm, remove from the heat and add the smoked paprika. Whisk to combine.

3. Leave for 30–40 minutes to steep before use.

4. Store in a sterilized jar or bottle. Keep the oil for up to 3 months, stored at room temperature and away from direct sunlight.

Variation
To make **Chili Red Oil** add 1 scotch bonnet or habanero chili, slit almost in half, to the oil in step 1 and simmer for 5 minutes. Mix the smoked paprika with 1 tablespoon of water in a small bowl until smooth, then stir into the chili oil. Remove the pan from the heat and leave to infuse. Remove the pepper after 5 minutes, or leave in for longer for extra heat.

Scotch Bonnet & Turmeric Oil

MAKES ABOUT 150ML

125ml olive or vegetable oil
2 scotch bonnet peppers (1 red and 1 yellow), pierced and left whole
1 tsp ground turmeric

YOU WILL NEED
1 sterilized jar or bottle

This chili oil is a store-cupboard staple in my home. Great for drizzling over salads, adding more warmth or heat to dishes and especially useful when chili is omitted from the main dish, for example, when cooking for small children and you want to add heat to an individual serving. The longer the chilies infuse in the oil, the hotter and sweeter the oil will become. On the other hand, you could scoop out the seeds and membrane to quell the heat.

1. Gently warm the oil in a small saucepan. Place the scotch bonnets in the oil, stir well and leave to infuse for 5–7 minutes over a low heat.

2. Press the chilies to release some of their natural oils and stir gently.

3. Remove from the heat and leave to cool completely.

4. Add the turmeric and mix well to combine.

5. Pick out the chilies and pour the oil into a sterilized jar or bottle. Keep the oil for up to 3 months, stored at room temperature and away from direct sunlight.

Parsley & Baobab Herb Oil

Citrus notes of baobab with peppery, herbaceous and slightly bitter parsley are a delightful combination. I created this finishing oil to use up leftover parsley. Drizzle this green oil over soups and sauces in need of a bit of zing, and use it when you are short on fresh herbs.

MAKES ABOUT 200ML

1 bunch of flat-leaf parsley (about 35g)
1 bunch of spring onions (about 35g), trimmed and roughly chopped
125ml olive or sunflower oil
1 tbsp baobab powder

1. Start by preparing an ice bath with a liter of water and ice cubes.

2. In a medium saucepan, bring a liter of water and a teaspoon of fine sea salt to a boil. Remove the pan from the heat and plunge the parsley and spring onions into the hot salted water. Ensure the leaves are completely covered and blanch for 10–15 seconds, then swiftly transfer the herbs to the ice bath to cool.

3. Drain and squeeze dry using a clean kitchen towel or a salad spinner. Chop the parsley and spring onions roughly, then place in a food processor and whizz thoroughly with the oil and baobab powder until the oil is a glowing green.

4. Place a cheesecloth over a strainer, and place the strainer over a bowl. Pour in the herb oil and strain, squeezing the herbs to remove all the oil. (A strainer on its own is perfectly all right, but the added cheesecloth will ensure a smoother finish.)

5. Pour the oil into an airtight jar, store in the fridge and use within 5 days. You can freeze the leftover herbs and spring onions and add them to soups or sauces to avoid waste.

Ras el Hanout Butter or Oil

Ras el hanout is one of my favorite spice blends and even after cooking with it, I yearn for more. Brush this over sizzling hot kefta, on your favorite roasts or drizzle over salads to bring them alive.

MAKES 1 TBSP

1 tbsp unsalted butter or oil
1 tsp **Imperial Ras el Hanout Spice Blend** (see page 269) or store-bought

1. Melt the butter or warm the oil in a small saucepan over a medium heat.

2. Add the Ras el hanout and mix well.

3. Use to finish roasts or grills, or to drizzle onto salads.

Niter Kibbeh
Ethiopian Spiced Clarified Butter

MAKES 500G

A spiced butter with a wonderful depth of flavor, this is used to cook the famous *doro wot* (see page 86) and many other regional recipes. I love adding it to tomato sauces, such as in my **Juicy Berbere Meatballs in Tomato Sauce** (see page 96). I have omitted several traditional ingredients that may not be easy to find outside the region. If you have a local Ethiopian or Eritrean supplier, you may be able to source ready-made spiced butter. Use it to enrich pasta sauces, stir fries, rice and for roasted vegetables.

1 cinnamon stick
1 tsp Ethiopian cardamom seeds (*korerima*) or 8 black cardamom pods, slightly smashed
3 cloves
1 tsp black peppercorns
2 tsp cumin seeds
1 tsp fenugreek seeds
500g unsalted butter
1 medium onion, peeled and sliced
3 large garlic cloves, peeled and slightly smashed
2 tbsp grated fresh ginger
¼ tsp ground turmeric
¼ tsp ground nutmeg
1 bay leaf

YOU WILL NEED
1 sterilized jar

1. Place a frying pan over a medium heat and toast the whole spices until fragrant.

2. Transfer to a saucepan and add the butter and all other ingredients. Place over a low heat to melt the butter. Once melted, leave to simmer for 20–40 minutes. (The butter will transform, creating a white layer, separating the milk solids, which will begin to foam as the moisture evaporates after 15–20 minutes. Be careful not to let the butter boil and burn.)

3. Once the bubbling reduces, and the foaming is clearer, the butter should be clarified and golden. I like to cook it for a further 10–15 minutes for a darker liquid and a richer flavor. Remove from the heat and pick out the aromatics.

4. Place a cheesecloth over a strainer and place the strainer over a bowl. Pour in the clarified butter, squeezing the cheesecloth to get all the liquid out. Repeat a few times with a clean cheesecloth for a finer liquid. Discard the used whole spices and aromatics.

5. Pour the clarified butter into a sterilized jar and cover tightly with a lid. The butter will keep at room temperature for 2 weeks or, once cooled, it will solidify and keep for up to 3 months in the fridge. Bring up to room temperature to soften before use.

Amlou
Almond & Honey Paste

MAKES 225G

Amlou is a most indulgent nut butter made with roasted almonds and golden argan oil. Argan oil is a treasured oil from the kernels of the argan tree. Highly prized for its health, beauty and culinary benefits, this mildly nutty oil is adored not only in Morocco, but across the world. The first time I was introduced to *amlou*, it was at breakfast where it was served in a small jar with **Honeycomb Pancakes** (see page 236), alongside other irresistible Moroccan pastries. I was immediately enchanted and investigated further in typical fashion. Despite the expense of argan oil, it is worth making this for a real treat. You can replace argan oil with peanut oil, walnut oil or milder oils, or simply use olive oil. Drizzle over salads, serve for dipping with **Medina Bread** (see page 194) or spread onto toast and pastries for the most enchanting African afternoon tea.

150g whole almonds (with or without skins)
40–90ml argan oil (or walnut or peanut oil)
2 tbsp honey or agave syrup
½ tsp ground cinnamon

1. Preheat the oven to 350°F.

2. Spread the almonds in a single layer on a large baking tray and roast for about 15 minutes, turning a few times, until the nuts are just lightly toasted.

3. Tip the nuts into a bowl and season with a pinch of fine sea salt. Leave to cool slightly.

4. Place the nuts in a food processor and pulse to break them up into smaller pieces. Pulse again to blend, adding the oil a little at a time, until smooth. This can take up to 10 minutes, depending on the strength of your blender. Add more oil for a more traditional and runnier nut butter.

5. Finally, add the honey or agave and cinnamon and blend to combine. Scoop the paste into a bowl and season with a generous pinch of sea salt flakes.

6. Store in an airtight jar and keep in the fridge for up to 3 months.

Smoky Selim Salt

Add this wonderful smoky salt to your cooking or use as a finishing salt for its intensely aromatic and unique fragrance.

MAKES ABOUT 2 TBSP

4–5 selim pods
2 tbsp sea salt flakes

1. Grind the selim pods in a mortar and pestle, or place in a spice or coffee grinder and pulse to a fine powder.

2. Tip the sea salt flakes into a jar, add the selim powder and shake to combine.

Hibiscus Salt

Use as a finishing salt to add a mildly tart and fruity flavor to salads, roasts, fish dishes and even popcorn, like in **Spiced Chocolate & Coffee Mousse with Hibiscus Glazed Popcorn** (see page 244).

MAKES ABOUT 4 TBSP

2 tbsp ground dried hibiscus, 20g dried hibiscus, ground, or 2 tbsp hibiscus tea
2 tbsp sea salt flakes

1. If using ground hibiscus, place in a spice or coffee grinder and pulse in a few short bursts with the salt. If using hibiscus tea or dried hibiscus, place the hibiscus in a spice or coffee grinder and pulse to a fine powder before adding the salt. Pulse again in short bursts until fine.

2. Store in an airtight jar.

Hibiscus Sugar

This pink snow is such a delight scattered over hot chocolate or yogurt or used to top doughnuts like my **Christmas Pudding Puff Puffs** (see page 242).

MAKES 4 TBSP

2 tbsp ground dried hibiscus, 20g dried hibiscus, ground, or 2 tbsp hibiscus tea
2 tbsp granulated sugar

1. If using ground hibiscus, place in a spice or coffee grinder and pulse in a few short bursts with the sugar. If using hibiscus tea or dried hibiscus, place the hibiscus in a spice or coffee grinder and pulse to a fine powder before adding the sugar. Pulse again in short bursts until fine.

2. Store in an airtight jar.

Hibiscus Syrup

MAKES ABOUT 300ML

1 tbsp ground dried hibiscus
Zest of 1 lemon, plus 1 tbsp juice
200ml mild-flavored honey
   (see below for variation
   with sugar)

YOU WILL NEED
1 sterilized jar

I adore hibiscus, with its dashing crimson and mildly lip-puckering flavor. Hibiscus and honey syrup is an important condiment used in several recipes across this book. Once I created this versatile syrup, I increasingly found new dishes to cook and adorn it with. I always keep a jar in the fridge to drizzle over ice cream or pancakes, and to enliven roasts and salads.

1. Place the ground hibiscus, 125ml water and the lemon zest and juice in a saucepan over a medium-low heat and bring to a simmer.

2. Add the honey and whisk thoroughly to combine. Simmer gently for about 5 minutes to thicken. When ready, the syrup should bubble a little and lightly coat the back of a wooden spoon. Although your hot syrup might be runnier than honey, it will thicken as it cools.

3. Pour into a sterilized jar while still hot and set aside to cool completely before use.

Variation
For **Hibiscus Sugar Syrup**, place the ground hibiscus, 200g sugar, 60ml water and the juice of 1 lemon in a small saucepan and bring to a simmer over a medium heat. Watch closely as the syrup dissolves and thickens for up to 5 minutes. Pour into a sterilized jar. Keep in the fridge and use within a month. Makes about 250ml syrup.

Smoky African Curry Spice

This is the curry spice used in the **Plantain & Coconut Curry** on page 83, a smoky and sweet blend I created to enchant you. The addition of selim pepper and paprika is crucial to the nuanced smoky flavors that create a curry that is out of this world.

MAKES ABOUT 3–4 TBSP

1 tsp fennel seeds
1 tsp cumin seeds
6 allspice berries or ½ tsp ground
  allspice
1 tsp ground cumin
1 tsp ground coriander
1 tsp ground turmeric
1 tsp smoked paprika
½ tsp ground ginger
½ tsp cayenne pepper
½ tsp ground selim pepper (about
  2 pods)

OR

1 tbsp Caribbean or mild curry
  powder
1 tsp smoked paprika
½ tsp cayenne pepper
½ tsp ground selim pepper (about
  2 pods)

1. Toast the seeds in a hot pan until fragrant.

2. Remove from the heat to cool.

3. Place in a pestle and mortar or spice or coffee grinder and blitz to a fine or coarse powder.

4. Combine all the spices in a bowl and mix well.

5. Store in an airtight jar away from direct sunlight for up to 3 months, for the most fragrant spices.

Imperial Ras el Hanout Spice Blend

No single Ras el hanout spice blend is the same, as you'll discover if you explore the spice souks across North Africa. This recipe is my own special blend with spices and florals that I love in this peppery and fragrant mix. Feel free to play around with your combination until you create your favorite blend or try a different blend each time.

MAKES ABOUT 8 TBSP

1 tbsp fennel seeds
1 tbsp anise seeds
1 tbsp cumin seeds
1 tbsp coriander seeds
1 tbsp black peppercorns
1 whole nutmeg
4 cloves
6 cardamom pods, peeled to
  release the seeds
3 cinnamon sticks or 1 tbsp ground
  cinnamon
2 tsp grains of paradise
1 tbsp ground turmeric
1 tbsp ground allspice
1 tsp saffron strands
2 tsp dried lavender
15g dried edible rose petals

1. Place a large frying pan over a medium heat and, once hot, toast the whole spices for 3–4 minutes, swirling the pan constantly to avoid burning, until they release their individual wonderful fragrance.

2. Pour all the spices and florals into a spice or coffee grinder and grind until smooth. You can do this in batches, if necessary.

3. Store in an airtight jar away from direct sunlight for up to 3 months, after which time the spices will be useful but less fragrant.

Paradise Spice

Paradise spice is one of my treasured spice blends, created to add a burst of flavor to several recipes in this book and transport you to an African paradise. I combined some of our best produce—peppery ginger from Nigeria, the enchanting citrus notes in grains of paradise, healing turmeric, spicy cayenne and fragrant makrut lime leaves, which are loved in and around the East African archipelagos. I love the spellbinding fragrance and flavors of makrut limes and their leaves. The leaves can be bought fresh, dried or ground and can be stored in the freezer.

1 tbsp ground makrut lime leaves
  (see technique on page 274)
1 tsp ground ginger
1 tsp ground turmeric
½ tsp cayenne pepper
½ tsp ground grains of paradise

1. Combine all the ingredients in an airtight jar. Secure with a lid and give it a shake to mix.

2. Store away from direct sunlight for up to 3 months, for the most fragrant spices.

Mikelesha Ethiopian Finishing Spice

MAKES ABOUT 2 TBSP

Mikelesha is an aromatic finishing spice used in Berbere and a host of other Ethiopian and Eritrean recipes.

2 tsp Ethiopian black cardamom or
  black cardamom, smashed with
  seeds removed
1 cinnamon stick
1 clove
¼ tsp freshly grated nutmeg
1 tsp black peppercorns

1. Toast all the spices in a hot pan for about 3 minutes, or until fragrant.

2. Leave to cool, then grind to a fine powder using a spice or coffee grinder.

3. Store in an airtight jar away from direct sunlight for up to 3 months, for the most fragrant spices.

Pepper Soup Spice Blend

MAKES 2 TBSP

There are several indigenous spices and herbs ground together to make pepper soup spice blend. Some are harder to track down than others. Although ready-blended spices are available in shops selling African produce, because I love making my own blend at home, I created this simple version that embodies the smoky, fragrant and warming essence of the much-loved soup.

6 calabash nutmeg
15 pods of selim pepper
1 tsp fennel seeds (optional but wonderful)

1. If the calabash nutmeg is smooth and rounded, smash and peel off the outer layer. If it is rough, then it is already peeled and ready to use.

2. Toast all the spices in a hot pan for about 3 minutes, or until fragrant.

3. Leave to cool, then grind to a fine powder using a spice or coffee grinder.

4. Store in an airtight jar away from direct sunlight for up to 3 months, for the most fragrant spices.

Smoky African Spice Blend

MAKES ABOUT 8 TBSP

This is a staple spice blend I enjoy at home in numerous dishes. Use to add more flavor to your jollof, as a dry rub for steak or in vegetable roasts such as **Spiced Roasted Plantains** (see page 279).

2 tbsp paprika
2 tbsp garlic granules
1 tbsp onion granules
1 tbsp cayenne pepper
1 tbsp ground ginger
1 tbsp dried thyme

1. Combine all the ingredients in an airtight jar. Secure the lid and give it a good shake to mix.

2. Store away from direct sunlight for up to 3 months, for the most fragrant spices.

Suya Spice Blend

MAKES ABOUT 150G

100g unsalted roasted peanuts
10 pods of selim pepper (optional but wonderful)
5 tbsp ground ginger
2 tbsp garlic granules
2 tbsp onion granules
1 tbsp cayenne pepper (or ½ tbsp for less heat)
1 tsp fine sea salt
1 tbsp paprika (optional)

This nutty spice blend will enchant you, just as it has done so many who adore suya, the much loved grilled street food popular in Nigeria and across West Africa. Shower the spice blend over grills, such as in **Sizzling Suya** (see page 116), and in roasts like the **Coconut & Peanut Suya Roast Chicken** (see page 106).

1. Place the nuts in a coffee or spice grinder and blitz in 1-second short bursts, to a fine powder. Be careful not to grind for too long, as the nuts will quickly turn into peanut butter.

2. Transfer the nuts to a piece of muslin or clean kitchen towel and squeeze out as much oil as possible, until you are left with a cookie-dough-like texture. Tip into a bowl and break into fine crumbs using a fork.

3. Add all the spices and seasonings to the bowl with the peanuts and mix well.

4. Store in an airtight container or glass jar away from direct sunlight for up to 3 months. The spice blend can also be mixed into tomato sauces, vegetable and bean dips, or sprinkled onto salads and roasts. The possibilities are just endless and wonderful.

Lerato's Tip

If you have peanut powder, you can use the equivalent quantity of peanuts. Simply toast the powder in a dry frying pan over a medium heat for a few minutes, stirring continuously, until slightly darker golden in color.

While I love sharing recipes that are easily adaptable to suit varying diets, geographical locations and availability, I must tell you that for the true essence of suya, I consider ginger to be a very important spice. Replace peanuts with almonds or other nuts for those with tree nut allergies, or use toasted sesame seeds or tahini paste to achieve that rich, nutty flavor suya is known for.

Berbere Spice Blend

MAKES ABOUT 200G

Ethiopian and Eritrean Berbere is a wonderfully aromatic mix of spices, herbs and florals, some of which are more difficult to find outside the region—the bitter and strong fragrant spice korerima (also known as Ethiopian cardamom) being one. For the most authentic flavors, your best option is to do as Ethiopians and Eritreans do and buy the blends ready-made from Ethiopia and Eritrea. While we cannot all do that, my spice blend mimics the fragrance and heat of the traditional blend, with green cardamom used as a substitute for korerima. I often substitute whole dried chilies with half chili powder and half paprika as well. Play around with the chili, adding a little at a time to the mix until the blend is to your liking. I use mine in everything from meatballs and stews to roasted vegetables.

150g mix of dried red chilies:
  Anaheim (mild) and dried
  Mexican Guajillo (medium-hot),
  stemmed and deseeded
1 tbsp coriander seeds
1 tbsp carom seeds (*ajwain*)
4 cloves
2 tsp coriander seeds
1 cinnamon stick
1 tbsp Ethiopian black cardamom
  seeds (*korerima*) or 10 green
  cardamom pods, seeds only
5 allspice berries
2 tsp cumin seeds
2 tsp fenugreek seeds
2 tsp garlic granules
2 tsp ground ginger
2 tsp dried rosemary
2 tsp black peppercorns
½ tsp ground nutmeg
1 tsp ground turmeric
1 tsp fine sea salt

1. Toast the chilies in a hot pan for a few minutes to release their wonderful oils. Toss into a bowl and set aside.

2. Add the whole spices to the pan and toast until fragrant. Remove from the heat, toss into the bowl of chilies and leave to cool.

3. Place the chilies and spices into a spice or coffee grinder and blitz to a fine or coarse powder—you may need to do this in batches.

4. Add all the remaining ingredients to the chilies and spices and blitz to combine.

5. Store in an airtight container for up to 6 months, but preferably for only 3 months for the most fragrant spices.

Cook's Tips

These are tips to help you easily prepare some of the ingredients in this book

VEGETABLE & FRUIT TIPS

HOW TO BLANCH GREENS

With a wide variety to choose from, some greens are sturdier than others. If using sturdier greens, such as wild spinach, kale, Swiss chard or collard greens, blanch in hot water for 5–10 minutes to soften before squeezing out as much liquid as possible and adding to the pan.

SOAKING BEANS

I use dried beans or black-eyed peas most often in this book and I don't bother soaking them when cooking in slow-cooked recipes. I only soak the beans in recipes that call for blending, to achieve a smoother texture. Tip the beans into a bowl full of water and soak for 8 hours or overnight. Drain and rinse before using.

HOW TO SKIN BLACK-EYED PEAS

Soak the beans overnight in a bowl full of water. The beans will expand exponentially, and the skins will shrivel. Place your bowl in the sink and keep a sieve on hand. Using both hands, rub the beans vigorously in between your palms and under the water. Fill the bowl to the top with water, and as the skins float to the top, carefully pour them out into the sieve, holding back the skinned beans. Return any stray beans to your bowl and repeat the process 3–4 times until all the skins are removed. Before soaking, you can also pulse the beans with water in a blender or food processor to loosen the skins.

HOW TO ROAST NUTS

Preheat the oven to 350°F. Place the nuts onto a roasting tray and roast for 10–15 minutes, turning halfway through, until the nuts are fragrant and take on a light golden-brown color. Remove from the oven, then tip into a bowl and set aside to cool.

HOW TO PREPARE GROUND HIBISCUS

Place dried hibiscus in a colander and quickly rinse under cool running water. Drain quickly and spread onto kitchen paper to blot dry. Be careful because its crimson color will run a little. Preheat the oven to 200°F. Spread in a single layer on a baking tray lined with baking parchment. Place in the middle of the oven and leave for 15–20 minutes or until dried with the oven door slightly open. Place the dried hibiscus in a coffee or spice grinder and blitz to a fine powder. Strain the powder with a fine sieve to remove any hard stalks. Store in a jar away from sunlight.

HOW TO PREPARE MAKRUT LIME LEAVES

Tear the leaves from the fibrous center rib or use a paring knife to cut out the rib. Stack the leaves together and roll them up like a cigar. Slice as thinly as possible and add to the pan. Fresh leaves can be wrapped and stored in the fridge for a week. Leaves can also be wrapped and frozen for up to a year.

HOW TO GRIND MAKRUT LIME LEAVES

Preheat the oven to 200°F. Rinse and dry fresh leaves and spread in a single layer onto a baking tray lined with baking parchment. Place in the middle of the oven and leave for 20–30 minutes with the oven door slightly open, until the leaves are dry to a crisp. Place the leaves in a coffee or spice grinder and blitz to a fine powder. Store in a jar away from sunlight.

HOW TO SHUCK AN EAR OF CORN

Shucking, which means undressing corn from its husk, is easier than it seems. Place the corn in a large bowl or in the sink and "shuck" by tightly gripping the tip of the corn husk and pulling back in one strong motion. Pull out the husk and remove any remaining brown silk. Break or cut off the stem. Thoroughly rinse under cool running tap water before cooking.

HOW TO PREPARE A VANILLA POD

Place the vanilla pod on the chopping board and hold down the curved end. Use a paring knife to slice lightly into the top layer along the length of the pod. Open it up and flatten. Use the back of the knife to scrape the seeds out of the pod. Throw the pod into a jar of sugar to create vanilla-flavored sugar.

FISH & SEAFOOD TIPS

HOW TO CLEAN PRAWNS & LANGOUSTINES

Twist the head off, peel off the shell, then hold firmly and pull out the tail. Use a paring knife to gently slice into the back and pull out the dark vein. Rinse and set aside. Crush the shells with the back of your knife to flatten and set aside to make a concentrated fish stock.

HOW TO DEFROST FROZEN PRAWNS

Defrost prawns in the fridge a few hours before cooking or place them in a bowl filled with enough cold water to cover all the prawns. Leave for 15–20 minutes then drain. Pour into a colander under cold running water, rinse thoroughly and pat dry.

HOW TO PREPARE LOBSTER TAILS

Use heavy-duty kitchen shears or a large chef's knife to cut through the lobster shell. Crack the ribs of the shell and open to loosen the meat while leaving it attached. Cut along the top of the tail to check for veins. Pull out and discard.

GENERAL COOKING TIPS

HOW TO SPATCHCOCK A CHICKEN

Place the chicken breast-side down on a chopping board. Cut through the flesh and bones along both sides of the backbone using heavy-duty kitchen shears, if possible, either starting from the neck to the tail or vice versa and remove it. (You can reserve the backbone for a stock.) Make small incisions on the inside, then turn the chicken over and, using the bottom of your palm, firmly press down on to the breastbone to crack and flatten the bird.

HOW TO TELL WHETHER A CHICKEN IS COOKED THROUGH

Cut into the joint between the thigh and the leg; if the juice runs clear, the chicken is ready. The flesh can have a pink tinge even when cooked through, especially in organic or free-range chickens, so you could also use an internal thermometer for a safe-to-eat reading of 165˚F.

FLOUR SUBSTITUTIONS

In recipes containing flour for baking or for fritters, gluten-free flour can be used instead.

HOW TO STERILIZE YOUR JARS

Preheat the oven to 325˚F and wash the jar with warm soapy water. Rinse thoroughly and place the wet jar and its lid upside down on a clean oven dish or tray. Place in the oven for 20 minutes. Check brand specifications, as some jars and covers may require boiling and not dry heat.

HOW TO TELL IF OIL IS HOT ENOUGH

375˚F—For frying plantains, lower a cube of plantain into the oil. If it sizzles steadily, then the oil is hot enough. To test with a cube of bread, if it turns golden brown in less than 15 seconds, the oil is hot enough.

350°F—For general shallow to deep frying, drop a cube of bread into the oil. If it turns golden brown in 15 seconds then the oil is hot enough.

325˚F—Drop a cube of bread into the oil. If it turns golden brown in 30–35 seconds, then the oil is hot enough.

300°F—If a cube of bread begins to boil rather than crisp up, the oil is below 325˚F.

Check the precise temperature by using a sugar or deep-frying thermometer.

For indoor grilling, I use a grill within my oven and a coated cast iron and seasoned griddle pan, which means it has nonstick characteristics. For most recipes, I tend to brush the food with oil rather than put oil in the pan when grilling. This reduces the chance of smoking. When cooking very wet marinades, I may brush a little oil over the ridges of the griddle pan but, as long as the meat or vegetable is brushed with enough oil, leave it to cook and it should release itself before turning. When grilling in the oven, I brush the food and the grill rack or tray with oil. Also, make sure your kitchen is well ventilated.

USEFUL EQUIPMENT

A combination of **nonstick frying pans** and a range of different-sized **saucepans** and **sauté pans** are useful for everyday meals. I regularly cook with a **cast iron pot** or **Dutch oven** that can move from stove top to oven, and vice versa.

A **pestle and mortar** is very useful for crushing and grinding small quantities of spices and pastes. I do love the larger **Ghanaian** *asanka* with its ridges that cut through tomatoes, onions and peppers for quick sauces and marinades.

A set of **deep roasting trays** are essential for keeping roasts moist and catching those wonderful juices, **deep baking dishes** or **casseroles** are perfect for baked dishes, and **baking trays** are essential for baking plantain chips and more.

A **food processor** makes light work of chopping and preparing larger quantities of pastes.

A **blender** is essential for many purees, sauces and marinades in this book.

Brushes for glazing pastry and basting roasts are useful for many recipes in this book. I suggest stocking up on a few, such as a finer brush for pastry glazes, and larger silicone brushes for coarser marinades.

A **rolling pin** is a handy tool for our breads.

A **griddle pan** is most useful for indoor grilling. Although an oven grill is wonderful, you simply cannot beat the char from a **barbecue, outdoor grill** or a **griddle pan.** A **grill tray** or **heavy duty roasting tray with a grilling rack** is useful to keep the foods at a good height, to avoid them cooking in their own moisture.

A **steam pot** or a **steamer basket** is wonderful for my **African Grain Salad**, couscous, steamed fish and steamed bean cakes.

A **thermometer** is useful for accuracy when roasting large meat, chicken and fish.

The **aebleskiver** or dumpling pan is traditionally used for puffed rice cakes like *masa* in Nigeria, *mofogasy* in Madagascar or *vitumbua* in Kenya. Use it for the **Coconut & Cardamom Rice Cakes** (see page 234).

How to Cook Plantains

I have a great affection for plantains, and gladly I am not alone. They're incredibly versatile and wonderful, whether fried, roasted, grilled, boiled or mashed. Within *Africana* I have shared a variety of recipes for you to enjoy plantains in both traditional and surprising ways—as well as essential recipes that will help you master cooking this fruit.

Green and unripe—although notoriously difficult to peel and the least sweet form, these are wonderful in curries or stews. They require longer cooking times and are sometimes boiled and pounded into *fufu*. When cooking the unripe and less sweet green variety, an extra burst of flavor from crushed sea salt is wonderful.

Green plantains are also most commonly used for **Plantain Chips** (see page 280), as they crisp a lot more easily due to their higher starch content. Plantain chips are a great snack and a good alternative to croutons, as seen in the pepper soup recipes (see pages 68–9). Whether you make your own or buy them, you will find yourself endlessly pining for more.

Yellow and ripe—these are much more sweet and malleable than the green, unripe variety. This is my favorite stage of ripeness for frying, baking or roasting. I also like to use just-ripened and firm yellow plantains for curries such as **Plantain & Coconut Curry** (see page 83) or plantain chips. As they continue to ripen, dark patches will begin to appear, slowly taking over the yellow.

Black and overripe—this is the final ripening stage of the fruit. At their peak sweetness and softness, they are perfect for pancakes and fritters, such as the **Plantain & Prawn Cakes** (see page 60).

PEELING PLANTAINS

Top and tail the plantain and, using the tip of your knife, cut lightly into the peel lengthways. Use your thumb to pull the peel apart and discard.

Fried Plantains

SERVES 2

2 ripe yellow plantains, peeled (see
page 277) and sliced into
½-inch-thick diagonal strips
Vegetable oil, for frying

1. Heat at least ¾ inch of oil to 375°F degrees in a shallow frying pan. Once hot (see page 275), carefully place the plantain pieces into the hot oil without overcrowding. Leave to fry for a few minutes and use a turner or slotted spoon to peek at the underside. Once golden brown, swiftly turn over to fry the other side.

2. Remove when golden brown on both sides and drain on kitchen paper before sprinkling with sea salt flakes, if you like, to serve.

Boiled Plantains

SERVES 2

2 unripe green plantains, or very
firm just ripened yellow plantains,
washed and cut (with the skin)
into 2-inch chunks
1 tsp fine sea salt

1. Place the plantains in a saucepan and fill with enough water to cover. Add the salt and bring to a boil. Cook over a medium heat for 25–30 minutes, until the plantains (not the skin) is softened. If using just ripe or very ripe plantains, the cooking time will be significantly reduced. Use a fork or small knife to poke into the plantain—if it releases easily, then the plantains are cooked. Drain carefully and leave to cool.

2. To peel, score the skin and pull apart to release the cooked plantain. Discard the skin and serve.

Baked or Roasted Plantains

SERVES 2

2 ripe yellow plantains, peeled (see
page 277) and sliced into ½-inch
oblong shapes
1 tbsp vegetable, coconut or olive
oil

1. Preheat the oven to 400°C. Line a baking tray with baking parchment.

2. Place the plantains in a bowl, drizzle with the oil and mix well to coat, or use a brush. Arrange the plantains in a single layer on the lined baking tray and bake for 25–30 minutes, checking after 15 minutes and turning them over, until softened and golden brown.

3. Remove from the oven and sprinkle with sea salt flakes to serve.

Variation
You could also slice the plantains lengthways in half, brush with oil and roast in the oven, grill or cook on the barbecue.

Kelewele
Spiced Roasted Plantains

These irresistibly spiced and roasted plantains are inspired by a fried version that is a staple in Ghana. I prefer roasting or baking plantains and this recipe allows much of the marinade to adhere to the plantains without all the oil required for deep frying.

SERVES 2–4

2 tbsp vegetable, peanut or coconut oil

2 ripe plantains (yellow and slightly soft or yellow with some black patches), peeled (see page 277) and sliced into 1-inch chunks, then each chunk sliced in half lengthways

FOR THE MARINADE

1 small red onion, peeled and roughly chopped

4 garlic cloves, peeled and roughly chopped, or ½ tsp garlic granules

1-inch piece of ginger, peeled and grated

1 tbsp **Smoky African Spice Blend** (see page 271)

1 tsp sea salt flakes or ½ tsp fine sea salt

¼ tsp freshly ground black pepper

3 sprigs of thyme, leaves picked

½ tsp ground cinnamon (optional)

¼ tbsp ground nutmeg (optional)

1. Place all the marinade ingredients in a food processor, reserving some thyme leaves for later, and blend to a smooth paste. Tip the paste into a bowl, drizzle with the oil and mix well. Add the plantains to the marinade, mix well and, if you have time, leave to marinate for 30 minutes.

2. Preheat the oven to 400°F and line a baking tray with baking parchment.

3. Shake off any excess marinade and place the plantains in a single layer on the prepared baking tray. Roast in the oven for 30–35 minutes, checking after 15 minutes and turning halfway, until the plantains are soft and golden brown with charred edges.

4. Remove from the baking tray and sprinkle with the reserved thyme leaves to serve.

Plantain Chips

MAKES 1 500ML JAR

2 large green (unripe) or 2 yellow
  plantains (ripe but must be firm),
  peeled (see page 277)
1 tbsp coconut or vegetable oil
  (if oven baking), or more (if deep
  frying)
½ tsp paprika
¼ tsp cayenne pepper (optional)

Variation

Season your chips with a variety
of spices for a different treat
every time. Try garlic and onion
granules with paprika for
barbecue-inspired flavors, or my
favorite which is a light pinch of
ground nutmeg, cinnamon,
ginger and clove for a festive
treat at Christmas. You could
also throw in bruised fresh
rosemary and thyme leaves for a
wonderful herb infusion. The
possibilities are endless.

1. If using unripe green plantains, use a mandolin to cut
   them into thin slices. For ripe and yellow plantains, try
   cutting with a mandolin but if it sticks, use a small
   sharp knife.

2. Place in a bowl and sprinkle over a generous pinch of
   salt if using unripe plantains.

Oven method

a. Preheat the oven to 350°F and line a baking tray with
   baking parchment.

b. Drizzle with the oil and mix well. (I prefer to lay the
   plantain slices on the lined baking tray and brush
   with a little oil on both sides.) Place the slices on the
   prepared tray in one layer and roast for 20–25
   minutes, until crispy and golden.

c. Remove from the oven and tip into a large bowl to
   cool.

Deep frying method

a. Pour oil into a medium, heavy-based saucepan to fill
   ¾ inch deep and heat to 375°F (see page 275).

b. Carefully and swiftly drop one piece of plantain into
   the hot oil at a time. After about 30 seconds, stir
   frequently, using a slotted spoon, until golden.

c. Scoop out the chips and spread onto a wide plate
   lined with kitchen paper to drain any excess oils.

3. Finally, season whilst still warm with sea salt flakes.
   And for a little kick, sprinkle with freshly ground
   pepper, paprika and cayenne pepper, if you like. Toss
   to mix evenly. If you are fortunate to resist the urge to
   devour all the chips in an instant, keep in an airtight
   container or jar to retain that wonderful crispness.

Universal Conversion Chart

Oven Temperature Equivalents

250°F = 120°C

275°F = 135°C

300°F = 150°C

325°F = 160°C

350°F = 180°C

375°F = 190°C

400°F = 200°C

425°F = 220°C

450°F = 230°C

475°F = 240°C

500°F = 260°C

Measurement Equivalents

Measurements should always be level unless directed otherwise.

⅛ teaspoon = 0.5 mL

¼ teaspoon = 1 mL

½ teaspoon = 2.5 mL

1 teaspoon = 5 mL

1 tablespoon = 3 teaspoons = ½ fluid ounce = 15 mL

2 tablespoons = ⅛ cup = 1 fluid ounce = 30 mL

4 tablespoons = ¼ cup = 2 fluid ounces = 60 mL

5⅓ tablespoons = ⅓ cup = 3 fluid ounces = 80 mL

8 tablespoons = ½ cup = 4 fluid ounces = 120 mL

10⅔ tablespoons = ⅔ cup = 5 fluid ounces = 160 mL

12 tablespoons = ¾ cup = 6 fluid ounces = 180 mL

16 tablespoons = 1 cup = 8 fluid ounces = 240 mL

Index

For my mother, Stella Uche—who blessed me with great curiosity and the audacity to live out my dreams. And for my grandma Theresa Ebonne, I think she would have loved this book.

Acknowledgments

I thank God for this great opportunity and for the support of so many wonderful people. Thank you for holding *AFRICANA* in your hands as you embark on this journey with me. You have made my dreams come true!

To Seni Glaister and Jon Stefani, I am eternally grateful for your encouragement over the years, for believing in me from the very beginning.

Deepest gratitude to my publisher Lisa Milton—thank you for believing in me. And the fantastic team at HQ and HarperCollins including Kate Fox, Nancy Adimorah, Nira Begum—thank you all for your support and dedication to this dream.

To my agent, Bev James, thank you for inspiring me always to be purposeful and powerful with my message. To Tom Wright, Aoife Rice-Murphy, Emily Prosser and the dynamic team at Bev James Management, thank you all for all that you do.

To the wonderful team who brought *AFRICANA* to life in spectacular color and pizazz, Jo Roberts-Miller, Anita Mangan, Esther Clark, Caitlyn Macdonald, Tara Fisher, and Tabitha Hawkins, my deepest gratitude to you for such beauty.

To Eva Sonaike, thank you for the most exquisite selection of fabric, and to Afoke Bakpa of Ellelyne for the gorgeous tie-dye napkins celebrating African design.

To Mboni Kibelloh, Angela Yankson—thank you for gifting me with stories passed down from your mothers and grandmothers. Chef Nti,

Vanessa Mehri, Pierre Tham, Tinsae Elsdon, thank you for sharing your stories and passion for Africa with me.

Deepest gratitude to: Joy Baldwin, Maeve Simpson, Marina Del-Gaudio, Lisa Oladejo, Angela Brooks, Bo Obuks-Ebuehi, April Pearson, Amy Zamarripa Solis, Leslie Leigh, Susan Shyllon, Dupe & Aitua Ekhaese, Gilli Clare, Nicola Bamford, Dale Blackford, Leila Zadeh, Nicola Bamford, Mark Seifert, Antony and Zena Maturi, Beatriz Nunez, Stuart Aspden, John Paul-Raad, Justin, Natasha Jones, Vanessa Ferreira, Robin Van Creveld, Martin Nathan, Joy Ventour, Andrew McNamara, Sudi Pigott, Jessica Weston, Gordana Glam, Annalynne Cooke, Tosin Oyekole, Julia Jepp, Uchenna Udeh, Chinedu Udeh-Momoh, Ndidi Emefiele, Pauline Thomas, who have all cooked with me, sat at my table and who have all supported Lerato Foods over the years.

To my dear family and friends: Valéry and Deborah Shaylor, Frank and Christine Shaylor, Emily Akanimoh, Tonia and Teun Karman, Tenyin Ikpe Etim, Ade Ologunro, Zeze Oriaikhi-Sao, Becky Obozuwa, Louise Akrofi, Paul Corney and Ana Aguilar-Corney, Bella Kuffour and Marian Okogwu, Pauline Cox, Fiona Dunlop, Adam Piper and Jennifer Choi. I appreciate you all.

To Ingrid—my mutti, thank you for your unwavering support and love. And to my husband Thurston—"my rock," thank you for keeping me sane and for making my dreams yours.